Everyman, I will go with thee,
and be thy guide

THE EVERYMAN
LIBRARY

The Everyman Library was founded by J. M. Dent in 1906. He chose the name Everyman because he wanted to make available the best books ever written in every field to the greatest number of people at the cheapest possible price. He began with Boswell's 'Life of Johnson'; his one-thousandth title was Aristotle's 'Metaphysics', by which time sales exceeded 40 million.

Today Everyman paperbacks remain true to J. M. Dent's aims and high standards, with a wide range of titles at affordable prices in editions which address the needs of today's readers. Each new text is reset to give a clear, elegant page and to incorporate the latest thinking and scholarship. Each book carries the pilgrim logo, the character in 'Everyman', a medieval mystery play, a proud link between Everyman past and present.

William Shakespeare

JULIUS CAESAR

Edited by
JOHN F. ANDREWS

Foreword by
SIR JOHN GIELGUD

EVERYMAN
J. M. DENT · LONDON
CHARLES E. TUTTLE
VERMONT

First published in Everyman by J. M. Dent 1993
Published by permission of GuildAmerica Books, an imprint of Doubleday Book and Music Clubs, Inc.

Photoset by Deltatype Ltd, Ellesmere Port, Cheshire
Printed in Great Britain by
The Guernsey Press Co. Ltd, Guernsey, C.I.
for
J. M. Dent
Orion Publishing Group
Orion House
5 Upper St Martin's Lane
London WC2H 9EA
and
Charles E. Tuttle Co.
28 South Main Street
Rutland, Vermont
05701 – USA

British Library Cataloguing-in-Publication-Data is available upon request

ISBN 0 460 87396 2

CONTENTS

NOTE ON AUTHOR AND EDITOR

William Shakespeare is held to have been born on St George's Day, 23 April 1564. The eldest son of a prosperous glove-maker in Stratford-upon-Avon, he was probably educated at the town's grammar school.

Tradition holds that between 1585 and 1592, Shakespeare first became a schoolteacher and then set off for London. By 1595 he was a leading member of the Lord Chamberlain's Men, helping to direct their business affairs, as well as being a playwright and actor. In 1598 he became a part-owner of the company, which was the most distinguished of its age. However, he maintained his contacts with Stratford, and his family seem to have remained there.

From about 1610 he seems to have grown increasingly involved in the town's affairs, suggesting a withdrawal from London. He died on 23 April 1616, in his 53rd year, and was buried at Holy Trinity Church on the 25th.

John F. Andrews has recently completed a 19-volume edition, *The Guild Shakespeare*, for the Doubleday Book and Music Clubs. He is also the editor of a 3-volume reference set, *William Shakespeare: His World, His Work, His Influence*, and the former editor (1974–85) of the journal *Shakespeare Quarterly*. From 1974 to 1984, he was director of Academic Programs at the Folger Shakespeare Library in Washington and Chairman of the Folger Institute.

CHRONOLOGY OF SHAKESPEARE'S LIFE

Year[1]	*Age*	*Life*
1564		Shakespeare baptized 26 April at Stratford-upon-Avon
1582	18	Marries Anne Hathaway
1583	19	Daughter, Susanna, born
1585	21	Twin son and daughter, Hamnet and Judith, born
1590–1	26	*The Two Gentlemen of Verona* & *The Taming of the Shrew*
1591	27	2 & 3 *Henry VI*
1592	28	*Titus Andronicus* & 1 *Henry VI*
1592–3		*Richard III*
1593	29	*Venus and Adonis* published
1594	30	*The Comedy of Errors*. *The Rape of Lucrece* published
1594–5		*Love's Labour's Lost*
1595	31	*A Midsummer Night's Dream*, *Romeo and Juliet*, & *Richard II*. An established member of Lord Chamberlain's Men
1596	32	*King John*. Hamnet dies
1596–7		*The Merchant of Venice* & 1 *Henry IV*
1597	33	Buys New Place in Stratford
		The Lord Chamberlain's Men's lease to play at the Theatre expires; until 1599 they play mainly at the Curtain

1 It is rarely possible to be certain about the dates at which plays of this period were written. For Shakespeare's plays, this chronology follows the dates preferred by Stanley Wells and Gary Taylor, the editors of the Oxford Shakespeare. Publication dates are given for poetry and books.

CHRONOLOGY OF HIS TIMES

Year	*Literary Context*	*Historical Events*
1565–7	Golding, Ovid's *Metamorphoses*, tr.	Elizabeth I reigning
1574	*A Mirror for Magistrates* (3rd ed.)	
1576	London's first playhouse built	
1578	John Lyly, *Euphues*	
1579	North, Plutarch's *Lives*, tr. Spenser, *Shepherd's Calender*	
1587	Marlowe, *I Tamburlaine*	Mary Queen of Scots executed
1588	Holinshed's *Chronicles* (2nd ed.)	Defeat of Spanish Armada
1589	Kyd, *Spanish Tragedy* Marlowe, *Jew of Malta*	Civil war in France
1590	Spenser, *Faerie Queene*, Bks I–III	
1591	Sidney, *Astrophel and Stella*	Proclamation against Jesuits
1592	Marlowe, *Dr Faustus* & *Edward II*	Scottish witchcraft trials Plague closes theatres from June
1593	Marlowe killed	
1594	Nashe, *Unfortunate Traveller*	Theatres reopen in summer
1594–6		Extreme food shortages
1595	Sidney, *An Apologie for Poetry*	Riots in London
1596		Calais captured by Spanish Cadiz expedition
1597	Bacon, *Essays*	

Year	*Age*	*Life*
1597–8		*The Merry Wives of Windsor* & *2 Henry IV*
1598	34	*Much Ado About Nothing*
1598–9		*Henry V*
1599	35	*Julius Caesar*. One of syndicate responsible for building the Globe in Southwark, where the Lord Chamberlain's Men now play
1599–1600		*As You Like It*
1600–1		*Hamlet*
1601	37	*Twelfth Night*. His father is buried in Stratford
1602	38	*Troilus and Cressida*. Invests £320 in land near Stratford[2]
1603	39	*Measure for Measure*. The Lord Chamberlain's Men become the King's Men. They play at court more than all the other companies combined
1603–4		*Othello*
c.1604	40	Shakespeare sues Philip Rogers of Stratford for debt
1604–5		*All's Well That Ends Well*
1605	41	*Timon of Athens*. Invests £440 in Stratford tithes
1605–6		*King Lear*
1606	42	*Macbeth* & *Antony and Cleopatra*
1607	43	*Pericles*. Susanna marries the physician John Hall in Stratford
1608	44	*Coriolanus*. The King's Men lease Blackfriars, an indoor theatre. His only grandchild is born. His mother dies
1609	45	*The Winter's Tale*. 'Sonnets' and 'A Lover's Complaint' published
1610	46	*Cymbeline*
1611	47	*The Tempest*
1613	49	*Henry VIII*. Buys house in London for £140
1613–14		*The Two Noble Kinsmen*
1616	52	Judith marries Thomas Quiney, a vintner, in Stratford. On 23 April he dies, and is buried two days later
1623		Publication of the First Folio. His widow dies in August

2 A schoolmaster would earn around £20 a year at this time.

Year	*Literary Context*	*Historical Events*
1598	Marlowe and Chapman, *Hero and Leander*	Rebellion in Ireland
	Jonson, *Every Man in his Humour*	
1599	Children's companies begin playing	Essex fails in Ireland
	Thomas Dekker's *Shoemaker's Holiday*	
1601	'War of the Theatres'	Essex rebels and is executed
	Jonson, *Poetaster*	
1602		Tyrone defeated in Ireland
1603	Florio, Montaigne's *Essays*, tr.	Elizabeth I dies, James I accedes
		Raleigh found guilty of treason
1604	Marston, *The Malcontent*	Peace with Spain
1605	Bacon, *Advancement of Learning*	Gunpowder plot
1606	Jonson, *Volpone*	
1607	Tourneur, *The Revenger's Tragedy*, published	Virginia colonized
		Enclosure riots
1609		Oath of allegiance
		Truce in Netherlands
1610	Jonson, *Alchemist*	
1611	Authorised Version of the Bible	
	Donne, *Anatomy of the World*	
1612	Webster, *White Devil*	Prince Henry dies
1613	Webster, *Duchess of Malfi*	Princess Elizabeth marries
1614	Jonson, *Bartholomew Fair*	
1616	Folio edition of Jonson's plays	

Biographical note, chronology and plot summary compiled by John Lee, University of Bristol, 1993.

FOREWORD TO JULIUS CAESAR

One of the first serious problems one faces in planning a production of *Julius Caesar* is the question of the Roman mob. How many players can be afforded, and how much time allotted to manipulate them, not only in the Forum Scene, but also at the opening of the play, the murder scene, and the episode of the lynching of Cinna the Poet?

Brutus is evidently the protagonist of the play, but it is very difficult for even the most skilful actor to prevent him from being outshone by the players of Mark Antony and Cassius. Though he has many great scenes and speeches (some of them foreshadowing Hamlet and Macbeth) and, on paper, dominates the action, he is entirely without humour and may easily seem dull and priggish.

Antony has brilliant youthfulness and vitality; Cassius, a feverish, spiteful urgency. The text gives wonderful opportunities for contrasting orchestration in the acting and speaking of these three superb characters.

Casca, with his one fine scene in prose after the Games, is certainly the best of the minor parts, and his opportunity for comedy is something of a relief after the sonorous stretches of verse in which most of the play is written.

Caesar himself is merely an imposing figurehead, with few opportunities for the actor (as I know myself from having attempted the part several times on both stage and screen), except for his short scene with Calphurnia. His appearance as the ghost in the tent scene is strikingly effective, but his speeches in the Senate-house, just before the murder, are trite and pompous, as Shakespeare seems to have intended.

Portia is, of course, extremely sympathetic, but has only two short scenes to arouse our interest. I always feel that more could be made of the boy Lucius, who has evidently been a surrogate son to the childless couple. His presence in the tent scene when he falls asleep over his instrument as he is singing, and reminding us of Portia just when Brutus alludes so movingly to her death, should be one of the most touching episodes in the whole play.

In 1952 I played the part of Cassius in the Hollywood film of *Julius Caesar*, and Marlon Brando made a striking success of Mark Antony in his only appearance in a classical role. I still think that this production was one of the best renderings ever given of the play. The film, produced by John Houseman and directed by Joseph L. Mankiewicz, still holds up with considerable effect after all these years, and succeeds when so many stage productions (including several in which I have acted myself) have failed.

It is a great pity, however, that in the battle scenes of the film, the last two acts were carelessly strung together on the cheap, for these scenes particularly should have benefited by the more ample expanses of the screen. But the later scenes are, in any case, apt to be something of an anticlimax once the tent scene is over, and the death scenes, first of Cassius, then of Brutus, fail in their writing to compare with the magnificent poetry so vividly achieved in the first three acts, while Antony must make do with a few conventional speeches to finish off the play.

In America, the Mercury Theatre's 1937 production of the play by Orson Welles is still remembered and spoken of as having been sensationally successful, but Welles' ingenious innovation of dressing the characters as Mussolini Blackshirts, which seemed brilliantly appropriate at that particular time, has encouraged fatal mistakes in more recent stage productions. It is most important, of course, that the characters should appear in civilian costumes during the first three acts of the play, and the plotting and carrying out of the murder can only make its proper impact if one is made to feel the lurking secrecy of a swarming city, rife with dangerous intrigue in high places, and threatened by a lawless mob.

Actors are traditionally wary of wearing togas, but, if worn with ease and confidence, they should seem becoming and graceful and indeed easier to wear than the constricting armour, kilted tunics, and helmets which the actors must appear in for the battle scenes. It has been suggested that the tragedy be staged in Elizabethan costume, and there is a possible excuse for this idea in some of the anachronisms in the text. But ruffs and trunk hose would hardly, I believe, be very successful, and these costumes are equally difficult for actors to wear.

I saw the play for the first time when I was only twelve years old. My recollection of the event has always reminded me of one of my most cherished memories.

The play was performed in 1916 at the Drury Lane Theatre for a single performance only – to celebrate Shakespeare's Tercentenary – and was acted by a large and distinguished cast consisting of all the leading players then in London. The part of Cassius was superbly acted by H. B. Irving, the eldest son of the late Sir Henry. His eminent father had always dismissed the possibility of staging the play, because he thought it impossible to decide which of the three principal parts he should, as actor-manager, choose for himself.

Once, I believe in America, the Booth brothers appeared in it together. Sir Herbert Beerbohm Tree, who succeeded to leadership of the profession after Irving's death, staged an elaborate spectacle, with a large crowd and handsome pictorial scenery by Alma-Tadema, a greatly admired Royal Academician of the period. This production had three fine actors in the three great parts, though Tree himself was not greatly praised for his Mark Antony, and his casting of Lady Tree as the boy Lucius cannot have been a very wise or happy choice. Tree's scenery, which must have been stored in the intervening years, was used again at the Drury Lane matinée, and of course I thought it very grand and effective. But, apart from the acting of Cassius, I also admired greatly an electrifying performance of Mark Antony by the young Henry Ainley. His subsequent playing of the same part in a production of his own at the St James's Theatre, some four years later, seemed to me far less striking.

Above all I remember the tremendous effect of the crowd scenes. In the souvenir programme, which I still possess, I find that these scenes were directed by Harley Granville-Barker, whom I came to admire so greatly when I became an actor. The few rehearsals I had under his direction, and a number of letters he wrote me at various times, are among my most precious reminders of his genius.

But, alas, the intervention of the 1914–18 War, and his second marriage to a lady who beguiled him away from the theatre, robbed a whole generation of a superb master of the stage. His preface on *Julius Caesar* is typically sensitive and I have always found it an inspiration when studying the play.

Sir John Gielgud

SIR JOHN GIELGUD's first stage appearance was playing the role of the Herald in *Henry V*. He has since appeared in such diverse Shakespearean roles as Hamlet, Shylock, Antony, King Lear, Prospero, Julius Caesar, and Richard II, and directed productions of *Hamlet*, *Romeo and Juliet*, *The Merchant of Venice*, and *Twelfth Night*, among many others.

EDITOR'S INTRODUCTION TO JULIUS CAESAR

Shakespeare probably wrote *Julius Caesar* in 1599, shortly after he produced *Henry V*, the ninth of his ten 'chronicle histories' about the dynastic struggles in late medieval England, and shortly before he completed *Hamlet*, the first of what commentators now refer to as the four 'great tragedies'. He probably wrote *Antony and Cleopatra*, the thematic sequel to *Julius Caesar*, in late 1606 or early 1607, shortly after he finished *Othello*, *King Lear*, and *Macbeth*, the other pillars of his 'big four', and shortly before he began directing most of his attention to the tragicomic romances with which he would gather his labours to a close between 1608 and 1613.

Approached in terms of their position in Shakespeare's career, *Julius Caesar* and *Antony and Cleopatra* bracket the artistic period for which he is most widely celebrated today. The earlier of the 'Roman plays' is sometimes described as the drama that charts Shakespeare's ascent to his creative summit; the later one is frequently discussed as the work that signals his transition from a preoccupation with tragedy to a new exploration of what might be called 'divine comedy', a transfiguring theatrical form that permitted the playwright to examine those values that enable human beings to surmount their trials and seek fulfilment in a sphere beyond the vicissitudes of earthly Fortune. Whereas *Julius Caesar* can be seen as an outgrowth of the English history plays, transposing to a more remote classical setting the same problems that Shakespeare had been pondering in dramas like *Richard II* and the two segments of *Henry IV*, *Antony and Cleopatra* can be viewed as a foreshadowing of the emphasis on reunion, reconciliation, and renewal in 'late plays' like *Pericles*, *Cymbeline*, *The Winter's Tale*, and *The Tempest*.

Stylistically, *Julius Caesar* and *Antony and Cleopatra* seem galaxies apart. The earlier work strikes us as clear, focused, and straightforward; it is one of the shortest of Shakespeare's plays, and the elegance of its elocution has carved many of its phrases into our collective memory. The later tragedy, by contrast, is elusive, panoramic, and convoluted; it is one of the longest of Shakespeare's dramas, and its figurative language is at times so extravagant and multifaceted that different interpreters can emerge with quite disparate readings of its more complex passages. *Julius Caesar* impresses us as the achievement of an assured playwright who is just beginning to attain his full scope as a thinker and as a writer of tragedy; *Antony and Cleopatra* impresses us as the effort of a more mature dramatist who has scaled the heights in tragedy several times over and is now beginning to experiment with increasingly innovative techniques in his ongoing quest for loftier realms to survey.

For all their differences, however, *Julius Caesar* and *Antony and Cleopatra* have a great deal in common. They both derive from the same narrative source, Sir Thomas North's 1579 English translation of Plutarch's *Lives of the Noble Grecians and Romans*. They both address philosophical and political questions that would have engaged the interest of Shakespeare's English contemporaries. And they both concern themselves with one of the major themes of Renaissance culture: the significance and continued pertinence of Europe's Graeco-Roman heritage.

Like many of his fellow writers and intellectuals, Shakespeare was deeply curious about the meaning of the classical past, and he seems to have conceived of *Julius Caesar* and *Antony and Cleopatra* as the centrepieces of a four-part theatrical meditation on 'the matter of Rome'. He had begun his exploration of antiquity in the early 1590s with *Titus Andronicus*, a melodrama about a mythical general in the fourth century AD whose torments Shakespeare depicted as an adumbration of the collapse of Roman civilization. Yet to come in his dramatic corpus, probably in 1607 or 1608, was *Coriolanus*, a tragedy about another legendary warrior, whose agonizing strife in the fifth century BC was a precondition to the flowering of a nascent Republic. In between lay *Julius Caesar* and *Antony and Cleopatra*, the first a chronicle of the dissolution of republican institutions through the rise and fall of Rome's most famous conqueror, the second a drama about the consolidation of empire through the decline and demise of Mark Antony and the ascendancy of Julius Caesar's nephew and adopted son, Octavius.

Just how Shakespeare construed the critical period he anatomized in *Julius Caesar* (44–42 BC) and *Antony and Cleopatra* (40–30 BC) remains debatable, but we can be sure that he was aware of many different ways of looking at it. He would have known, for example, that to Roman writers such as Cato, Lucan, and Cicero, who brought a republican perspective to the events that led to the Ides of March in 44 BC, Julius Caesar was a despot whose disregard of civil liberties had made his assassination imperative. He would also have known that a number of Renaissance thinkers, among them Sir Philip Sidney and Ben Jonson, shared his anti-authoritarian attitude towards the military genius who'd crossed the Rubicon and ensconced himself in the Capitol as a dictator.

Meanwhile, Shakespeare would probably have been even more acutely aware that the writer on whom he drew as his principal source, Plutarch of Charonea (AD 46–120), a Greek historian who had lived in Rome during the most decadent years of the Empire, portrayed Caesar as a *de facto* monarch who had brought a season of respite to a society ravaged by more than a century of civil war. According to Plutarch, Caesar was an exemplary leader who wielded power justly and responsibly and whose one fault, a vanity that made him wish to be crowned king, was a small price to pay for the oversight he provided for a body politic in desperate need of a head. Plutarch's view of the topic was the one favoured by imperial historians such as Livy and Suetonius and by medieval writers such as Chaucer and Dante (who had placed Brutus and Cassius in the same circle as the treacherous Judas in the bleakest depths of his *Inferno*), and Shakespeare would have also found it reflected, implicitly if not explicitly, in many of the official proclamations of a Tudor establishment committed to the maintenance of social and political order in the England of his own day. Through exhortations such as the 'Homily against Disobedience and Wilfull Rebellion', Elizabethans were regularly warned that monarchy was the only form of government that could ensure domestic tranquillity. What the Apostle Paul referred to as 'the powers that be' were to be revered as ministers 'ordained of God' (Romans 13:1) to shield their people from all the perils of internecine conflict. To rebel against the existing hierarchy was to risk a return to the kind of anarchy that had ripped England asunder during the fifteenth-century Wars of the Roses, whose horrors Shakespeare had himself depicted in three English history plays on the troubled reign of Henry VI and a fourth play on the bloody tyranny of Richard III.

In addition to what he found in sources that would have informed his thinking about the political issues involved in 'the matter of Rome', Shakespeare would also have known a broad range of other writings that addressed the subject in ethical or theological terms. He would have been familiar with the critique of Roman Stoicism in Book XIV of St Augustine's *City of God* (AD 426), where the adherents of Rome's most influential school of philosophy are described as so prone to 'ungodly pride' that they are virtually indistinguishable from the self-righteous Pharisees of the Gospels. And he would have been aware of similar observations in Montaigne's *Essays* (1580, 1588) and in Erasmus' *In Praise of Folly* (1509), where the typical Stoic is derided as 'a stony semblance of a man, void of all sense and common feeling of humanity, . . . a man dead to all sense of nature and common affections, and no more moved with love or pity than if he were a flint or rock; whose censure nothing escapes; that commits no errors himself, but has a lynx's eye upon others; measures everything by an exact line, and forgives nothing; pleases himself with himself only; the only rich, the only wise, the only free man.'

Meanwhile Shakespeare would also have known the traditional Christian doctrine that the Pax Romana, the 'Universal Peace' that had been ushered in by Caesar Augustus (as we are reminded in a passage about Octavius Caesar in IV.v.3 of *Antony and*

Cleopatra), was an epoch providentially arranged to afford a suitable setting for the advent of another 'Prince of Peace'. What this meant, in the language of the title-page to a 1578 English edition of Appian's *Civil Wars*, was that the 'action' represented in *Julius Caesar* and *Antony and Cleopatra* could be discerned in golden hindsight as a 'prophane Tragedie, whereof flowed our diuine Comoedie'. In other words, a sequence of events that meant one thing to a pre-Christian Roman such as Brutus, Antony, or Octavius could have a radically different significance to a later era accustomed to explaining all of human history in the light of a divine plan in which even God's enemies were constrained to play a role in fulfilling his designs.

There are in fact biblical echoes in both plays that hint at the cosmic irony this Christian vantage on pagan Antiquity would seem to imply. And it may well be that that angle of vision accounts in part for the phenomenon Tony Randall remarks upon in his delightful and thought-provoking foreword to the Everyman edition of *Antony and Cleopatra*. For if in some fundamental sense even 'the Noblest Roman of them all' is limited by the mere fact that he *is* what Hamlet's friend Horatio calls 'an antique Roman', there may be sound reasons for an audience's sense that plays like *Julius Caesar* and *Antony and Cleopatra* provide us, in Randall's words, with no one 'to root for'.

In both tragedies we find ourselves in the presence of grandiose figures whose behaviour distresses us. In *Julius Caesar*, for example, we concentrate much of our attention on Brutus, a man who seems to be unanimously applauded for his virtues, and a man whose lineage can be traced to an ancestor (the legendary Lucius Junius Brutus) who expelled kingship from Rome and founded the Republic in 509 BC. At a time when survival of the kind of representative government initiated by his forebear appears to be in grave jeopardy, Marcus Junius Brutus is naturally the statesman to whom his concerned compatriots turn for another deliverance. We see him deliberate over his decision to join a conspiracy that goes against his better nature. We observe the scrupulous distinctions he insists upon in his desire to sanctify a deed that must inevitably appear brutal. We admire the integrity with which he essays to keep his cause pure: free of self-serving motives, free of unnecessary bloodshed, free of demagoguery, free of corruption. We respond to the solicitude he shows his pageboy Lucius. And we note the devotion he inspires in his comrades and in his courageous wife Portia. At the same time, however, we cannot help noticing that this Brutus is a man who often comes across as lacking in feeling, a man who must always have his own way even though he invariably turns out to be wrong, and a man who seems incapable of imagining that he is susceptible to error. What we find, in short, is a character whose high-minded 'constancy' seems remarkably similar to that of the would-be king whose arrogance blinds him to the fact that, for all the authority he wields, he is 'but a Man'.

Because we keep hearing about Brutus' moral and political stature, we tend to assume that in some fundamental sense he really must be the paragon that Mark Antony eulogizes at the end of the play. If, however, we find it difficult to square our perceptions of Brutus with the praise that even his erstwhile enemies bestow upon him, before we conclude that the fault is in ourselves we should consider the possibility that Shakespeare *wants* us to feel puzzled, uneasy, and dismayed – that a crucial element of his strategy as a dramatist, indeed, is to make his audience uncomfortable with discrepancies between what a character like Brutus says about himself or has said about him, and what his thoughts and actions reveal him to be in actuality.

The kind of disappointment we are likely to feel about Brutus, and in different ways about Shakespeare's other Romans, is the discontent that issues, quite literally, from disillusionment – from our discovery that a character we want to 'root for', a person who seems to be endowed with almost superhuman talents, is fatally deficient in some quality that is essential to his or her full realization of that vast potential. In Shakespearean tragedy, the defect that vitiates a protagonist's gifts is usually a lapse in self-knowledge (which results in impaired judgement) or a lapse in self-control (which results in perverted will-power) or both.

Frequently a failure of reason causes or is accompanied by a breakdown of will; just as frequently a failure of will (such as a habitual surrender to the vices of the flesh) either leads to or is associated with a breakdown of reason. In either case, the key to a play's effect – to the fulfilment of its 'purpose', as Hamlet would put it – lies in the audience's ability to respond intelligently and sensitively to all the clues Shakespeare provides about his characters, and on that basis to perceive any flaws or follies in even the most elevated and attractive of them.

The personalities we encounter in *Julius Caesar* and *Antony and Cleopatra* occupy a setting and live in a time that has a great deal to do with who they are, how they think of themselves, and what they do. As they note on numerous occasions, the stage they march across is pregnant with consequence, and what is at stake upon it is not just Rome, and not just the Roman Empire; it is nothing less than what one of Caesar's near-contemporaries would later refer to as 'the whole world' (Matthew 16:26).

As Brutus observes in one of many such images in the Roman plays, 'There is a Tide in the affairs of Men' (*Julius Caesar*, IV.iii.220), and the person who can crest it to victory will enjoy all the benefits of 'Fortune'. Brutus thinks it possible to master that 'Tide', but events prove Cassius to be a better judge of its ebb and flow. Later, prompted by Cleopatra, Mark Antony trusts his fortunes to the tide in a less figurative sense; because of his dependence on his Siren-like Queen, however, he too founders. In the meantime, like Pompey the Great, who had been overthrown by Julius Caesar, a younger Pompey falls victim to an even wilier Caesar. And as might have been predicted, the ineffectual Lepidus never regains his land legs after the poor, drunken 'Third part o' the World' is carried ashore from Pompey's galley in II.vii of *Antony and Cleopatra*. What prevails, then, is 'the Spirit of Caesar' (*Julius Caesar*, II.i.165), a ghostly presence that hovers over the last half of the play that bears his name, and one that then becomes embodied anew in the Octavius who methodically dispatches his rivals in *Antony and Cleopatra*.

As she weighs the meagre options that remain to her after the defeat and death of her partner, Cleopatra observes that ''Tis paltry to be Caesar: / Not being Fortune, he's but Fortune's Knave' (V.ii.2–3). In these words we hear the self-consoling rationalizations of a loser – here a Circean temptress whose baleful influence on a potential Aeneas has 'unqualited' Antony (III.xi.43) and made him defenceless against the 'Fullest Man' (III.xiii.85) of the age. But what we should also recognize in Cleopatra's comment is something that would have been even more apparent to the audiences for whom Shakespeare wrote his Roman plays: the fact that the same tide that is now at the flood will eventually recede, taking with it both Caesar and the Empire that he and his contemporaries have so painstakingly assembled out of the 'Clay' (I.i.35) from which mortal kingdoms are moulded.

The Caesar who arrives to consummate his victory at the end of *Antony and Cleopatra* is almost as puffed up with 'Glory' (V.ii.359) as the earlier Caesar who compared himself to 'Olympus' (*Julius Caesar*, III.ii.75) at what he mistakenly believed to be the apogee of his supremacy. There is no suggestion that Octavius' stay at the top will be as short-lived as that of his predecessor. But in subtle, wry ways Shakespeare makes it clear that even so august an Emperor as the second Caesar has now become is neither omniscient nor omnipotent.

Whether the 'Immortal Longings' that have concluded Cleopatra's part in the pageant a few moments earlier in *Antony and Cleopatra* (V.ii.279) will yield her an eternity in the embrace of the paramour she calls 'the Crown o' th' Earth' (IV.xv.63) is anything but certain. And whether her suicide, any more than those of Cassius, Brutus, and Antony, would have impressed Shakespeare's original audiences as a triumph over Fortune and its 'vile Conquest' (*Julius Caesar*, V.v.38) is equally problematic. But of one thing there can be no doubt: the 'Greatness' of Cleopatra's grandiloquent exit has assured her of a theatrical immortality that can only be described as transcendent. Like the poetry she speaks and the rapture she evokes in those she charms, it alone is sufficient to assure that audiences and readers, if not Fortune, will ever award the palm to Egypt rather than to Rome.

Julius Caesar has none of the verbal pyrotechnics that set *Antony and Cleopatra* apart from the other Roman plays. But it has enjoyed a life in performance and in the classroom that is more than equal to that of the later play. Cinema-lovers continue to laud the stunning 1952 film in which Sir John Gielgud played Cassius to James Mason's Brutus and Marlon Brando's Mark Antony. And as Sir John notes in his informative foreword to this volume of *The Everyman Shakespeare*, *Julius Caesar* was once performed by the Booth brothers in a production that precipitated a turning point in the history of the United States.

The occasion was a benefit to raise funds for the Shakespeare statue that had been commissioned for New York's Central Park on the three-hundreth anniversary of the playwright's birth, and the one-night event took place in the Winter Garden Theatre on 25 November 1864. By this point Edwin Booth had already won acclaim as the foremost New World actor of his generation, and he took the role of Brutus. His older brother, Junius Brutus, named for their imposing father, a tragedian who had been a rival to Edmund Kean before he emigrated from England in 1821, played Cassius. Meanwhile his younger brother, John Wilkes, named after a radical eighteenth-century Lord Mayor of London whose support for the secessionist rebels on the far side of the Atlantic had made him a hero to America's founding fathers, gave a memorable performance as Mark Antony. Though the youngest Booth was cast in what would turn out to be the wrong part for him, he may well have known even then, less than five months before the gloomy Good Friday at Ford's Theatre in Washington when he shot a President he accused of monarchial ambitions and then leapt to the stage with the shout 'Sic Semper Tyrannis', that he was in the right play. And with what keen alertness he must have listened as he heard a latter-day Junius Brutus, playing Cassius, say

> How many Ages hence
> Shall this our lofty Scene be acted over
> In States unborne and Accents yet unknown?

John F. Andrews, 1993

[illegible]

[illegible]

[illegible]

THE TEXT OF THE EVERYMAN SHAKESPEARE

Background

THE EARLY PRINTINGS OF SHAKESPEARE'S WORKS

Many of us enjoy our first encounter with Shakespeare when we are introduced to *Julius Caesar* or *Macbeth* at school. It may therefore surprise us that neither of these tragedies could have been read, let alone studied, by most of the playwright's contemporaries. Along with seventeen other titles that never saw print during Shakespeare's lifetime, they made their inaugural appearance as 'literary' works seven years after his death, in the 1623 collection we know today as the First Folio.

The Folio contained thirty-six titles in all. Of these, half had been issued previously in the small paperbacks we now refer to as quartos.* Like several of the plays first published in the Folio, the most trustworthy of the quarto printings appear to have been set either from the dramatist's own manuscripts or from faithful copies of them. It's not impossible that the poet himself prepared some of them for the press, and it's intriguing to imagine him reviewing proof-pages as the words he'd written for actors to speak and embody were being transposed into the type that readers would filter through their eyes, minds, and imaginations. But, alas, there's no indisputable evidence that Shakespeare had any direct involvement with the publication of these early texts of his plays.

What about the plays that appeared in print for the first time in the Folio? Had Shakespeare taken any steps to give them the

* Quartos derived their name from the four-leaf units of which these small books were comprised: large sheets of paper that had been folded twice after printing to yield four leaves, or eight pages. Folios, volumes with twice the page-size of quartos, were put together from two-leaf units: sheets that had been folded once after printing to yield four pages.

permanency of book form before he died in 1616? We don't know. All we can say is that when he became fatally ill in 1616, Shakespeare was denied any opportunities he might have taken to ensure that his 'insubstantial Pageants' survived their creator, who was now slipping into the 'dark Backward and Abysm of Time'.

Fortunately, two of the playwright's collegues felt an obligation, as they put it, 'to procure his Orphans Guardians'. Sometime after Shakespeare's death John Heminge and Henry Condell made arrangements to preserve his plays in a manner that would keep them vibrant for posterity. They dedicated their endeavour to two noblemen who had helped England's foremost acting company through some of its most trying vicissitudes. They solicited several poetic tributes for the volume, among them a now-famous eulogy by fellow writer Ben Jonson. They commissioned a portrait of Shakespeare to adorn the frontispiece. And they did their utmost to display the author's dramatic works in a style that would both dignify them and and make them accessible to 'the great Variety of Readers'.

As they prepared Shakespeare's plays for the compositors who would set them in stately Folio columns, Heminge and Condell (or editors designated to carry out their wishes) revised and augmented many of the entrances, exits, and other stage directions in the manuscripts. They divided most of the plays into acts and scenes.* For a number of plays they appended 'Names of the Actors', or cast of characters. Meanwhile they made every effort to ensure that the Folio printers had reliable copy-texts for each of the titles: authoritative manuscripts for the plays that had not been published previously, and good quarto printings (annotated in some instances to insert staging details, mark script changes, and add supplementary material) for those issued prior to the Folio. For several titles they supplied texts that were substantively different from, if not always demonstrably superior to, the quarto versions that preceded them.

* The early quartos, reflecting the unbroken sequence that probably typified Elizabethan and Jacobean performances of the plays, had been printed without the structural demarcations usual in Renaissance editions of classical drama.

Like even the most accurate of the earlier printings, the Folio collection was flawed by minor blemishes. But it more than fulfilled the purpose of its generous-minded compilers: 'to keep the memory of so worthy a Friend and Fellow alive as was our Shakespeare'. In the process it provided a publishing model that remains instructive today.

MODERN EDITIONS OF THE PLAYS AND POEMS

When we compare the First Folio and its predecessors with the usual modern editions of Shakespeare's works, we're more apt to be impressed by the differences than by the similarities. Today's texts of Renaissance drama are normally produced in conformity with twentieth-century standards of punctuation and usage; as a consequence they look more neat, clean, and, to our eyes, 'right' than do the original printings. Thanks to an editorial tradition that extends back to the early eighteenth century, most of the rough spots in the early printings of Shakespeare have long since been smoothed away. Textual scholars have ferreted out redundancies and eradicated inconsistencies. They have emended what they've perceived to be errors and oversights in the author's playscripts, and they have systematically attended to what they've construed as misreadings by the copyists and compositors who transmitted those playscripts to posterity. They've added '[Within]' brackets and other theatrical notations. They've revised stage directions they've judged incomplete or inadequate in the initial printings. They've regularized disparities in the speech headings. They've gone back to the playwright's sources and reinstated the proper forms for many of the character and place names a presumably hasty or inattentive author got 'wrong' as he conferred identities on his dramatis personae and stage locales. They've replaced obsolete words like *bankrout* with their modern heirs (in this case *bankrupt*). And in a multitude of other ways they've accommodated Shakespeare to the tastes, interests, and expectations of latter-day readers.

The results, on the whole, have been splendid. But interpreting the artistic designs of a complex writer is always problematical, and the task is especially challenging when that writer happens to have been a poet who felt unconstrained by many of the 'rules' that more conventional dramatists respected. The undertaking becomes further complicated when new rules, and new criteria of linguistic and social correctness, are imposed by subsequent generations of artists and critics.

To some degree in his own era, but even more in the neoclassical period (1660–1800) that came in its wake, Shakespeare's most ardent admirers thought it necessary to apologize for what Ben Jonson hinted at in his allusion to the 'small Latin, and less Greek' of an untutored prodigy. To be sure, the 'sweet Swan of Avon' sustained his popularity; in fact his esteem rose so steadily that by the end of the eighteenth century he'd eclipsed Jonson and his other coevals and become the object of universal Bardolatry. But in the theatre most of his plays were being adapted in ways that were deemed advisable to tame their supposed wildness and bring them into conformity with the taste of a society that took pride in its refinement. As one might expect, some of the attitudes that induced theatre proprietors to metamorphose an unpolished poet from the provinces into something closer to an urbane man of letters also influenced Shakespeare's editors. Persuaded that the dramatist's works were marred by crudities that needed expunging, they applied their ministrations to the canon with painstaking diligence.

Twentieth-century editors have moved away from many of the presuppositions that guided a succession of earlier improvers. But a glance at the textual apparatus accompanying virtually any modern edition of the plays and poems will show that emendations and editorial procedures deriving from such forebears as the sets published by Nicholas Rowe (1709), Alexander Pope (1723–25, 1728), Lewis Theobald (1733, 1740, 1757), Thomas Hanmer (1743–45, 1770–71), Samuel Johnson (1765), Edward Capell (1768), George Steevens (1773) retain a strong hold on today's renderings. The result is a 'Shakespeare' who offers the tidiness we've come to expect in our libraries of classical authors, but not necessarily the playwright a 1599 reader of the Second Quarto of *Romeo and Juliet* would recognize as a contemporary.

OLD LIGHT ON THE TOPIC

Over the last two decades we've learned from art curators that paintings by old Masters such as Michelangelo and Rembrandt look much brighter when centuries of grime are removed from their surfaces – when hues dulled with soot and other extraneous matter are restored to their pristine luminosity. Conductors like Christopher Hogwood have shown the aesthetic rewards to be gained from a return to the scorings and instruments with which Renaissance and Baroque musical compositions were first presented. Twentieth-century experiments in the performance of Shakespeare's plays have shown that an open, multi-level stage analogous to that on which the scripts were originally enacted does more justice to their dramaturgical techniques than does a proscenium auditorium devised for works that came later in the development of Western theatre. And archaeological excavations in London's Bankside have revealed that the foundations of playhouses such as the Rose and the Globe look rather different from what many historians had expected. And we're now learning from a close scrutiny of Shakespeare's texts that they too look different, and function differently, when we accept them for what they are and resist the impulse to 'normalize' features that strike us initially as quirky, unkempt, or unsophisticated.

The Aims that Guide the Everyman Text

Like other modern editions of Shakespeare's plays and poems, The Everyman Shakespeare owes an incalculable debt to the scholarship that has led to so many excellent renderings of his works. But in an attempt to draw fresh inspiration from the spirit that animated those remarkable achievements at the outset, the Everyman edition departs in a number of respects from the usual post-Folio approach to the presentation of Shakespeare's texts.

RESTORING SOME OF THE NUANCES OF RENAISSANCE PUNCTUATION

In its punctuation Everyman tries to give equal emphasis to sound and sense. In places where Renaissance practice calls for heavier punctuation than we'd normally employ – to mark the caesural pause in the middle of a line of verse, for instance – Everyman sometimes retains commas that other modern editions omit. Meanwhile, in places where current practice usually calls for the inclusion of commas – after vocatives and interjections such as 'O' and 'alas', say, or before 'Madam' or 'Sir' in phrases such as 'Ay Madam' or 'Yes Sir' – Everyman follows the original printings and omits them.

Occasionally the absence of a comma has a significant bearing on what an expression means, or can mean. At one point in *Othello*, for example, Iago tells The Moor 'Marry patience' (IV.i.90). Inserting a comma after 'Marry', as most of today's editions do, limits Iago's utterance to one that says 'Come now, have patience.' Leaving the clause as it stands in the Folio, the way the Everyman text does, permits Iago's words to have the additional, agonizingly ironic sense 'Be wed to Patience'.

The early texts generally deploy exclamation points quite sparingly, and the Everyman text follows suit. Everyman also follows the early editions, more often than not, when they use question marks in places that seem unusual by current standards: at the ends of what we'd normally treat as exclamations, for example, or at the ends of interrogative clauses in sentences that we'd ordinarily denote as questions in their entirety.

The early texts make no orthographic distinction between simple plurals and either singular or plural possessives, and there are times when the context doesn't indicate whether a word spelled *Sisters*, say, should be rendered *Sisters*, *Sisters'*, or *Sister's* in today's usage. In such situations the Everyman edition prints the words in the form modern usage prescribes for plurals.

REVIVING SOME OF THE FLEXIBILITY OF RENAISSANCE SPELLING

Spelling had not become standardized by Shakespeare's time, which meant that many words could take a variety of forms. Like James Joyce and some of the other innovative prose and verse stylists of our own century, Shakespeare revelled in the freedom a largely unanchored language provided, and with that in mind Everyman retains original spelling forms (or adaptations of those forms that preserve their key distinctions from modern spellings) whenever there is any reason to suspect that they might have a bearing on how a word was intended to be pronounced or on what it meant, or could have meant, in Shakespeare's day. When there is any likelihood that multiple forms of the same word could be significant, moreover, the Everyman text mirrors the diversity to be found in the original printings.

In many cases this practice affects the personalities of Shakespeare's characters. One of the heroine's most familiar questions in *Romeo and Juliet* is 'What's in a Name?' For two and a half centuries readers – and as a consequence actors, directors, theatre audiences, and commentators – have been led to believe that Juliet was addressing this query to a Romeo named 'Montague'. In fact 'Montague' *was* the name Shakespeare found in his principal source for the play. For reasons that will become apparent to anyone who examines the tragedy in detail, however, he changed his protagonist's surname to 'Mountague', which plays on both 'mount' and 'ague' (fever). Setting aside an editorial practice that began with Lewis Theobald in the middle of the eighteenth century, Everyman resurrects the name Shakespeare himself gave Juliet's lover.

Readers of *The Merchant of Venice* in the Everyman edition will be amused to learn that the character modern editions usually identify as 'Lancelot' is in reality 'Launcelet', a name that calls attention to the clown's lusty 'little lance'. Like Costard in *Love's Labour's Lost*, another stage bumpkin who was probably played by the actor Will Kemp, Launcelet is an upright 'Member of the Commonwealth'; we eventually learn that he's left a pliant wench 'with Child'.

Readers of *Hamlet* will find that 'Fortinbras' (as the name of the Prince's Norwegian opposite is rendered in the First Folio and in most modern editions) appears in the earlier, authoritative 1604 Second Quarto of the play as 'Fortinbrasse'. In the opening scene of that text a surname that meant 'strong in arms' in French is introduced to the accompaniment of puns on *brazen*, in the phrase 'brazon Cannon', and on *metal*, in the phrase 'unimprooued mettle'. In the same play readers of the Everyman text will encounter 'Ostricke', the ostrich-like courtier who invites the Prince of Denmark to participate in the fateful fencing match that draws *Hamlet* to a close. Only in its final entrance direction for the obsequious fop does the Second Quarto call this character 'Osrick', the name he bears in all the Folio text's references to him and in most modern editions of Shakespeare's most popular tragedy.

Readers of the Everyman text of *Macbeth* will discover the fabled 'Weird Sisters' appear only as the 'weyward' or 'weyard' Sisters. Shakespeare and his contemporaries knew that in *Chronicles of England, Scotland, and Ireland* Raphael Holinshed had used the term 'weird sisters' to describe the witches who accost Macbeth and Banquo on the heath; but because he wished to play on *wayward*, the playwright changed their name to *weyward*. Like Samuel Johnson, who thought punning vulgar and lamented Shakespeare's proclivity to seduction by this 'fatal Cleopatra', Lewis Theobald saw no reason to retain the playwright's 'weyward' spelling of the witches' name. He thus restored the 'correct' form from Holinshed, and editors ever since have generally done likewise.

In many instances Renaissance English had a single spelling for what we now define as two separate words. For example, *humane* combined the senses of 'human' and 'humane' in modern English. In the First Folio printing of *Macbeth* the protagonist's wife expresses a concern that her husband is 'too full o'th' Milke of humane kindnesse'. As she phrases it, *humane kindnesse* can mean several things, among them 'humankind-ness', 'human kindness', and 'humane kindness'. It is thus a reminder that to be true to his or her own 'kind' a human being must be 'kind' in the sense we now attach to 'humane'. To disregard this logic, as the protagonist and his wife will soon prove, is to disregard a principle as basic to the cosmos as the laws of gravity.

In a way that parallels *humane*, *bad* could mean either 'bad' or 'bade', *borne* either 'born' or 'borne', *least* either 'least' or 'lest', *lye* either 'lie' or 'lye', *powre* either 'pour' or 'power', *then* either 'than' or 'then', and *tide* either 'tide' or 'tied'.

There were a number of word-forms that functioned in Renaissance English as interchangeable doublets. *Travail* could mean 'travel', for example, and *travel* could mean 'travail'. By the same token *deer* could mean *dear* and vice-versa, *dew* could mean *due*, *hart* could mean *heart*, and (as we've already noted) *mettle* could mean *metal*.

A particularly interesting instance of the equivocal or double meanings some word-forms had in Shakespeare's time is *loose*, which can often become either 'loose' or 'lose' when we render it in modern English. In *The Comedy of Errors* when Antipholus of Syracuse compares himself to 'a Drop / of Water that in the Ocean seeks another Drop' and then says he will 'loose' himself in quest of his long-lost twin, he means both (a) that he will release himself into a vast unknown, and (b) that he will lose his own identity, if necessary, to be reunited with the brother for whom he searches. On the other hand, in *Hamlet* when Polonius says he'll 'loose' his daughter to the Prince, he little suspects that by so doing he will also lose his daughter.

In some cases Shakespeare employs word-forms that can be translated into words we wouldn't think of as related today: *sowre*, for instance, which can mean 'sour', 'sower', or 'sore', depending on the context. In other cases he uses forms that do have modern counterparts, but not counterparts with the same potential for multiple connotation. For example, *onely* usually means 'only' in the modern sense; but occasionally Shakespeare gives it a figurative, adverbial twist that would require a nonce word such as 'one-ly' to replicate in current English.

In a few cases Shakespeare employs word-forms that have only seeming equivalents in modern usage. For example, *abhominable*, which meant 'inhuman' (derived however incorrectly, from *ab*, 'away from', and *homine*, 'man') to Shakespeare and his contemporaries, is not the same word as our *abominable* (ill-omened, abhorrent). In his advice to the visiting players Hamlet complains about incompetent actors who imitate 'Humanity so abhominably' as to make the characters they depict seem unrecognizable as men. Modern readers who don't realize the distinction between Shakespeare's word and our own, and who see *abominable* on the page before them, don't register the full import of the Prince's satire.

Modern English treats as single words a number of word-forms that were normally spelled as two words in Shakespeare's time. What we render as *myself*, for example, and use primarily as a reflexive or intensifying pronoun, is almost invariably spelled *my self* in Shakespeare's works; so also with *her self*, *thy self*, *your self*, and *it self* (where *it* functions in the way that *its* does today).

Often there is no discernible difference between Shakespeare's usage and our own. At other times there is, however, as we are reminded when we come across a phrase such as 'our innocent self' in *Macbeth* and think how strained it would sound in modern parlance, or when we note how naturally the self is objectified in the balanced clauses of the Balcony Scene in *Romeo and Juliet*:

> Romeo, doffe thy name,
> And for thy name, which is no part of thee,
> Take all my selfe.

Yet another manifestation of the differences between Renaissance orthography and our own can be exemplified with words such as *today*, *tonight* and *tomorrow*, which (unlike *yesterday*) were treated as two words in Shakespeare's time. In *Macbeth* when the Folio prints 'Duncan comes here to Night', the unattached *to* can function either as a preposition (with *Night* as its object, or in this case its destination) or as the first part of an infinitive (with *Night* operating figuratively as a verb). Consider the ambiguity a Renaissance reader would have detected in the original publication of one of the most celebrated soliloquies in all of Shakespeare:

> To morrow, and to morrow, and to morrow,
> Creeps in this petty pace from day to day,
> To the last syllable of Recorded time:
> And all our yesterdayes, have lighted Fooles
> The way to dusty death.

Here, by implication, the route 'to morrow' is identical with 'the way to dusty death', a relationship we miss if we don't know that for Macbeth, and for the audiences who first heard these lines spoken, *to morrow* was not a single word but a potentially equivocal two-word phrase.

RECAPTURING THE ABILITY TO HEAR WITH OUR EYES

When we fail to recall that Shakespeare's scripts were designed initially to provide words for people to hear in the theatre, we sometimes overlook a fact that is fundamental to the artistic structure of a work like *Macbeth*: that the messages a sequence of sounds convey through the ear are, if anything, even more significant than the messages a sequence of letters, punctuation marks, and white spaces on a printed page transmit through the eye. A telling illustration of this point, and of the potential for ambiguous or multiple implication in any Shakespearean script, may be found in the dethronement scene of *Richard II*. When Henry Bullingbrook asks the king if he is ready to resign his crown, Richard replies 'I, no no I; for I must nothing be.' Here the punctuation in the 1608 Fourth Quarto (the earliest text to print this richly complex passage) permits each *I* to signify either 'ay' or 'I' (*I* being the usual spelling for 'ay' in Shakespeare's time). Understanding *I* to mean 'I' permits additional play on *no*, which can be heard (at least in its first occurrence) as 'know'. Meanwhile the second and third soundings of *I*, if not the first, can also be heard as 'eye'. In the context in which this line occurs, that sense echoes a thematically pertinent passage from Matthew 18:9: 'if thine eye offend thee, pluck it out'.

But these are not all the implications *I* can have here. *I* can also represent the Roman numeral for '1', which will soon be reduced, as Richard notes, to 'nothing' (0), along with the speaker's title, his worldly possessions, his manhood, and eventually his life. In Shakespeare's time, to become 'nothing' was, *inter alia*, to be emasculated, to be made a 'weaker vessel' (1 Peter 3:7) with 'no thing'. As the Fool in *King Lear* reminds another monarch who has abdicated his throne, a man in want of an 'I' is impotent, 'an O without a Figure' (I.iv.207). In addition to its other dimensions, then, Richard's reply is a statement that can be formulated mathematically, and in symbols that anticipate the binary system behind today's computer technology: '1, 0, 0, 1, for 1 must 0 be.'

Modern editions usually render Richard's line 'Ay, no; no, ay; for I must nothing be.' Presenting the line in that fashion makes good sense of what Richard is saying. But as we've seen, it doesn't make total sense of it, and it doesn't call attention to Richard's paradoxes in the same way that hearing or seeing three undifferentiated *I*s is likely to have done for Shakespeare's contemporaries. Their culture was more attuned than ours is to the oral and aural dimensions of language, and if we want to appreciate the special qualities of their dramatic art we need to train ourselves to 'hear' the word-forms we see on the page. We must learn to recognize that for many of what we tend to think of as fixed linkages between sound and meaning (the vowel 'I', say, and the word 'eye'), there were alternative linkages (such as the vowel 'I' and the words 'I' and 'Ay') that could be just as pertinent to what the playwright was communicating through the ears of his theatre patrons at a given moment. As the word *audience* itself may help us to remember, people in Shakespeare's time normally spoke of 'hearing' rather than 'seeing' a play.

In its text of *Richard II*, the Everyman edition reproduces the title character's line as it appears in the early printings of the tragedy. Ideally the orthographic oddity of the repeated *I*s will encourage today's readers to ponder Richard's utterance, and the play it epitomizes, as a characteristically Shakespearean enigma.

OTHER ASPECTS OF THE EVERYMAN TEXT

Now for a few words about other features of the Everyman text.

One of the first things readers will notice about this edition is its bountiful use of capitalized words. In this practice as in others, the Everyman exemplar is the First Folio, and especially the works in the Folio sections billed as 'Histories' and 'Tragedies'.* Everyman makes no attempt to adhere to the Folio printings with literal exactitude. In some instances the Folio capitalizes words that the Everyman text of the same passage lowercases; in other instances Everyman capitalizes words not uppercased in the Folio. The objective is merely to suggest something of the flavour, and what appears to have been the rationale, of Renaissance capitalization, in the hope that today's audiences will be made continually aware that the works they are contemplating derive from an earlier epoch.

Readers will also notice that instead of cluttering the text with stage directions such as '[Aside]' or '[To Rosse]', the Everyman text employs unobtrusive dashes to indicate shifts in mode of address. In an effort to keep the page relatively clear of words not supplied by the original printings, Everyman also exercises restraint in its addition of editor-generated stage directions. Where the dialogue makes it obvious that a significant action occurs, the Everyman text inserts a square-bracketed phrase such as '[Fleance escapes.]'. Where what the dialogue implies is subject to differing interpretations, however, the Everyman text provides a facing-page note to discuss the most plausible inferences.

* The quarto printings employ far fewer capital letters than does the Folio. Capitalization seems to have been regarded as a means of recognizing the status ascribed to certain words (*Noble*, for example, is almost always capitalized), titles (not only King, Queen, Duke, and Duchess, but Sir and Madam), genres (tragedies were regarded as more 'serious' than comedies in more than one sense), and forms of publication (quartos, being associated with ephemera such as 'plays', were not thought to be as 'grave' as the folios that bestowed immortality on 'works', writings that, in the words of Ben Jonson's eulogy of Shakespeare, were 'not of an age, but for all time').

Like other modern editions, the Everyman text combines into 'shared' verse lines (lines divided among two or more speakers) many of the part-lines to be found in the early publications of the plays. One exception to the usual modern procedure is that Everyman indents some lines that are not components of shared verses. At times, for example, the opening line of a scene stops short of the metrical norm, a pentameter (five-foot) or hexameter (six-foot) line comprised predominantly of iambic units (unstressed syllables followed by stressed ones). In such cases Everyman uses indentation as a reminder that scenes can begin as well as end in mid-line (an extension of the ancient convention that an epic commences *in medias res*, 'in the midst of the action'). Everyman also uses indentation to reflect what appear to be pauses in the dialogue, either to allow other activity to transpire (as happens in *Macbeth*, II.iii.87, when a brief line 'What's the Business?' follows a Folio stage direction that reads '*Bell rings. Enter Lady.*') or to permit a character to hesitate for a moment of reflection (as happens a few seconds later in the same scene when Macduff responds to a demand to 'Speak, speak' with the reply 'O gentle Lady, / 'Tis not for you to hear what I can speak').

Everyman preserves many of the anomalies in the early texts. Among other things, this practice pertains to the way characters are depicted. In *A Midsummer Night's Dream*, the ruler of Athens is usually identified in speech headings and stage directions as 'Theseus', but sometimes he is referred to by his title as 'Duke'. In the same play Oberon's merry sprite goes by two different names: 'Puck' and 'Robin Goodfellow'.

Readers of the Everyman edition will sometimes discover that characters they've known, or known about, for years don't appear in the original printings. When they open the pages of the Everyman edition of *Macbeth*, for example, they'll learn that Shakespeare's audience were unaware of any woman with the title 'Lady Macbeth'. In the only authoritative text we have of the Scottish tragedy, the protagonist's spouse goes by such names as 'Macbeth's Lady', 'Macbeth's Wife', or simply 'Lady', but nowhere is she listed or mentioned as 'Lady Macbeth'. The same is true of the character usually designated 'Lady Capulet' in modern editions of *Romeo and Juliet*. 'Capulet's Wife' makes appearances as 'Mother', 'Old Lady', 'Lady', or simply 'Wife'; but she is never called 'Lady Capulet', and her husband never treats her with the dignity such a title would connote.

Rather than 'correct' the grammar in Shakespeare's works to eliminate what modern usage would categorize as solecisms (as when Mercutio says 'my Wits faints' in *Romeo and Juliet*), the Everyman texts leaves it intact. Among other things, this principle applies to instances in which archaic forms preserve idioms that differ slightly from related modern expressions (as in the clause 'you are too blame', where 'too' functions as an adverb and 'blame' is used, not as a verb, but as an adjective roughly equivalent to 'blameworthy').

Finally, and most importantly, the Everyman edition leaves unchanged any reading in the original text that is not manifestly erroneous. Unlike other modern renderings of Shakespeare's works, Everyman substitutes emendations only when obvious problems can be resolved by obvious solutions.

The Everyman Text of *Julius Caesar*

The only authoritative text of *Julius Caesar* is the one an eminent bibliographer has dubbed the 'best-printed play' in the 1623 First Folio (F1). From all indications the copy for the Folio printing was either the theatre promptbook or an accurate transcript thereof.

The Folio punctuation for Shakespeare's tragedy is somewhat heavier than is normal today, but F1's abundant commas, colons, and semicolons can usually be defended on dramatic or rhetorical grounds. Question marks occasionally crop up in what we would regard as mid-sentence positions; the Folio also employs interrogatives in places where modern grammar would call for exclamation points. Meanwhile, full stops or colons appear in situations where current usage would opt for question marks. More often than do most twentieth-century editions, *The Everyman Shakespeare* preserves the peculiarities of Folio punctuation, hoping thereby to recapture some of the inflections Elizabethan and Jacobean actors would have brought to their lines as they spoke them on the stage of the Globe.

In phrases with compound adjectives, the Folio *Julius Caesar* tends to insert one more hyphen than we would: 'high-sighted-Tyranny' (II.i.116), for example, or 'honey-heavy-Dew' (II.i.228), or 'low-crooked-Curtsies' (III.i.43). In these instances Everyman does what most modern editions do: it drops the final hyphen.

Although the Folio text is segmented into acts, it contains no scene divisions. Most of the scene demarcations to be found in modern printings derive from the editions of Nicholas Rowe (1709) or Edmund Capell (1768). Everyman's one departure from the segmentation that has become standard occurs in Act IV, where Alexander Pope's editions (1723–25, 1728) denoted a new scene, IV.iii, to signal that the quarrel between Cassius and Brutus has taken them inside Brutus' tent. As it happens, the stage is never cleared; so, unlike most of today's texts, *The Everyman Shakespeare* overrides Pope and treats as a single scene, IV.ii, what editors have long acknowledged to be a seamless dramatic sequence.

Everyman follows the Folio spellings for *Murellus* (*Marullus* in North's Plutarch and in most modern editions), *Claudio* (*Claudius* in Plutarch), and *Varrus* (*Varro* in Plutarch); it also retains the Folio's Italianate variations for *Antony* (*Antonio*, rather than the *Antonius* Latin would give us) and *Octavius* (which appears twice as *Octavio*). There is no reason to doubt that these spellings represent conscious authorial modifications of the forms Shakespeare found in his sources, and it would be presumptuous to 'correct' them.

In a few instances the Everyman edition accords with other modern printings and alters the text to be found in the First Folio. For each of the emendations listed below, the first entry, in boldface type, is the Everyman reading and the second is the reading to be found in the Folio. Where the Everyman version of the text derives from a later seventeenth-century edition of *Julius Caesar*, the first entry is followed by a parenthesis identifying that edition. In this roster F2 designates the Second Folio (1623), F3 the Third Folio (1663–64), and F4 the Fourth Folio (1685).

I.ii.	23	***Manent*** *Manet* (so also in IV.ii.47)
	136	**some time** (F3) sometime
	140	**yours?** (F2) yours
	269	**Rogues.** Rogues,
I.iii.	10	**dropping Fire** dropping-fire (comparable instances occur in II.i.116, 228, III.i.43)
II.i.	116	**sighted Tyranny** sighted-Tyranny
	120	**Women, then** Women. Then
	134	**Oath; when** Oath. When
	155	**Caesar:** Caesar,
	228	**heavy Dew** heavy-Dew
	265	**his** (F2) hit
	272	**Self, your Half,** selfe; your halfe
	278	**the** (F2) tho
III.i.	43	**crooked Curtsies** crooked-Curtsies
	114	**States** (F2) State
	116	**lies** (F2) lie
	226	**you, Antony** you Antony
III.ii.	110	**art** (F2) are
IV.i.	32	**on,** on:
	36	**barren-spirited** barren spirited
	37	**Imitations,** Imitations.
	41	**Brutus** (F2) Brntus
IV.ii.	52	**Man,** (F2) man
	160	**temper'd** (F2) remper'd
	215	**Outlawry** (F4) Outlarie
	222	**Proscription.** (F3) Proscription
	252	**off,** off.
	309	**Slumber** (F3) Slumbler
	335	**Lucius** (F2) Lucus
V.i.	65	***Exeunt*** *Exit*
V.iv.	26	**Brutus, Friend** (F4) Brutus Friend
V.v.	33	**thee too,** thee, to
	63	**Master,** (F3) Master
	76	**With all** Withall

In a number of instances the Everyman text differs from many, if not most, of today's editions in its adherence to the reading in the First Folio. For each of the passages listed below, the first entry, in boldface type, is the Everyman version of the text, derived from the Folio, and the second is the emendation to be found in at least some modern editions.

I.i. 16 **Souls** soles (from F4)
36 **Holy-day** (so also in I.ii.55) holiday
43 **Pompey many** Pompey? Many
oft? oft
45 **Windows?** windows,
66 **where** whe'er (so also in V.iii.96, V.iv.30)
Mettle metal

I.ii. 5 **Lord.** lord?
12 **Ha?** Ha!
70 **Laughter** laugher
83 **ought** aught
122 **loose** lose (compare IV.ii.266, V.v.36)
123 **I** Ay (so also in I.ii.213, 295, III.iii.10–12, IV.ii.300, 326, V.v.62)
bad bade (so also in I.iii.151, III.i.126)
157 **Divel** Devil (so also in IV.ii.321)
160 **too** to
163 **not so (with** not (so with
177 **sowre** sour
187 **Caesar.** Caesar?
219 **a Shouting** a-shouting
242 **howted** hooted *or* shouted (compare I.iii.28)
253 **like** like;
264 **Heard** herd
278 **away.** away?
299 **be?** be!

I.iii. 10 **Tempest-dropping** tempest dropping
28 **Howting** Hooting
33 **strange disposed** strange-disposed
42 **this?** this!
50 **blew** blue
70 **Fear, and Warning** fear and warning
84 **Yoke, and Sufferance,** yoke and sufferance
94 **air-less** airless
108 **Rome?** Rome,

109 **Offal?** offal,
111 **Caesar.** Caesar!
124 **honourable dangerous** honourable-dangerous
125 **know by this,** know, by this
129 **Is Favours,** in favour's
137 **this?** this! (compare I.iii.42)
153 **yet, ere Day,** yet ere day
161 **Him, . . . Worth, . . . him,** Him . . . worth . . . him

II.i.
1 **ho?** ho!
3 **say?** say!
5 **Lucius?** Lucius!
15 **Crown him that,** Crown him? – that; –
18 **dis-joins** disjoins
23 **Climber upward** climber-upward
28 **least** lest (so also in III.i.88, 93, V.iii.105)
40 **first** ides
51 **What Rome?** What, Rome?
66 **State of a Man** state of man
82 **path thy** path, thy
88 **Men,** men
113 **Times** time's
126 **it.** it?
134 **Oath. When** oath, when *or* oath; when
156 **shrew'd** shrewd
211 **eight** eighth
244 **wafter** wafture
263 **Night?** night,
293 **reputed:** reputed,
307 – **Lucius . . . knocks?** Most editions place this line before the entrance direction that precedes it in the Folio and here.
313 **Kerchief?** kerchief!

II.ii.
23 **do** did
46 **hear** are
84 **Vision,** vision
89 **Reliques** relics
105 **Calphurnia?** Calpurnia!

II.iv.
3 **doest** dost
18 **bussling** bustling
37 **Man, almost, to** man almost to
41 **is?** is!

III.i.	27	Cimber, let Cimber? Let
	39	Lane law *or* line
	62	true fix'd true-fix'd
	114	unborne unborn (compare V.i.57, 71)
		unknown? unknown!
	117	Dust? dust!
	183	strook struck
	199	Foes? foes,
	200	Corse, corse? *or* corse!
	203	then than (so also in III.ii.25, 40, V.iv.29)
	209	Hart heart
	210	stroken strucken
	211	lie? lie!
	236	utter. utter?
	284	Passion I see is Passion, I see, is
		catching from catching, for
	286	Began Begin
	293	Course corse
III.ii.	7	rend'red rendered (so also in III.ii.10)
	48	not. not?
	74	here? here!
	99	Ambitious: ambitious,
	107	am, am
	137	Which pardon Which, pardon
	162	Will. will?
	192	Countrymen? countrymen!
	203–4	Revenge . . . live. Many editions reassign this passage to ALL.
	218	Writ wit
III.iii.	38	Brutus Brutus'
		Cassius Cassius'
	40	Ligarius Ligarius'
IV.i.	49	bayed bay'd
IV.ii.	45	Lucilius Lucius
	47	Lucius Lucilius
	59	Palm? palm!
	79	not Cassius not, Cassius
	101	You . . . Brutus. Many editions reassign this line to Brutus.
	106	not. not?
	146	Pluto's Plutus'

159 **ill temper'd** ill-temper'd (so also in line 160)
165 **forgetful.** forgetful?
176 **rime?** rime!
213 **Tenure** tenor
239 **presently.** presently?
251 **new added** new-added
252 **off.** off *or* off,
271 **say.** say?
272 ***Enter Lucius.*** Many editions delay this stage direction until after Brutus says 'Lucius my Gown' (line 273).
335 **Lord.** Lord?
340 **Lord.** Lord?
Lord. Lord?

V.i. 4 **Battailes** (compare V.i.16, 96, 107; V.iii.107)
35 **too.** too?
41 **Teeths** teeth (F3)
101 **himself, . . . how:** himself – . . . how,
104 **Life,** life –

V.ii. 4 ***Octavio's*** *Octavius'*

V.iii. 103 **Tharsus** Thasos
107 **Labio** Labeo

V.iv. 0 ***Cato*** *young Cato*
17 **thee** the

V.v. 33 **to thee, to Strato, Countrymen:** to thee too, Strato. – Countrymen,
40 **Live's** life's

JULIUS CAESAR

NAMES OF THE ACTORS

JULIUS CAESAR

OCTAVIUS CAESAR
MARK ANTONY
M. AEMILIUS LEPIDUS } Triumvirs after Caesar's death

CICERO
PUBLIUS
POPILIUS LENA } Senators

MARCUS BRUTUS
CASSIUS
CASCA
TREBONIUS
CAIUS LIGARIUS
DECIUS BRUTUS
METELLUS CIMBER
CINNA } Conspirators against Julius Caesar

CALPHURNIA, Wife to Caesar
PORTIA, Wife to Brutus
FLAVIUS and MURELLUS, Tribunes
ARTEMIDORUS OF CNIDOS, a Teacher of Rhetoric
SOOTHSAYER
CINNA, a Poet
ANOTHER POET

LUCILIUS TITINIUS MESSALA YOUNG CATO VOLUMNIUS FLAVIUS	Friends to Brutus and Cassius
VARRUS CLITUS CLAUDIO STRATO DARDANIUS	Soldiers in Brutus' Army

LUCIUS, Servant to Brutus
PINDARUS, Servant to Cassius

GHOST OF CAESAR

SENATORS, CITIZENS, GUARDS, ATTENDANTS, etc.

I.i This opening scene occurs on a street in Rome. Flavius and Murellus are a pair of Tribunes (magistrates with a special duty to protect the rights of the plebeians – the common people – from being violated by the aristocratic patricians). They are disturbed to see a large number of plebeians taking a day off to celebrate the latest victories of a general who seems to the Tribunes to be amassing too much power and popularity for the good of the Roman republic.

1 **Idle Creatures** The plebeians are described as 'idle' because they are parading in the streets on a day when they should be working.

3 **Mechanical** craftsmen, working-class people. Compare the expression 'rude Mechanicals' in *A Midsummer Night's Dream*, III.ii.9.

4–5 **the Sign / Of your Profession** the tools and apparel of your trade.

7 **Rule** measuring tool, ruler.

8 **What dost thou with** what are you doing with.
Best Apparel finest clothes, as opposed to the clothes workmen would normally wear on a working day.

10–11 **in . . . Cobbler** The Cobbler (a man who repairs shoes) plays on another sense of *cobbler*: a clumsy fellow who botches things up, rather than a 'fine Workman'. Here *in respect of* means 'with respect to the idea of'.

16 **bad Souls** This spelling, derived from the First Folio printing, involves wordplay on 'Conscience' (line 15). What the Cobbler does for a living, of course, is mend bad *soles*. As is usual in his comic scenes with clowns, Shakespeare here touches lightly on themes that will be explored more seriously elsewhere in the play. Later we will hear frequent reference to souls that need mending or are in danger.

19, 20 **out** The Cobbler plays on two meanings: (a) out of sorts, angry; and (b) out of your shoes, because of holes in them. *Out* can also mean 'out of your assigned role', as with an actor who has forgotten his lines or is unable to deliver them properly. In the next scene we will hear that Murellus and Flavius are 'put to Silence' (I.ii.289), beyond the point where the Cobbler can 'mend' their speech.

ACT I

Scene 1

Enter Flavius, Murellus, and certain Commoners over the Stage.

FLAVIUS Hence: home, you Idle Creatures, get you home.
Is this a Holiday? What, know you not,
Being Mechanical, you ought not walk
Upon a Labouring Day without the Sign
Of your Profession? – Speak, what Trade art thou?

CARPENTER Why Sir, a Carpenter.

MURELLUS Where is thy Leather Apron, and thy Rule?
What dost thou with thy Best Apparel on?
– You Sir, what Trade are you?

COBBLER Truly Sir, in respect of a fine Workman, I am but, as you would say, a Cobbler.

MURELLUS But what Trade art thou? Answer me directly.

COBBLER A Trade, Sir, that I hope I may use with a safe Conscience, which is indeed, Sir, a Mender of bad Souls.

FLAVIUS What Trade, thou Knave? Thou naughty Knave, what Trade?

COBBLER Nay I beseech you, Sir, be not out with me; yet if you be out, Sir, I can mend you.

MARCELLUS What mean'st thou by that? Mend me, thou saucy Fellow?

COBBLER Why Sir, cobble you.

FLAVIUS Thou art a Cobbler, art thou?

26 **Awl** a pointed tool for boring holes in leather or wood. In lines 25 and 27 the Cobbler puns on *Awl* in 'all . . . with' and 'withal' (for all that), and he gives it a sexual twist when he alludes to the use of such an instrument for meddling (messing around or 'cobbling') with 'Women's matters'. He continues the innuendo with 'old Shoes'; compare *The Two Gentlemen of Verona*, II.iii.15–20, where Launce compares his mother to 'this Shoe with the Hole in it', the one with 'the worser Sole'.

29 **recover** both (a) re-cover, and (b) cure or rescue.

30 **Neat's Leather** cowhide. Compare *The Tempest*, II.ii.76, where Stephano uses the same expression; and see the note on 'Neat's Tongue' in *The Merchant of Venice*, I.i.111.

37 **Triumph** victory celebration. According to Plutarch, Shakespeare's principal source for the play, Caesar's triumph over Cneius and Sextus, the sons of Cneius Pompeius, Pompey the Great, was widely resented, both because it put down fellow Romans rather than foreign foes and because it destroyed the heirs of 'the noblest man of Rome'. Caesar had defeated Pompey in 48 BC, after which Pompey was murdered, and he defeated Pompey's sons in 45 BC, roughly a year before Caesar's own assassination.

39 **Tributaries** captives who must pay tribute to the victor.

43 **Knew you not** did you not acknowledge and celebrate?
Pompey . . . oft Most editions alter the Folio syntax, reproduced here, by placing a question mark after *Pompey* and treating the clause that follows (to the end of line 48) as a declarative sentence. Not only is such an emendation unnecessary; it interrupts a sequence of rhetorical questions. The phrase *many a time and oft* means 'on numerous and frequent occasions'.

52 **replication** reverberation, echo. Murellus is using hyperbole to emphasize how universally and loudly the Roman populace once cheered a legitimate hero.

53 **concave Shores** overhanging, curved banks.

55 **Cull out** pick out, as one does when selecting flowers from a bunch.
Holy-day both (a) holy day (see line 72 and I.ii.8), and (b) holiday (vacation from work).

57 **Pompey's Blood** the blood of Pompey's bloodline (his sons).

COBBLER Truly Sir, all that I live by is with the Awl: I meddle with no Tradesman's matters, nor Women's matters. But withal I am indeed, Sir, a Surgeon to old Shoes: when they are in great Danger, I recover them. As proper Men as ever trod upon Neat's Leather have gone upon my Handy-work.

FLAVIUS But wherefore art not in thy Shop to day?
Why dost thou lead these Men about the Streets?

COBBLER Truly Sir, to wear out their Shoes, to get my self into more Work. But indeed, Sir, we make Holy-day to see Caesar, and to rejoice in his Triumph.

MURELLUS Wherefore rejoice? What Conquest brings he home?
What Tributaries follow him to Rome,
To grace in Captive Bonds his Chariot Wheels?
You Blocks, you Stones, you worse than Senseless Things:
O you Hard Hearts, you Cruel Men of Rome,
Knew you not Pompey many a time and oft?
Have you climb'd up to Walls and Battlements,
To Tow'rs and Windows? Yea, to Chimney Tops,
Your Infants in your Arms, and there have sate
The livelong Day, with patient Expectation,
To see great Pompey pass the Streets of Rome:
And when you saw his Chariot but appear,
Have you not made an universal Shout,
That Tiber trembled underneath her Banks
To hear the replication of your Sounds,
Made in her concave Shores? And do you now
Put on your Best Attire? And do you now
Cull out a Holy-day? And do you now
Strew Flowers in his way that comes
In Triumph over Pompey's Blood? Be gone,
Run to your Houses, fall upon your Knees,

59 **intermit** forestall or delay.

61 **Fault** breach (the literal meaning), misdeed.

62 **sort** [artisan] class.

65 **most exalted Shores** highest banks, those the river reaches in flood times.

66 **where** whether (often spelled *whe'er* in modern editions).

Basest Mettle the ignoble character of the lowest members of society. Flavius puns on 'base metal', the kinds of elements alchemists attempted to transform into gold (with a further pun on *gilt* and *guilt* in the following line), and suggests that the fickle mob can be worked on just as readily by political 'alchemists' such as Caesar. Compare the wordplay on *Guilt* in *Macbeth*, II.ii.52–54.

69 **Images** Plutarch tells us that Caesar's followers put statues of him around the city, some of them decked with crowns, wreaths, or other ornaments hinting at royalty. Moreover, Plutarch says, those who sought Caesar's favour went around the city 'in the night-time' and 'put diadems upon the heads of his images, supposing thereby to allure the common people to call him King instead of Dictator'. Shakespeare omits any mention of Plutarch's statement that after Caesar had won his 'civil wars', when 'Pompey's images had been thrown down, he caused them to be set up again'.

70 **Ceremonies** symbols of state, such as scarves or diadems.

72 **Feast of Lupercal** a fertility festival held in mid-February in honour of Lupercus, a deity sometimes identified with the Greek god Pan. Here Shakespeare treats the Lupercalia as if it occurred a month later, and he associates it with the triumphs the historical Caesar actually held the previous October, following his victory over the sons of Pompey in March of 45 BC. As we will see later, Shakespeare also associates the season with two non-Roman feasts that occur in the spring: Passover and Easter. See the note to line 55.

74 **Trophies** ornaments of victory or tribute.

75 **the Vulgar** the common rabble.

Pray to the Gods to intermit the Plague
That needs must light on this Ingratitude.

FLAVIUS Go, go, good Countrymen, and for this Fault
Assemble all the Poor Men of your sort;
Draw them to Tiber banks, and weep your Tears
Into the Channel till the lowest Stream
Do kiss the most exalted Shores of all.

Exeunt all the Commoners.

– See where their Basest Mettle be not mov'd;
They vanish Tongue-tied in their Guiltiness.
Go you down that way towards the Capitol,
This way will I. Disrobe the Images,
If you do find them deck'd with Ceremonies.

MURELLUS May we do so?
You know it is the Feast of Lupercal.

FLAVIUS It is no matter; let no Images
Be hung with Caesar's Trophies. I'll about
And drive away the Vulgar from the Streets;
So do you too where you perceive them thick.
These growing Feathers, pluck'd from Caesar's Wing,

78 **Pitch** the height of a bird's flight. Flavius' image suggests that unless Caesar's wings are clipped, he is likely to become a bird of prey, such as a hawk, eagle, or falcon, soaring in the sky above and threatening to swoop down on those below him who fly at an 'ordinary Pitch'. Lines 77–78 echo *Richard II*, IV.i.108, where York announces that 'Plume-pluck'd Richard' is ready to resign his crown to the rival who will become King Henry IV.

I.ii This scene occurs in a street or other public place in Rome. Most editions add 'Citizens' to those who enter to begin this scene. But whether a crowded stage would in fact need additional actors to suggest a 'Throng' (line 20) is not clear.

4 **his Course** Antony is about to participate in the 'Holy Chase' (line 8) of the Lupercalian feast. During this festival the runners coursed naked, and they carried goatskin 'thongs' (either phalluses or replicas thereof). Women cursed with infertility sought to be touched by one of the thongs in the hope that its magic powers would make them fruitful.

7 **Calphurnia** The name of Caesar's wife is often spelled *Calpurnia*; the spelling adopted here is the one found in the First Folio. The *ph* was probably not pronounced as an *f* sound, but the *h* may have been sounded as a slight aspirant. Calphurnia's barrenness would have reminded Elizabethans of the plight of Sarah (Sarai), and of God's promise that through her Abraham (Abram) would be 'a father to many nations' (Genesis 17:1–9).

11 **leave no Ceremony out** omit no detail of the ritual; leave out nothing that might make its magic effectual. Many editions add a '*Flourish*' stage direction after this line; in his next speech (line 15) Caesar refers to 'Music'.

14 **press** jostling throng.

17 **the Ides of March** 15 March. In the ancient Roman calendar, the ides (*idus*) of March, May, July, and October fell on the 15th day of the month; the ides of the other months fell on the 13th. Debts, interest, and other payments were often due on the ides, so it became known, at least in a fiscal sense, as a day of reckoning.

Will make him fly an ordinary Pitch,
Who else would soar above the view of Men
And keep us all in servile Fearfulness. *Exeunt.*

Scene 2

Enter Caesar, Antony for the Course, Calphurnia, Portia, Decius, Cicero, Brutus, Cassius, Casca, a Soothsayer; after them Murellus and Flavius.

CAESAR Calphurnia.
CASCA Peace ho, Caesar speaks.
CAESAR Calphurnia.
CALPHURNIA Here, my Lord.
CAESAR Stand you directly in Antonio's way
When he doth run his Course. – Antonio.
ANTONY Caesar, my Lord.
CAESAR Forget not in your speed, Antonio,
To touch Calphurnia: for our Elders say,
The Barren touched in this Holy Chase
Shake off their sterile Curse.
ANTONY I shall remember,
When Caesar says 'Do this'; it is perform'd.
CAESAR Set on, and leave no Ceremony out.
SOOTHSAYER Caesar.
CAESAR Ha? Who calls?
CASCA Bid every Noise be still: peace yet again.
CAESAR Who is it in the press that calls on me?
I hear a Tongue shriller than all the Music
Cry 'Caesar.' Speak, Caesar is turn'd to hear.
SOOTHSAYER Beware the Ides of March.
CAESAR What Man is that?
BRUTUS A Soothsayer bids you beware the Ides of
March.

23 **Dreamer** Caesar appears to mean one who believes in the prophetic powers of dreams. Caesar claims to be sceptical about what others regard as signs of divine intervention in human affairs. His phrasing echoes Genesis 37:19 where Joseph's brothers refer to him contemptuously as 'this dreamer'. It turns out, of course, that Joseph's dreams, and his interpretations of Pharaoh's dream (see Genesis 41), are prophetic. Compare Jeremiah 23:23–30, Daniel 2, and Joel 2:28–29.

S.D. **Sennet** a trumpet flourish to signal ceremonial entrances and exits.

Manent the Latin plural for 'remain'. The singular form, *Manet*, occurs at I.ii.210.

24 **the order of the Course** how the race proceeds.

26 **Gamesome** playful, frivolous.

27 **quick** lively. Here Brutus seems to combine three meanings of the word: (a) alive, (b) speedy, and (c) alert and playful.

32 **shew** show, display.

as . . . have that I am accustomed to having. According to North's translation of Plutarch, relations between Cassius and Brutus became strained ('strange') after Caesar chose Brutus over Cassius for the position of Praetor (chief magistrate). 'Cassius' friends' urged Brutus 'to beware of Caesar's enticements and to fly his tyrannical favours; the which they said Caesar gave him, not to honour his virtue but to weaken his constant mind, framing it to the bent of his bow'. Shakespeare's only hint is in Cassius' allusion to Brutus as a special favourite of Caesar's (line 317).

33 **Strange** unfamiliar, unfriendly, estranging; lacking in intimacy. Here *stubborn* means 'hard', 'harsh', and 'inflexible'.

33–34 **a Hand / Over your Friend** By implication Cassius is comparing Brutus to a rider who bears a 'hard Rein' over a horse (*King Lear*, III.i.27–28). Cassius' phrasing is significant: it literally accords Brutus the upper hand.

37 **my self** Most modern editions print *myself*, but Shakespeare always renders as two words *my self*, *thy self*, and *your self*. The difference between his spelling and ours is frequently meaningful.

38 **Passions of some Difference** conflicting emotions. *Difference* can also mean 'quarrel' (see the note to *King Lear*, I.iv.97), and that sense will soon prove pertinent.

CAESAR Set him before me, let me see his Face.
CASSIUS Fellow, come from the Throng; look upon
Caesar.
CAESAR What sayst thou to me now? Speak once again.
SOOTHSAYER Beware the Ides of March.
CAESAR He is a Dreamer, let us leave him. Pass.
Sennet. Exeunt. Manent Brutus and Cassius.
CASSIUS Will you go see the order of the Course?
BRUTUS Not I.
CASSIUS I pray you do.
BRUTUS I am not Gamesome: I do lack some part
Of that quick Spirit that is in Antony.
Let me not hinder, Cassius, your Desires;
I'll leave you.
CASSIUS Brutus, I do observe you now of late:
I have not from your Eyes that Gentleness
And shew of Love as I was wont to have;
You bear too Stubborn and too Strange a Hand
Over your Friend that loves you.
BRUTUS Cassius,
Be not deceiv'd: if I have veil'd my Look,
I turn the Trouble of my Countenance
Merely upon my self. Vexed I am
Of late, with Passions of some Difference,

39 **onely** only, solely.
proper to pertaining to.

40 **Soil** blemish, discolouration.

43 **construe** interpret; here, as is usual in Shakespeare, the accent falls on the first syllable.

44 **with . . . War** Brutus described a 'psychomachia' (soul-battle) between two conflicting impulses in his mind and heart. It will emerge that he speaks more accurately than he suspects; see the notes to lines 60, 66.

48 **Cogitations** thoughts.

56 **Shadow** reflected image.

57 **of the best Respect** both (a) of the most respected, and (b) of the most reflective sort (with *Respect* meaning 'thought' or 'wisdom', as in *Hamlet*, III.i.65–66.

58 **immortal** Cassius is being sardonic. But although Caesar the man will prove to be mortal, the name he bears will become immortal; see the note to line 195.

60 **his** Here *his* probably refers to each of the 'many' alluded to in line 57. But *his Eyes* can also mean 'Brutus' eyes': that is, Brutus' ability to perceive what other respected Romans see.

66 **Glass** mirror. Here *Reflection* carries an abstract sense (mental reflection, meditation) as well as the obvious physical sense.

67 **modestly** truthfully, without flattery or exaggeration.
discover disclose, uncover.

69 **jealous on me** suspicious of me.

70 **a common Laughter** a frivolous person, a jester not to be taken seriously. *Laughter* can also mean 'laughing stock'.

Conceptions onely proper to my self,
Which give some Soil, perhaps, to my Behaviours.
But let not therefore my good Friends be griev'd
(Among which number, Cassius, be you one),
Nor construe any further my Neglect
Than that poor Brutus, with himself at War,
Forgets the Shews of Love to other Men.

CASSIUS Then Brutus, I have much mistook your Passion,
By means whereof this Breast of mine hath buried
Thoughts of great Value, worthy Cogitations.
Tell me, good Brutus, can you see your Face?

BRUTUS No, Cassius, for the Eye sees not it self
But by Reflection, by some other things.

CASSIUS 'Tis just,
And it is very much lamented, Brutus,
That you have no such Mirrors as will turn
Your hidden Worthiness into your Eye,
That you might see your Shadow. I have heard,
Where many of the best Respect in Rome
(Except immortal Caesar), speaking of Brutus,
And groaning underneath this Age's Yoke,
Have wish'd that Noble Brutus had his Eyes.

BRUTUS Into what Dangers would you lead me, Cassius?
That you would have me seek into my self
For that which is not in me?

CASSIUS Therefore, good Brutus, be prepar'd to hear:
And since you know you cannot see your self
So well as by Reflection, I your Glass
Will modestly discover to your self
That of your self which you yet know not of.
And be not jealous on me, gentle Brutus:
Were I a common Laughter, or did use

71 **To stale with ordinary Oaths** to cheapen (make *stale*) with common declarations. One meaning of *ordinary* is 'tavern', so Cassius' image may allude to oaths exchanged by drunkards over stale brew.

72 **Protester** one who professes love.

74 **scandal** slander, speak disrespectfully. Here *after* means 'afterwards'.

75 **Banqueting** indulging in gluttony and other vices of the flesh.

76 **the Rout** the vulgar (compare I.i.75), the common herd.
Dangerous treacherous, a threat to you. Caesar will soon be calling Cassius dangerous because he does *not* engage in the activities enumerated here (see lines 188–206).

81 **wherefore** why.

83 **ought toward** anything pertaining to. Here *toward* is probably to be pronounced as a two-syllable word; in I.i.68, on the other hand, *towards* is to be treated as a one-syllable word.
the general Good the welfare of the commonweal. Compare *Hamlet*, II.ii.466–73, where 'General' refers to 'the Million' without refinement or discretion, what Flavius refers to in I.i.75 as 'the Vulgar' and what Cassius calls 'the Rout' in line 76.

85 **indifferently** impartially, objectively; literally, without seeing any difference.

86 **speed** prosper.

89 **Favour** both (a) face, appearance, and (b) good will, kind demeanour.

90 **Story** discourse, narrative.

93 **as lief** as soon.

95 **borne** both (a) carried, and (b) born.

99 **chafing with** rubbing against, like an enraged animal. Compare *King Lear*, IV.vi.20–22.

103 **Accoutred** dressed and armed.

104 **bad** the past tense of *bid*; bade. Compare line 123.

To stale with ordinary Oaths my Love
To every new Protester; if you know
That I do fawn on men, and hug them hard,
And after scandal them; or if you know
That I profess my self in Banqueting
To all the Rout, then hold me Dangerous.

Flourish, and Shout.

BRUTUS What means this Shouting? I do fear the People
Choose Caesar for their King.

CASSIUS Ay, do you fear it?
Then must I think you would not have it so.

BRUTUS I would not, Cassius, yet I love him well:
But wherefore do you hold me here so long?
What is it that you would impart to me?
If it be ought toward the general Good,
Set Honour in one Eye, and Death i'th' other,
And I will look on both indifferently:
For let the Gods so speed me as I love
The name of Honour more than I fear Death.

CASSIUS I know that Virtue to be in you, Brutus,
As well as I do know your outward Favour.
Well, Honour is the subject of my Story.
I cannot tell what you and other men
Think of this Life; but for my single self,
I had as lief not be as live to be
In awe of such a thing as I my self.
I was borne free as Caesar, so were you;
We both have fed as well, and we can both
Endure the Winter's Cold as well as he.
For once, upon a raw and gusty Day,
The troubled Tiber chafing with her Shores,
Caesar said to me, 'Dar'st thou, Cassius, now
Leap in with me into this angry Flood
And swim to yonder Point?' Upon the word,
Accoutred as I was, I plunged in
And bad him follow; so indeed he did.

107 **Controversy** rivalry, contention. Cassius seems to be referring primarily to the two men's struggle against the current; but of course he is also thinking about their competition with each other. Suetonius and Plutarch say that Caesar was a powerful swimmer. Shakespeare appears to have invented this episode to characterize both Cassius and Caesar: see the notes to lines 180, 208–9, for other indications that Shakespeare chose to portray Caesar as a man more vulnerable than he was reputed to be.

108 **arrive** arrive at, reach.

110–13 **I . . . Caesar** In Book II of the *Aeneid* Virgil describes how Aeneas, the legendary founder of Rome, escaped from the burning citadel of Troy with his enfeebled father, Anchises, riding on his shoulders. According to Plutarch, Caesar swam a quarter of a mile in the harbour of Alexander, all the while holding 'divers books' aloft to prevent them from getting wet, as he eluded a troop of Egyptian pursuers. Here *I* can mean 'Ay' (yes) as well as 'I'.

115 **bend his Body** bow in obeisance.

116 **carelessly** both (a) offhandedly, nonchalantly, and (b) uncaringly, without affection.

118 **the Fit** Caesar was afflicted with epilepsy, later referred to as 'the Falling Sickness' (line 253). But what Cassius seems to be referring to here is another kind of seizure, the chills of a person in the throes of a high fever.

119 **this God did shake** Cassius is drawing a contrast between Caesar the ordinary mortal and the Caesar who now commands the kind of reverence normally reserved for deities. Compare the use of *shake* in *King Lear*, I.i.40.

120 **His . . . fly** Here Cassius is using a military metaphor to describe Caesar's wan complexion. *Colour* refers to the flag (the colours) of a troop of soldiers, in this case cowardly ones who have fled. By implication, Caesar is just as fearful as other men, if not more so.

121 **Bend** a look or glance fixing on a particular person. *Bend* can mean 'aim', 'tautness', or 'firmness' (as in *King Lear*, I.i.144, and *Macbeth*, I.vii.79–80). But it can also have the opposite meaning, as in line 115. See the Plutarch quotation in the note to line 32.

The Torrent roar'd, and we did buffet it
With lusty Sinews, throwing it aside
And stemming it with Hearts of Controversy.
But ere we could arrive the Point propos'd,
Caesar cried 'Help me, Cassius, or I sink.'
I, as Aeneas, our great Ancestor,
Did from the Flames of Troy upon his Shoulder
The old Anchises bear, so from the Waves of Tiber
Did I the tired Caesar. And this Man
Is now become a God, and Cassius is
A wretched Creature and must bend his Body
If Caesar carelessly but nod on him.
He had a Fever when he was in Spain,
And when the Fit was on him I did mark
How he did shake; 'tis true, this God did shake,
His Coward Lips did from their Colour fly,
And that same Eye whose Bend doth awe the World

122 **loose** both (a) set loose, release, and (b) lose.

124 **Mark** take note of, pay attention to.

127 **feeble Temper** physical and emotional weakness. *Temper* refers to both (a) self-control (one's ability to keep one's passions in check), and (b) strength (the hardness of metals that have been 'tempered', or treated with extremes of heat and cold to make them durable and flexible).

128 **get the Start** outstrip, as in a race for the palm traditionally awarded the victor in a competition. Compare line 144.

133 **Colossus** Cassius probably alludes to a gigantic bronze statue of Apollo at Rhodes that was said to have bestridden the harbour for more than five decades in the third century BC; it was toppled by an earthquake in 224 BC.

136–38 **Men . . . Underlings** Cassius alludes to the widely held view that those whose minds rule their bodies and emotions (the parts of a human being subject to influence from the 'Stars') are in control of their own wills and destinies. See the note to *Romeo and Juliet*, III.i.143.

140 **sounded** both (a) spoken, and (b) plumbed for depth (a nautical term). Compare II.i.139.

142 **become** suit, befit.

144 **start a Spirit** cause a spirit to appear at the bidding of a conjurer. *Start* can also mean 'ignite', and in lines 172–73 Cassius expresses satisfaction that he has managed to 'start a Spirit' in Brutus.

147 **Great** both (a) large, and (b) distended, like a tumescent male member.

149 **the great Flood** Cassius refers to the deluge sent by Zeus to destroy a degenerate human race. The only mortals spared were Deucalion, the King of Pithia, and his wife Pyrrha. Elizabethans would also have thought of Noah's flood described in the book of Genesis.

153 **Rome, Room** Cassius puns on two words whose sounds would probably have been quite similar in Shakespeare's time.

154 **onely** only (as in line 39). Here the unusual word order calls attention to the pun on *one*. Cassius is saying that Caesar regards himself as the only 'one-ly' ('Great') Man in Rome. See the note to line 313.

Did loose his Lustre. I did hear him groan,
I, and that Tongue of his, that bad the Romans
Mark him, and write his Speeches in their Books,
Alas, it cried 'Give me some Drink, Titinius,'
As a Sick Girl. Ye Gods, it doth amaze me
A Man of such a feeble Temper should
So get the Start of the majestic World
And bear the Palm alone. *Shout. Flourish.*

BRUTUS Another general Shout?
I do believe that these Applauses are
For some new Honours that are heap'd on Caesar.

CASSIUS Why man, he doth bestride the narrow World
Like a Colossus, and we petty Men
Walk under his huge Legs, and peep about
To find our selves dishonourable Graves.
Men at some time are Masters of their Fates.
The Fault, dear Brutus, is not in our Stars,
But in our Selves, that we are Underlings.
'Brutus' and 'Caesar': what should be in that 'Caesar'?
Why should that Name be sounded more than yours?
Write them together: yours is as Fair a Name.
Sound them, it doth become the Mouth as well;
Weigh them, it is as Heavy; conjure with 'em,
'Brutus' will start a Spirit as soon as 'Caesar'.
Now in the Names of all the Gods at once,
Upon what Meat doth this our Caesar feed,
That he is grown so Great? – Age, thou art sham'd;
Rome, thou hast lost the breed of Noble Bloods.
When went there by an Age, since the great Flood,
But it was fam'd with more than with one Man?
When could they say, till now, that talk'd of Rome,
That her wide Walks encompass'd but one Man?
Now is it Rome indeed, and Room enough,
When there is in it but one onely Man?
O! you and I have heard our Fathers say,

156 **Brutus** Cassius refers to Lucius Junius Brutus, whom Marcus Brutus claimed as an ancestor. The earlier Brutus had led a successful revolt against the corrupt and tyrannical Tarquins, driving them from Rome in 509 BC and thereby establishing republican government in place of kingship. The survival of that form of goverment is what is now at stake.

156–58 **that . . . King** Cassius is saying that the legendary Brutus would have tolerated (*brook'd*) the Devil's rule as readily as he would put up with that of a king.

159 **nothing jealous** in no way doubtful. Compare line 69.

160 **work me too** Most editors alter the Folio spelling here to *to*. But it may be that *work me* has the force of 'work me to' (persuade me of), and thus that *too* here means 'also'.

Aim notion, idea. Brutus has 'some Aim' in a sense that puts him a step ahead of Cassius. Although he is playing hard to get, and thus forcing Cassius into the role of wooer, if not seducer, Brutus is in control here and will soon be the 'onely Man' among the conspirators, the one whose 'Aim' (purpose) will aim (direct) the course the others take.

163 **so** thus, in this manner.

164 **mov'd** urged. Compare I.i.66.

168 **chew** ruminate, meditate.

169 **Villager** a provincial, rather than a proud citizen of the world's most important metropolis.

171 **hard Conditions** adverse circumstances, imposing the 'Yoke' (line 59) of hard labour as a condition of survival. See the note to I.iii.146.

as that.

172 **like** likely.

177 **sowre** both (a) sour (pungent, sullen), and (b) sore (irritable, chafing). Compare *Macbeth*, II.i.55.

178 **worthy note** worthy of notice. Here *note to day* can imply more than the phrase means when *to day* is modernized to *today*.

There was a Brutus once that would have brook'd
Th' eternal Divel to keep his State in Rome
As easily as a King.

BRUTUS That you do love me, I am nothing jealous;
What you would work me too, I have some Aim;
How I have thought of this, and of these Times,
I shall recount hereafter. For this present,
I would not so (with Love I might entreat you)
Be any further mov'd. What you have said
I will consider; what you have to say
I will with Patience hear, and find a Time
Both meet to hear and answer such high things.
Till then, my Noble Friend, chew upon this:
Brutus had rather be a Villager
Than to repute himself a Son of Rome
Under these hard Conditions as this Time
Is like to lay upon us.

CASSIUS I am glad
That my weak Words have struck but thus much shew
Of Fire from Brutus.

Enter Caesar and his Train.

BRUTUS The Games are done, and Caesar is returning.

CASSIUS As they pass by, pluck Casca by the Sleeve,
And he will, after his sowre fashion, tell you
What hath proceeded worthy note to day.

BRUTUS I will do so. But look you, Cassius,

180 **Angry Spot** Brutus probably refers to a birthmark that became enflamed when Caesar was moved to anger. There is no reference to such a spot in Plutarch, so Shakespeare probably included this detail to remind his audience of the 'mark' on the forehead which identified those who had fallen under the control of 'the Beast' (a symbol of Antichrist) in Revelation 13:11–18.

181 **a chidden Train** an entourage of scolded followers.

183 **ferret** Cicero's eyes are small and red like those of a ferret.

185 **Conference** parliamentary debate.

195 **Yet . . . Fear** Caesar has become so caught up in the public image he has tried to create that he assumes himself to be identical with it. His suspicions of Cassius, however, indicate that he retains some doubts about whether that persona can withstand the scrutiny of a penetrating eye. According to Plutarch, Caesar confessed that ' "As for those fat men and smooth-combed heads, . . . I never reckon of them; but these pale-visaged and carrion-lean people, I fear them most," meaning Brutus and Cassius.'

my Name By Shakespeare's time, the name *Caesar* had long been synonymous with *King* (a fact preserved in such titles as Kaiser and Czar). This was not yet the case when Julius Caesar was alive. The association derived from Caesar's adopted son Octavius, who took on the name Augustus when he became Emperor and who established a precedent whereby those who succeeded him were known as Caesar. It is one of the ironies of the play that 'always I am Caesar' (line 208) is spoken by the one Caesar whose destiny is *not* to be Caesar in the sense he aspires to.

200 **he hears no Music** It was proverbial that those who disliked music were lacking in inner harmony and were thus disposed to disturb social harmony. Lorenzo alludes to this commonplace in *The Merchant of Venice*, V.i.83–88. Shakespeare's depiction of Antony derives from Plutarch, who says that 'In his house they did nothing, but feast, dance, and mask: and himself passed away the time in hearing of foolish plays.' At a time when Elizabethan Puritans accused the Bankside players of encouraging vice, and Court authorities were on the alert for material 'Dangerous' to the state, Shakespeare and his colleagues probably enjoyed Caesar's portrayal of the play-loving Antony as a regular fellow who could be trusted.

The Angry Spot doth glow on Caesar's Brow,
And all the rest look like a chidden Train;
Calphurnia's Cheek is pale, and Cicero
Looks with such ferret and such fiery Eyes
As we have seen him in the Capitol
Being cross'd in Conference by some Senators.

CASSIUS Casca will tell us what the matter is.

CAESAR Antonio.

ANTONY Caesar.

CAESAR Let me have Men about me that are Fat,
Sleek-headed Men, and such as Sleep a-nights.
Yond Cassius has a Lean and Hungry Look,
He thinks too much: such Men are Dangerous.

ANTONY Fear him not, Caesar, he's not Dangerous;
He is a Noble Roman, and well given.

CAESAR Would he were fatter. But I fear him not:
Yet if my Name were liable to Fear,
I do not know the Man I should avoid
So soon as that spare Cassius. He reads much,
He is a great Observer, and he looks
Quite through the Deeds of Men. He loves no Plays,
As thou dost, Antony; he hears no Music;
Seldom he smiles, and smiles in such a sort
As if he mock'd himself, and scorn'd his Spirit
That could be mov'd to smile at any thing.
Such Men as he be never at Heart's Ease
Whiles they behold a Greater than themselves,
And therefore are they very Dangerous.
I rather tell thee what is to be fear'd
Than what I fear: for always I am Caesar.

208–9 **for . . . Deaf** Caesar claims constancy and hints at immortality in a line in which he unwittingly echoes the name of God ('I am') as disclosed to Moses in Exodus 3:14. Then, in ironic juxtaposition, Caesar refers to one of those infirmities that mark him as a mortal like other men. Plutarch says nothing about Caesar's deafness, so this is another trait that Shakespeare invented, possibly because he associated the malady with epilepsy.

213 **I** both (a) Ay, and (b) I [would].

214 **Sad** serious, in this case because of his displeasure and apprehensiveness.

217 **Crown** At this point in his 'Life of Caesar', Plutarch describes a 'laurel crown' with 'a royal band or diadem wreathed about it'.

225 **marry** indeed. This expression originated in an oath that referred to the Virgin Mary.

226 **gentler than other** more tentatively than the one that preceded it.

227 **honest Neighbours** a common term of respect, usually used by the lower classes to refer to ordinary law-abiding folk (compare *A Midsummer Night's Dream*, III.i.146–47, where Bottom uses the phrase to refer to peacemakers). Here Casca employs the term with the condescension of an aristocrat contemptuous of 'the Rabblement' (line 242). Casca, Brutus, and Cassius are all members of the Senate, the patrician body of the republic, and Casca and Cassius are more openly scornful of the plebeians than are the Tribunes who have scolded them for their fickleness in the opening scene.

232 **mere Foolery** pure hypocritical miming. Here *Foolery* means 'mockery'.
mark it pay attention to it.

235 **Coronets** Casca probably refers to a small, inferior 'crownet', presumably the most 'royal' object that Caesar and Antony are willing to risk toying with at this stage in their dealings with the populace. Compare *King Lear*, I.i.140.

237 **would fain have had it** would have liked to have it.

238 **put it by** pushed it aside.

Come on my Right Hand, for this Ear is Deaf,
And tell me truly what thou think'st of him.
Sennet. Exeunt Caesar and his Train. [*Manet Casca.*]

CASCA You pull'd me by the Cloak, would you speak with me?

BRUTUS I, Casca, tell us what hath chanc'd to day
That Caesar looks so Sad.

CASCA Why you were with him, were you not?

BRUTUS I should not then ask Casca what had chanc'd.

CASCA Why there was a Crown offer'd him; and being offer'd him, he put it by with the back of his Hand thus, and then the People fell a Shouting.

BRUTUS What was the second Noise for?

CASCA Why for that too.

CASSIUS They shouted thrice: what was the last Cry for?

CASCA Why for that too.

BRUTUS Was the Crown offer'd him thrice?

CASCA Ay marry was't, and he put it by thrice, every time gentler than other; and at every putting by, mine honest Neighbours shouted.

CASSIUS Who offer'd him the Crown?

CASCA Why Antony.

BRUTUS Tell us the Manner of it, gentle Casca.

CASCA I can as well be hang'd as tell the manner of it: it was mere Foolery, I did not mark it. I saw Mark Antony offer him a Crown, yet 'twas not a Crown neither, 'twas one of these Coronets; and as I told you, he put it by once; but for all that, to my thinking, he would fain have had it. Then he offered it to him again; then he put it by again; but to my thinking, he was very loath to lay his Fingers off it. And then he offered it the third time; he put it the third time by, and still as he

242 **howted** hooted, shouted.

243 **chopt** chapped, rough from manual labour.

247 **swounded** swooned (sometimes spelled *swoonded*).

250 **soft** hush, hold it.

253 **'Tis . . . Sickness** Most modern editions insert a stop (a colon or a semicolon) after *like*, assuming that Brutus is already certain of Caesar's epilepsy. The Folio line lacks even so much as a comma. Here *like* means 'likely'.

255 **Falling Sickness** Cassius is using the term metaphorically, with reference to 'Underlings' who bow to Caesar (see lines 113–22).

259–60 **as they use to do** as they are used to doing to. *True* means 'honest', law-abiding.

260 **Players** Casca suggests that Caesar's 'Foolery' (line 232) is in fact a kind of theatrical role-playing. Compare lines 199–203.

264 **Heard** herd. The Folio spelling is a reminder of how often the common herd are heard, not only in this scene but elsewhere in the play. Despite the Patricians' contempt for them, the plebeians have a significant voice in the affairs of Rome's government.

265 **pluck'd me ope** pulled open. The *me* construction is short for 'for me', and it is usually employed when a speaker is being familiar or colloquial.

his Doublet a chose-fitting jacket worn by Elizabethan men. This and other evidence would suggest that when the play was performed in Shakespeare's lifetime, the Romans were dressed not in togas, but in ordinary Elizabethan attire. But in a different context (described in note 272) North's Plutarch refers to Caesar's 'doublet collar'.

266–68 **And . . . Word** Here Casca seems to be saying that if he had been a real man, of any occupation whatever, he would have taken Caesar at his word. *And* (line 266) means 'if'.

refus'd it the Rabblement howted, and clapp'd their chopt Hands, and threw up their sweaty Night-caps, and utter'd such a deal of stinking Breath, because Caesar refus'd the Crown, that it had, almost, chok'd Caesar; for he swounded, and fell down at it. And for mine own part, I durst not laugh, for fear of opening my Lips and receiving the bad Air.

CASSIUS But soft I pray you: what, did Caesar swound?

CASCA He fell down in the Market-place, and foam'd at Mouth, and was speechless.

BRUTUS 'Tis very like he hath the Falling Sickness.

CASSIUS No, Caesar hath it not; but you, and I,
And honest Casca, we have the Falling Sickness.

CASCA I know not what you mean by that, but I am sure Caesar fell down. If the tag-rag People did not clap him, and hiss him, according as he pleas'd and displeas'd them, as they use to do the Players in the Theatre, I am no True Man.

BRUTUS What said he when he came unto himself?

CASCA Marry, before he fell down, when he perceiv'd the common Heard was glad he refus'd the Crown, he pluck'd me ope his Doublet, and offer'd them his Throat to cut. And I had been a man of any Occupation, if I would not have taken him at a Word, I would I might go to Hell among the Rogues. And so he fell. When he came to himself again, he said if he had done or said any thing amiss he desir'd their

272 **his Infirmity** the weakness or illness that has caused him to swoon. It is not necessary to infer that Shakespeare's Caesar was referring specifically to his epilepsy. Plutarch's Caesar uses this pretext to 'excuse' his 'folly' to 'the magistrates of the commonwealth', imputing his disdainful refusal to rise when they entered 'to his disease, saying that their wits are not perfect which have his disease of the falling evil, when standing on their feet they speak to the common people, but are soon troubled with a trembling of their body and a sudden dimness and giddiness'.

283 **and** if.

286–87 **it was Greek to me** By Shakespeare's time this was already a proverbial expression for a statement that a person found incomprehensible. It is in keeping with the blunt character Shakespeare gives Casca, but in fact it is a departure from the character of the conspirator depicted by Plutarch, who tells us that the historical Casca spoke in Greek when he struck the first blow of the assassination. Casca's rough-edged personality is emphasized in this scene by the fact that he alone speaks prose.

289 **put to Silence** removed from participation in public discourse. According to Plutarch, Caesar deprived them of their Tribuneships. Shakespeare's phrasing makes their fate sound more ominous.

295 **I** both (a) Ay, and (b) I [will]. Compare line 213.
your Mind hold you don't change your mind.

296 **Dinner** the midday meal (as distinguished from supper).

300 **Quick Mettle** intelligent, lively. In the following line Cassius is probably punning on *mettle/metal* as he thinks about the swords that will be employed in the 'Execution' (carrying out) of the 'Enterprise' he has hinted at in his conversation with Brutus. Compare I.i.66, I.ii.27.

303 **this Tardy Form** this pretence of being ignorant and slow of wit. Cassius is playing on 'Quick Metal', with the implication that Casca appears similar to a piece of metal that is slow to take form (such as that of a sword) as it is heated and cooled in the tempering process. Compare line 127.

Worships to think it was his Infirmity. Three or four Wenches where I stood cried 'Alas, good Soul,' and forgave him with all their Hearts. But there's no heed to be taken of them; if Caesar had stabb'd their Mothers, they would have done no less.

BRUTUS And after that, he came thus sad away.

CASCA Ay.

CASSIUS Did Cicero say any thing?

CASCA Ay, he spoke Greek.

CASSIUS To what effect?

CASCA Nay, and I tell you that, I'll ne'er look you i' th' Face again. But those that understood him smil'd at one another, and shook their Heads. But for mine own part, it was Greek to me. I could tell you more News too: Murellus and Flavius, for pulling Scarfs off Caesar's Images, are put to Silence. Fare you well. There was more Foolery yet, if I could remember it.

CASSIUS Will you sup with me to night, Casca?

CASCA No, I am promis'd forth.

CASSIUS Will you dine with me to morrow?

CASCA I, if I be alive and your Mind hold, and your Dinner worth the eating.

CASSIUS Good, I will expect you.

CASCA Do so; farewell both. *Exit.*

BRUTUS What a Blunt Fellow is this grown to be?
He was Quick Mettle when he went to School.

CASSIUS So is he now, in Execution
Of any bold or noble Enterprise,
How-ever he puts on this Tardy Form.

304 **Rudeness** coarseness. Cassius implies that Casca's apparent lack of good manners, his incivility, is 'mere Foolery' (line 232), not unlike the 'Tardy Form' Caesar has displayed in his refusal to take the crown he desires. Brutus too, has donned a 'Tardy Form' (see the note to line 160). According to Plutarch, 'they that desired change . . . wished Brutus only their prince and governor above all other'. And 'Cassius, finding Brutus' ambition stirred up . . . did prick him forward. . . .' In many ways Cassius is to Brutus what Antony is to Caesar: a flattering bad angel who inflates his ego and thereby facilitates what the proud Brutus is already prone to do without external persuasion.

309 **home to you** to your house.

310 **wait for you** receive you, entertain you.

313 **Thy Honourable Mettle may be wrought** Again Cassius is playing on *mettle* (virtue, character) and *metal* (compare line 300). His implication is that Brutus, for all his apparent constancy, is susceptible to being bent or moulded (*wrought*) to something that would seem to go against his natural disposition. What Cassius suggests is that an 'Honourable Mettle' can be transformed, by a perversion of alchemical or tempering processes, into the 'Basest Mettle' of those who without Brutus, would 'vanish Tongue-tied in their Guiltiness' (I.i.66–67). But whether Brutus really needs to be 'seduc'd' (line 316) by Cassius is anything but clear. According to Plutarch, Cassius was urged by the other conspirators to win Brutus over. 'For they told him that so high an enterprise' required 'a man of such estimation as Brutus, to make every man boldly think, that by his only presence the fact were holy and just'. See the notes to lines 154, 160, 304.

314 **meet** fitting.

315 **likes** minds of similar nobility. Cassius implicitly depicts his own mind as less than 'Noble'. *Likes* anticipates II.ii.128.

317 **bear me hard** have hard feelings about me, dislike me. *Hard* recalls I.i.42, I.ii.73, 170. It plays on *firm* in line 316. See the notes to I.ii.33, 34, 121, 154, 160.

This Rudeness is a Sauce to his good Wit,
Which gives men Stomach to digest his Words
With better Appetite.

BRUTUS And so it is.
For this Time I will leave you.
To morrow, if you please to speak with me,
I will come home to you; or if you will,
Come home to me, and I will wait for you.

CASSIUS I will do so: till then think of the World.

Exit Brutus.

Well Brutus, thou art Noble; yet I see
Thy Honourable Mettle may be wrought
From that it is dispos'd. Therefore it is meet
That Noble Minds keep ever with their likes:
For who so firm that cannot be seduc'd?
Caesar doth bear me hard, but he loves Brutus.

318–19 **If . . . me** Cassius' implication is that if Brutus were a man of prudence and personal ambition, he would attach himself to Caesar, who loves him, rather than join the conspiracy against Caesar. What this sentence suggests is that Cassius' motives are less than pure. He may be concerned about preserving the liberties of Rome's citizens now that he feels threatened by Caesar's power, but he might feel differently if Caesar favoured him the way he does Brutus.

320 **Hands** handwriting styles.

322 **tending to** both (a) pointing in the direction of, and (b) attending to (and thereby getting Brutus' attention).

324 **glanced** hinted; here pronounced as a two-syllable word.

325 **seat him sure** position himself securely.

326 **shake him** both (a) make him tremble (as in line 119), and (b) shake him down (like an overripe fruit on a branch). Compare *King Lear*, I.i.37–42.

I.iii The setting is a street in Rome. In all likelihood Casca and Cicero enter from different locations.

1 **even** evening.
Brought accompanied, escorted.

3 **all the sway of Earth** the whole world and its dominions. *Sway* means 'rule' or 'dominion'; but here it suggests another meaning that goes with *Shakes* (line 4, echoing I.ii.326). Compare the ambiguity of *sway* in *King Lear*, I.ii.55. *Mov'd* recalls I.ii.164.

6 **riv'd** split. *Unfirm* (line 4) echoes I.ii.316–17.

7 **ambitious Ocean** Casca describes the ocean as 'ambitious' because it seems to be threatening to overwhelm its shores. Compare the references to the Tiber in I.i.49–53, 63–65, I.ii.98–107.

8 **exalted with** lifted up to the same height as.

9 **to night** tonight.

10 **Tempest-dropping Fire** This is probably a reference to extraordinary displays of lightning, wind, and rain. Among 'the strange and wonderful signs that were seen before Caesar's death', Plutarch mentions 'fires in the element and spirits running up and down in the night'.

If I were Brutus now, and he were Cassius,
He should not humour me. I will this Night,
In several Hands, in at his Windows throw,
As if they came from several Citizens,
Writings, all tending to the great Opinion
That Rome holds of his Name: wherein obscurely
Caesar's Ambition shall be glanced at.
And after this, let Caesar seat him sure,
For we will shake him, or worse Days endure.

Exit.

Scene 3

Thunder and Lightning. Enter Casca and Cicero.

CICERO Good even, Casca. Brought you Caesar home?
Why are you breathless, and why stare you so?
CASCA Are you not mov'd, when all the sway of Earth
Shakes like a thing unfirm? O Cicero,
I have seen Tempests when the scolding Winds
Have riv'd the knotty Oaks, and I have seen
Th' ambitious Ocean swell, and rage, and foam,
To be exalted with the threat'ning Clouds;
But never till to night, never till now,
Did I go through a Tempest-dropping Fire.

11 **Civil . . . Heaven** insurrection in the sky. Compare I.ii.44, where Brutus describes an internal 'Strife'.

12 **saucy** insolent. A colloquial form of the word is 'sassy'. Lines 12–13 recall I.ii.149–50, 311.

13 **Incenses** enflames.

14 **any thing more wonderful** anything else to be wondered at. Plutarch mentions the 'slave of the soldiers that did cast a marvellous burning flame out of his hand' but suffered 'no hurt'. But Plutarch says nothing about a surly lion.

18 **sensible of** sensitive to, able to feel.

20 **Against** opposite, across from.

21 **glaz'd upon** gazed blankly at.

23 **ghastly** ghost-like, white-faced, 'scared to death'. Plutarch says nothing about 'ghastly Women'.

26 **Bird of Night** This is probably a reference to the screech-owl. Like the raven, it was thought to be a bird of ill omen. Plutarch refers only to 'the solitary birds'.

28 **Howting** hooting. Compare I.ii.242.
Prodigies supernatural occurrences, almost always assumed to be signs of Heaven's displeasure and thus of impending doom.

29 **conjointly meet** coincide.

31 **portentous** ominous (filled with omens).

32 **Climate** locale.

33 **strange disposed** Here Shakespeare's syntax hovers between 'strangely disposed' and 'strange-disposed'. The literal meaning of *disposed* is 'put apart' (arranged individually), but in Shakespeare it often means 'inclined to merriment' (as in *Love's Labour's Lost*, II.i.247, V.ii.465); here the word suggests that the Heavens are disposed to mock a 'World' that has become too 'saucy' (line 12).

34 **construe** interpret. Compare I.ii.43–44.
after their fashion in their own way. *Fashion* echoes I.ii.177.

35 **Clean from** completely away from, in a way that has nothing to do with.

39 **disturbed** For metrical reasons, this word is here pronounced as a three-syllable word.

Either there is a Civil Strife in Heaven
Or else the World, too saucy with the Gods,
Incenses them to send Destruction.

CICERO Why, saw you any thing more wonderful?

CASCA A common Slave (you know him well by sight)
Held up his left Hand, which did flame and burn
Like twenty Torches join'd; and yet his Hand,
Not sensible of Fire, remain'd unscorch'd.
Besides (I ha' not since put up my Sword)
Against the Capitol I met a Lion,
Who glaz'd upon me and went surly by
Without annoying me. And there were drawn
Upon a heap a hundred ghastly Women,
Transformed with their Fear, who swore they saw
Men, all in Fire, walk up and down the Streets.
And yesterday the Bird of Night did sit,
Even at Noon-day, upon the Market-place,
Howting and shrieking. When these Prodigies
Do so conjointly meet, let not men say
'These are their Reasons, they are Natural,'
For I believe they are portentous things
Unto the Climate that they point upon.

CICERO Indeed, it is a strange disposed Time;
But men may construe things after their fashion,
Clean from the purpose of the things themselves.
Comes Caesar to the Capitol to morrow?

CASCA He doth: for he did bid Antonio
Send word to you he would be there to morrow.

CICERO Good-night then, Casca. This disturbed Sky
Is not to walk in.

CASCA Farewell, Cicero. *Exit Cicero.*

Enter Cassius.

CASSIUS Who's there?

CASCA A Roman.

42 **what Night is this?** both (a) Does tonight fall on some portentous date? and (b) What kind of night is this? In most editions this line is rendered as an exclamation; the early texts of Shakespeare often place a question mark where an exclamation point is called for in modern usage. But Cassius' remark in the following line seems more likely to be a reply to a question. For similar constructions and punctuation, see I.i.43, 45; I.ii.12, 299; I.iii.108, 109, 137; II.i.1, 3, 263, 313; II.ii.105; II.iv.41, 114, 117, 211; III.ii.74, 192; IV.ii.59, 176.

43 **Honest** honourable, virtuous, truthful.

45 **Faults** Cassius probably means 'evils', but the word *fault* could be applied to any crack, breach, or deficiency. Compare I.i.61, I.ii.137.

48 **unbraced** unfastened, unprotected. Cassius probably refers to a doublet (tight-fitting jacket) that he has opened to bare his breast to the 'Breast of Heaven' (line 51). See the note to I.ii.265.

49 **Thunder-stone** thunderbolt.

50 **cross** Cassius probably means both (a) crossing in a zigzag pattern, and (b) thwarting, perverse, angry.
blew both (a) blue, and (b) blown. *Aim* (line 52) recalls I.ii.160.

53 **tempt** try, by showing disrespect to. Casca accuses Cassius of *hubris*, the arrogance that leads to an outrageous, defiant gesture and brings the Heavens down in retribution.

54 **It is the part of Men** It is Man's place. Unlike Cassius, Casca is a God-fearing man who believes in omens.

55 **Tokens** signs.

56 **dreadful Heralds** fright-inducing messengers.
astonish us overwhelm us with awe.

57 **dull** lacking in both spirit and intelligence.

58 **want** lack.

64 **from Quality and Kind** departing from the traits characteristic of their normal nature.

65 **calculate** prophesy. The word derives from astrology, and it originally referred to predictions derived from mathematical calculations of the positions of stars and planets.

CASSIUS Casca, by your Voice.
CASCA Your Ear is good. Cassius, what Night is this?
CASSIUS A very pleasing Night to Honest Men.
CASCA Who ever knew the Heavens menace so?
CASSIUS Those that have known the Earth so full of Faults.
For my part, I have walk'd about the Streets
Submitting me unto the perilous Night,
And thus unbraced, Casca, as you see,
Have bar'd my Bosom to the Thunder-stone:
And when the cross blew Lightning seem'd to open
The Breast of Heaven, I did present my self
Even in the Aim and very Flash of it.
CASCA But wherefore did you so much tempt the Heavens?
It is the part of Men to fear and tremble
When the most mighty Gods by Tokens send
Such dreadful Heralds to astonish us.
CASSIUS You are dull, Casca, and those Sparks of Life
That should be in a Roman you do want,
Or else you use not. You look Pale, and Gaze,
And put on Fear, and cast your self in Wonder,
To see the strange Impatience of the Heavens;
But if you would consider the true Cause,
Why all these Fires, why all these gliding Ghosts,
Why Birds and Beasts, from Quality and Kind,
Why Old Men, Fools, and Children calculate,

66 **their Ordinance** their ordained ('pre-formed') behaviour.

67 **Faculties** abilities and dispositions.

68 **Monstrous** unnatural or supernatural, and thus ominous. The word derives from *monere*, Latin for 'admonish' or 'warn', and in Shakespeare it usually refers to something that is to be interpreted as a sign of divine displeasure.

73 **Dreadful** causing dread, cosmic reverence. Compare line 56.

77 **personal Action** what he has done or can do in his own person (using his own abilities).
Prodigious Here Cassius is probably using the term in something approaching the modern sense: portentous because of its colossal size. Compare line 28.

78 **Eruptions** outbreaks of Nature, such as earthquakes, volcanoes, and extraordinary storms.

81 **Thews** sinews, muscles.
Ancestors This word could also be construed as possessive: *Ancestors'*.

84 **Yoke** harness, frame (such as that used for oxen). Compare I.ii.59.
Sufferance submission, willingness to suffer patiently.
Womanish a highly derogatory term in a culture dedicated entirely to the 'masculine virtues' associated with military valour. Later in the play Portia will try to win Brutus' attention by showing that she is capable of manly fortitude. And when Decius Brutus wishes to persuade Caesar to go to the Capitol on the Ides of March, the only thing he has to do is to suggest that if Caesar doesn't come he will be laughed at for yielding to womanish fears.

88 **save** except.

89 **where . . . Dagger** Cassius means that he will either slay Caesar or slay himself. In either case he assumes, he will 'deliver' himself to death. In Plutarch it is Brutus who says 'I mean not to hold my peace, but to withstand it, and rather die than lose my liberty.' Compare *Hamlet* I.ii.129–32, III.i.53–57.

93 **Nor . . . nor** neither . . . nor.

95 **Can be retentive to** can hold in or restrain.

96 **Bars** not only prison bars, but any kind of impediment.

Why all these things change from their Ordinance,
Their Natures, and pre-formed Faculties,
To Monstrous Quality, why you shall find
That Heaven hath infus'd them with these Spirits,
To make them Instruments of Fear, and Warning,
Unto some Monstrous State.
Now could I, Casca, name to thee a Man
Most like this Dreadful Night,
That thunders, lightens, opens Graves, and roars
As doth the Lion in the Capitol,
A Man no mightier than thy self, or me,
In personal Action, yet Prodigious grown
And fearful, as these strange Eruptions are.

CASCA 'Tis Caesar that you mean, is it not, Cassius?

CASSIUS Let it be who it is: for Romans now
Have Thews, and Limbs, like to their Ancestors;
But woe the while, our Fathers' Minds are dead,
And we are governed with our Mothers' Spirits;
Our Yoke, and Sufferance, shew us Womanish.

CASCA Indeed, they say the Senators to morrow
Mean to establish Caesar as a King;
And he shall wear his Crown by Sea, and Land,
In every place, save here in Italy.

CASSIUS I know where I will wear this Dagger then:
Cassius from Bondage will deliver Cassius.
Therein, ye Gods, you make the Weak most Strong;
Therein, ye Gods, you Tyrants do defeat.
Nor Stony Tower, nor Walls of beaten Brass,
Nor air-less Dungeon, nor strong Links of Iron,
Can be retentive to the Strength of Spirit;
But Life, being weary of these worldly Bars,
Never lacks Power to dismiss it self.

98 **know all the World** let all the world know.

99 **bear** carry, like a beast of burden. This word echoes I.ii.33–34, 110–14, 129, 317. Compare *Hamlet*, III.i.67–73.

S.D. **Thunder still.** The thundering continues.

102 **cancel** annul, render inoperative, put to an end.

106 **were** would be.
Hinds female deer. By extension, the term also meant (a) rustics, and (b) cowards. Compare *Romeo and Juliet*, I.i.68, where Tybalt refers to 'Hartless Hinds'.

109 **Offal** wood chips or shavings (literally 'off-fall').

110 **Base Matter** lowest form of material. Compare I.i.66.
illuminate give light to (by providing the material for a fire).

111 **vile** worthless.
oh This spelling often signifies a sigh or a groan. It thus carries an implication that differs from the vocative O.

114 **my . . . made** I must now act on my resolve [because you will betray me to the 'Tyrant'].

115 **indifferent** of no concern.

117 **fleering** sneering.

118 **Be . . . Griefs** form a faction or party to obtain satisfaction (retribution) for our grievances.

121 **mov'd** persuaded. Compare I.ii.164.

123 **undergo** undertake, bear (line 99).

125 **by this** either (a) by this time, or (b) by this heart (or head). If Cassius has the second meaning in mind, he probably gestures accordingly. Compare *King Lear*, I.i.117.
stay wait.

126 **Pompey's Porch** *Porticus Pompei*, the portico or colonnade of the theatre that Pompey built in 55 BC. It was near the Senate-house, also built by Pompey.

128 **Complexion of the Element** composition (condition) of the sky.

If I know this, know all the World besides,
That part of Tyranny that I do bear
I can shake off at Pleasure. *Thunder still.*

CASCA So can I;
So every Bondman in his own Hand bears
The Power to cancel his Captivity.

CASSIUS And why should Caesar be a Tyrant then?
Poor Man, I know he would not be a Wolf
But that he sees the Romans are but Sheep;
He were no Lion were not Romans Hinds.
Those that with haste will make a mighty Fire
Begin it with weak Straws. What Trash is Rome?
What Rubbish, and what Offal? when it serves
For the Base Matter to illuminate
So vile a thing as Caesar. – But oh Grief,
Where hast thou led me? I, perhaps, speak this
Before a willing Bondman: then I know
My Answer must be made. But I am arm'd,
And Dangers are to me indifferent.

CASCA You speak to Casca, and to such a Man
That is no fleering Tell-tale. Hold, my Hand:
Be factious for redress of all these Griefs,
And I will set this Foot of mine as far
As who goes farthest.

CASSIUS There's a Bargain made.
Now know you, Casca, I have mov'd already
Some certain of the Noblest-minded Romans
To undergo with me an Enterprise
Of honourable dangerous Consequence;
And I do know by this, they stay for me
In Pompey's Porch; for now this fearful Night
There is no stir, or walking in the Streets;
And the Complexion of the Element

129 **Is Favours** is a propitious sign of Heaven's face: its encouragement of, and assistance to, 'the Work we have in hand'. *Favours* may be a metrically elided form for either *favourous* or *favourish*, two obsolete words for 'favourable'. Most modern editions alter this line to 'In favour's like . . .'. Compare I.ii.88–89.

135–36 **one incorporate / To our Attempts** a party to our efforts. The phrase 'incorporate to' literally means 'of a body with'.

136 **stay'd for** awaited.

137 **I am glad on't** I'm pleased to say you are.
what . . . this? This echoes line 42.

143 **Praetor's Chair** At this time Brutus was the chief magistrate in Rome. The chair Cassius refers to is the *sella curulis*, in which Brutus would sit while presiding over disputes brought before him to judge.

144 **Where Brutus may but find it** either (a) where only Brutus may find it, or (b) where Brutus may happen upon it.

146 **old Brutus' Statue** the statue of Brutus' ancestor, Lucius Junius Brutus, the father of the Roman republic. See the note to I.ii.156. According to Plutarch, 'Marcus Brutus came of that Junius Brutus for whom the ancient Romans made his statue of brass to be set up in the Capitol with the images of the kings, holding a naked sword in his hand, because he had valiantly put down the Tarquins from their kingdom of Rome. But that Junius Brutus, being of a sour stern nature, not softened by reason, being like unto sword blades of too hard temper, was so subject to his choler and malice he bore unto the tyrants, that for their sakes he caused his own sons to be executed.'

148 **Decius** The historical figure was named *Decimus*; Shakespeare adopts the form he found in North's Plutarch.

150 **hie** go quickly. Compare line 157, and see the comparable wordplay on *hie* and *high* in *Romeo and Juliet*, II.iv.69–79, and *Macbeth*, I.v.22, 27.

Is Favours, like the Work we have in hand,
Most Bloody, Fiery, and most Terrible.

Enter Cinna.

CASCA Stand close a while, for here comes one in haste.
CASSIUS 'Tis Cinna, I do know him by his Gait,
He is a Friend. – Cinna, where haste you so?
CINNA To find out you. Who's that, Metellus Cimber?
CASSIUS No, it is Casca, one incorporate
To our Attempts. Am I not stay'd for, Cinna?
CINNA I am glad on't. What a fearful Night is this?
There's two or three of us have seen strange Sights.
CASSIUS Am I not stay'd for? Tell me.
CINNA Yes you are.
O Cassius, if you could but win the Noble
Brutus to our Party –
CASSIUS Be you content.
Good Cinna, take this Paper,
And look you lay it in the Praetor's Chair,
Where Brutus may but find it; and throw this
In at his Window; set this up with Wax
Upon old Brutus' Statue; all this done,
Repair to Pompey's Porch, where you shall find us.
Is Decius Brutus and Trebonius there?
CINNA All but Metellus Cimber, and he's gone
To seek you at your House. Well, I will hie

151 **bad** bade. Compare I.ii.104, 123. Cinna becomes one of the 'bad Souls' (I.i.16) who heed Cassius' calling. According to Plutarch, Brutus' friends 'by many bills also, did openly call and procure him to do that he did. For under the image of his ancestor Junius Brutus, that drave the kings out of Rome, they wrote: "Oh that it pleased the gods thou wert now alive, Brutus." . . . His tribunal, or chair, where he gave audience during the time he was Praetor, was full of such bills: "Brutus, thou art asleep, and art not Brutus indeed." '

152 **repair to** make your way to.

156 **Encounter** Cassius probably means (a) meeting, but he may also be thinking of (b) military engagement. Like *Countenance* (line 159), *Encounter* often plays on the Latin word *cunnus* (female pudendum). Here it recalls the imagery of seduction in I.ii.316. Compare *Troilus and Cressida*, III.iii.217–19, and *King Lear*, V.i.60–63.

159 **Countenance** both (a) approval, support, and (b) reputation. See the note to I.ii.313.

Alchemy a science (the forerunner of modern chemistry) whose objective was to transmute base metals like lead and iron into gold. In I.i.66–67 Flavius has used an alchemical metaphor to describe the 'Basest Mettle' they have just moved. Cassius has hinted at such a metaphor in I.iii.110, when he described Rome's citizens as 'Base Matter'. For other references to transmutation, see I.i.14–16, 27–28, 77–80; I.ii.8–9, 299–306, 312–16; I.iii.59–100, 103–11, 128–30.

162 **conceited** conceived, described through your apt 'conceit' (referring to Casca's rhetorical figure).

And so bestow these Papers as you bad me.
CASSIUS That done, repair to Pompey's Theatre.
Exit Cinna.
– Come, Casca, you and I will yet, ere Day,
See Brutus at his House; three Parts of him
Is ours already, and the Man entire
Upon the next Encounter yields him ours.
CASCA O he sits high in all the People's Hearts;
And that which would appear Offence in us
His Countenance, like richest Alchemy,
Will change to Virtue and to Worthiness.
CASSIUS Him, and his Worth, and our great Need of him,
You have right well conceited; let us go,
For it is after Mid-night, and ere Day
We will awake him and be sure of him. *Exeunt.*

II.i This scene takes place in the orchard of Brutus' house.

2 **progress . . . Stars** movement of the constellations. *Stars* recalls I.ii.137–38.

4 **Fault** deficiency, disability. Compare I.i.61, I.ii.137, I.iii.45. According to Plutarch, Brutus' sleeplessness was habitual. When he served in Pompey's army during the war in which Caesar overcame his chief rival for hegemony in Rome, Brutus 'did nothing but study all day long. . . . Furthermore, when others slept, or thought what would happen the morrow after, he fell to his book, and wrote all day long till night . . .' See the note to IV.ii.270.

7 **Taper** candle.

11 **spurn at him** object to him, reject him. The literal meaning of *spurn* was 'kick', so this phrase had a stronger implication in Shakespeare's day than it would carry today. *Cause* (which echoes I.iii.62) can here mean both (a) reason, and (b) case (another English word that derives from the Latin *causa*) in the legal sense.

12 **for the general** for the cause that concerns the common good. Compare I.ii.83–85, 129.

14 **Adder** a small poisonous snake.

15 **craves** requires, calls for.

17 **do Danger** threaten harm.

18–19 **Th' Abuse . . . Power** The abuse of authority occurs when the one who holds it wields power without compassion. The Folio spelling of *dis-joins* is orthographically apt; compare *dis-joint* in *Macbeth*, III.ii.16.

20 **Affections** feelings, passions.
sway'd exercised power. Compare I.iii.3. Brutus' own 'Affections' are 'sway'd', and they are 'More than his Reason' can keep under control.

21 **a common Proof** a fact well attested by experience.

ACT II

Scene I

Enter Brutus in his Orchard.

BRUTUS What, Lucius, ho?
– I cannot, by the progress of the Stars,
Give guess how near to Day. – Lucius, I say?
– I would it were my Fault to sleep so soundly.
– When, Lucius, when? Awake, I say: what,
Lucius?

Enter Lucius.

LUCIUS Call'd you, my Lord?
BRUTUS Get me a Taper in my Study, Lucius.
When it is lighted, come and call me here.
LUCIUS I will, my Lord. *Exit.*
BRUTUS It must be by his Death: and for my part,
I know no personal Cause to spurn at him,
But for the general. He would be crown'd:
How that might change his Nature, there's the
Question.
It is the bright Day that brings forth the Adder,
And that craves wary Walking. Crown him that,
And then I graunt we put a Sting in him,
That at his will he may do Danger with.
Th' Abuse of Greatness is when it dis-joins
Remorse from Power. And to speak truth of Caesar,
I have not known when his Affections sway'd
More than his Reason. But 'tis a common Proof

22 **Lowliness** humility or the appearance of it.

24 **upmost Round** top rung. In line 23 *upward* can go with *Climber* to form a compound, or it can modify *turns*. Most of today's editions eliminate the second option by hyphenating the phrase: 'climber-upward'.

26 **base Degrees** lower rungs.

28 **least** lest.

29 **bear no Colour for the thing he is** support no argument based on what he is. This image suggests both (a) the colours (banner) of a military unit, and (b) the changing colours of the chameleon. Compare I.ii.120.

30 **Fashion it thus** let it be presented this way. *Fashion* recalls I.iii.34–35, where Cicero says that 'men may construe things after their fashion, / Clean from the purpose of the things themselves.' Brutus is now illustrating the pertinence of Cicero's observation. He is dis-joining 'Remorse' from both Reason and 'Power' (lines 18–19).
augmented extended, added to, extrapolated.

31 **Would . . . Extremities** would lead to these and these extremes.

33 **kind** species, type. Brutus' egg image may have been suggested to Shakespeare by a passage in North's Plutarch: 'Cassius, finding Brutus' ambition stirred up the more by these seditious bills, did prick him forward and egg him on the more, for a private quarrel he had conceived against Caesar.'

35 **Closet** private chamber, in this case a study.

40 **first of March** Most editors assume that Brutus means *Ides* of March and that an error in transmission resulted in the Folio's *first*. Line 58 would seem to support this assumption. But it is also conceivable that Shakespeare has Brutus say 'first of March' in order to show how disturbed and distracted Brutus is at this time. Line 4 makes it clear that Brutus has been having difficulty sleeping; and the soliloquy we have just heard shows that he is so preoccupied with the 'Question' on his mind that he has difficulty focusing on anything else. It may also be pertinent that North's Plutarch says that Cassius asked Brutus 'if he were determined to be in the Senate-house the first day of March, because he heard say that Caesar's friends should move the council that day, that Caesar should be called King by the Senate.' Compare I.iii.42, 137.

That Lowliness is young Ambition's Ladder,
Whereto the Climber upward turns his Face;
But when he once attains the upmost Round,
He then unto the Ladder turns his Back,
Looks in the Clouds, scorning the base Degrees
By which he did ascend. So Caesar may:
Then least he may, prevent. And since the Quarrel
Will bear no Colour for the thing he is,
Fashion it thus: that what he is, augmented,
Would run to these and these Extremities.
And therefore think him as a Serpent's Egg,
Which, hatch'd, would as his kind grow mischievous,
And kill him in the Shell.

Enter Lucius.

LUCIUS The Taper burneth in your Closet, Sir.
Searching the Window for a Flint, I found
This Paper, thus seal'd up, and I am sure
It did not lie there when I went to Bed.
Gives him the Letter.

BRUTUS Get you to Bed again, it is not Day:
Is not to morrow, Boy, the first of March?

LUCIUS I know not, Sir.

BRUTUS Look in the Calendar,
And bring me word.

LUCIUS I will, Sir. *Exit.*

43 **Exhalations** Brutus probably refers to lightning, perhaps sheet lightning. But he may refer to meteors, either in the usual modern sense (shooting stars) or in the earlier sense (luminous gases to be found in marshy areas). Compare *Romeo and Juliet*, III.v.12–15.

45 **Brutus, thou Sleep'st** Shakespeare surely expects the audience to find this message ironic in the present context. See the note to I.iii.151.

50 **piece it out** In the following lines Brutus augments 'Shall Rome' in a way that parallels his reasoning in the soliloquy we have just heard. See lines 28–34.

53 **The Tarquin** the tyrannical Lucius Tarquinius. After his son Sextus Tarquinius had raped Lucrece, the chaste wife of Collatinus, an officer in the Roman army, Lucius Junius Brutus joined Collatinus and Lucrece's father, Publius Valerius, in a vow to rid Rome of the hated Tarquins forever. They persuaded the people to exile the Tarquins, and thereafter Rome was governed by consuls rather than kings. See the notes to I.ii.156–58, I.iii.146.

54 **redress** remedy, set right. Compare I.iii.118, and see the notes to I.i.16, 19, 20.

62–63 **Between . . . Motion** It is perhaps revealing that Brutus described this sequence in reverse chronological order. The 'first Motion' is the initial impulse that leads to an action; the 'Acting' is the performance of the deed prompted by that initial impulse. Compare *Macbeth*, I.v.45–48. Lines 62–68 have a number of parallels in *Macbeth*: see the notes to I.iii.82, 128–45, I.v.6, 22, 60, II.i.35, II.ii.51 of that text.

64 **Phantasma** hallucination, vision.

65 **Genius** the presiding spirit or soul of a person (that part of a human being which Brutus regards as immortal).

mortal Instruments the physical aspects of a person (the body and all the emotions and passions subject to influences on the body). Brutus' 'Instruments' will prove 'mortal' not only to Caesar but to himself.

BRUTUS The Exhalations, whizzing in the Air,
Give so much Light that I may read by them.
Opens the Letter and reads.
'Brutus, thou Sleep'st: Awake and see thy self.
Shall Rome, etc. Speak, strike, redress.'
'Brutus, thou Sleep'st: Awake.'
Such Instigations have been often dropp'd
Where I have took them up.
'Shall Rome, etc.' Thus must I piece it out:
Shall Rome stand under One Man's Awe? What
Rome?
My Ancestors did from the Streets of Rome
The Tarquin drive, when he was call'd a King.
'Speak, strike, redress.' Am I entreated
To speak, and strike? O Rome, I make thee Promise
If the Redress will follow, thou receivest
Thy full Petition at the hand of Brutus.

Enter Lucius.

LUCIUS Sir, March is wasted fifteen Days.
Knock within.
BRUTUS 'Tis good. Go to the Gate: some body knocks.
[*Exit Lucius.*]
– Since Cassius first did whet me against Caesar,
I have not slept.
Between the Acting of a Dreadful Thing
And the first Motion, all the Interim is
Like a Phantasma, or a hideous Dream:
The Genius and the mortal Instruments

66 **in Council** Brutus likens the makeup of a human being to the composition of the State (the Body Politic). In lines 65–68 he suggests that the 'Phantasma' or 'hideous Dream' a person experiences in a situation such as his is similar to a political 'Insurrection'. To an Elizabethan audience accustomed to thinking in terms of correspondences between the macrocosm (the political State) and the microcosm ('the State of a Man'), Brutus' analogy would have suggested that his higher reason is in the process of being overthrown by his lower passions. Shakespeare's audience would probably have gone on to infer that if such a microcosmic insurrection led to a macrocosmic insurrection (here the assassination plot Brutus is about to join), the result was almost certain to be the social and political equivalent of a 'hideous Dream', a nightmare for the Body Politic. Compare I.iii.3–13.

69 **brother** brother-in-law. As North's Plutarch put it, 'Cassius had married Junia, Brutus' sister.'

71 **moe** more.

75 **mark of Favour** Lucius probably means 'feature, facial characteristic'; but his phrasing also suggests 'good will' or 'friendliness'. As Brutus notes in line 77, these masked men look 'dang'rous'. *Favour* echoes I.ii.88–89, I.iii.129. Here *discover* (line 74, echoing I.i.28–29 and I.ii.64–68) means 'identify' or 'disclose'.

80 **Monstrous Visage** portentous face. See the notes to I.iii.68, 77.

82 **path** walk, tread softly.
Native Semblance natural appearance.

83 **Erebus** the dark region through which spirits had to pass on their way to Hades. It should not escape our attention that all of Brutus' images of Conspiracy in this passage associate it with evil and the underworld. Compare lines 76–84 with *Macbeth*, II.i.48–63.
dim lacking in light. *Prevention* echoes lines 27–28.

85 **bold upon your Rest** early in disturbing your sleep.

90–92 **and . . . you** Cassius' words recall what he has said to Brutus in I.i.49–60, 139–58, and about Brutus in I.i.312–24; compare I.iii.140–46, 157–62, II.i.45–57.

Are then in Council, and the State of a Man,
Like to a little Kingdom, suffers then
The nature of an Insurrection.

Enter Lucius.

LUCIUS Sir, 'tis your brother Cassius at the Door,
Who doth desire to see you.
BRUTUS Is he alone?
LUCIUS No, Sir, there are moe with him.
BRUTUS Do you know them?
LUCIUS No, Sir, their Hats are pluck'd about their Ears,
And half their Faces buried in their Cloaks,
That by no means I may discover them
By any mark of Favour.
BRUTUS Let 'em enter. *[Exit Lucius.]*
– They are the Faction. – O Conspiracy,
Sham'st thou to shew thy dang'rous Brow by Night,
When Evils are most free? O then, by Day
Where wilt thou find a Cavern dark enough
To mask thy Monstrous Visage? Seek none,
Conspiracy:
Hide it in Smiles and Affability.
For if thou path thy Native Semblance on,
Not Erebus it self were dim enough
To hide thee from Prevention.

Enter the Conspirators, Cassius, Casca, Decius, Cinna, Metellus, and Trebonius.

CASSIUS I think we are too bold upon your Rest:
Good morrow, Brutus, do we trouble you?
BRUTUS I have been up this Hour, awake all Night.
Know I these Men, that come along with you?
CASSIUS Yes, every Man of them; and no Man here
But honours you; and every one doth wish

97 **watchful Cares** cares that keep you from sleeping. *Watchful* can also mean 'suspicious' and 'preventive'. And for a Christian audience it carries implications of fidelity and obedience that reverberate ironically at this moment in Brutus' career; see the notes to *Macbeth*, II.ii.70, V.vii.96, and *King Lear*, II.ii.166.

97–98 **interpose themselves / Betwixt** place themselves between.

102 **fret** interlace, as in a Renaissance ceiling adorned with embossed or carved lines in a decorative pattern. Lines 99–109 provide time for Cassius to confer with Brutus. Meanwhile they echo the uncertainty Brutus has expressed in lines 40–42, and they remind us that one of Caesar's contributions, in Plutarch's words, was 'the ordinance of the calendar and the reformation of the year, to take away confusion of time, being calculated exactly by the mathematicans and brought to perfection'.

105 **growing on** approaching, tending toward.

106 **Weighing** considering, in view of.

112 **the Face of Men** the countenance and character of those who will stand up for themselves as men.

113 **Sufferance of our Souls** what our souls are now subjected to, but are unwilling to tolerate (suffer) any longer. Compare I.iii.84.
Times either (a) Time's, or (b) Times'.

114 **betimes** early, immediately.

116 **high-sighted Tyranny** another image relating to Caesar's 'Pitch' (I.i.78), the height from which a bird of prey can sight and swoop down on its intended victim. Compare the imagery in I.i.63–66, I.ii.132–35, 157, 165–67, II.i.21–27.

117 **by Lottery** by random chance, at the bird's whim.
these these motives for action.

119 **steel** Brutus is referring to the use of fire to make steel by melting iron and alloying it with carbon and other metals. His phrasing recalls I.i.66–67; I.ii.126–29, 169–72, 269–72, 299–303, 312–14; I.iii.82–84, 108–11, 158–60.

You had but that Opinion of your self
Which every Noble Roman bears of you.
This is Trebonius.

BRUTUS He is welcome hither.

CASSIUS This, Decius Brutus.

BRUTUS He is welcome too.

CASSIUS This, Casca; this, Cinna; and this, Metellus
Cimber.

BRUTUS They are all welcome.
What watchful Cares do interpose themselves
Betwixt your Eyes and Night?

CASSIUS Shall I entreat a word?

They whisper.

DECIUS Here lies the East: doth not the Day break here?

CASCA No.

CINNA O pardon, Sir, it doth; and yon grey Lines,
That fret the Clouds, are Messengers of Day.

CASCA You shall confess that you are both deceiv'd:
Here, as I point my Sword, the Sun arises,
Which is a great way growing on the South,
Weighing the youthful Season of the Year.
Some two Months hence, up higher toward the North
He first presents his Fire, and the high East
Stands as the Capitol, directly here.

BRUTUS Give me your Hands all over, one by one.

CASSIUS And let us swear our Resolution.

BRUTUS No, not an Oath. If not the Face of Men,
The Sufferance of our Souls, the Times Abuse;
If these be Motives weak, break off betimes,
And every Man hence, to his idle Bed.
So let high-sighted Tyranny range on
Till each Man drop by Lottery. But if these
(As I am sure they do) bear Fire enough
To kindle Cowards and to steel with Valour
To melting Spirits of Women, then Countrymen
What need we any Spur but our own Cause

122 **prick** spur, incite. See the note to line 33.

124 **palter** speak deceitfully or falteringly.

127 **Cautelous** cautious, deceitful. Ironically, this word can also refer to men who cauterize (burn with iron), as Brutus and his companions are now steeling and kindling themselves to do (lines 117–22). For another passage that is usually assumed to refer to cauterization, see *Timon of Athens*, V.ii.18 (V.i.133 in most editions). And for previous references to *Fire* (line 118), see I.ii.144, 172–74, 180–85, 299–303; I.iii.9–13, 15–25, 48–52, 57–78, 107–11, 128–30, 159–60; II.i.35–37.

128 **Carrions** men who are so lacking in energy or resistance that they seem like corpses.

Suffering submissive, willing to suffer patiently. Compare line 113.

131 **even** unwavering, constant.

132 **unsuppressive** incapable of being suppressed. *Mettle* recalls I.i.66–67, I.ii.300, 312–14.

133 **or . . . or** either . . . or.

136 **a several Bastardy** an act that severs him from the birthright that proves him to be a true Roman.

139 **sound him** sound him out, test him for his depth of interest. Compare I.ii.140.

142 **Silver Hairs** Metellus refers to Cicero's age and reputation for wisdom and integrity. But 'purchase' in the next line relates to another sense of *silver*: currency. An Elizabethan audience would have been reminded of the 'thirty pieces of silver' that Judas took from the 'chief priests and elders' in exchange for Jesus; see Matthew 26:14–16, 27:3–10. *Opinion* (repute, regard) echoes I.ii.322–23, II.i.89–92.

144 **commend** approve, praise.

147 **Gravity** solemnity, dignity, wisdom, integrity. Metellus' imagery anticipates the physical sense of *gravity* that relates to gravitation and the weight it imparts to heavy objects.

148 **break with him** open up our secret and our cause to him. In keeping with his name, Metellus has proposed another alchemical transmutation (see the references to *Mettle* in note 132). But the agent whose 'Countenance' signifies 'the richest Alchemy' (I.iii.159) declines to be alloyed with 'Silver'.

To prick us to Redress? What other Bond
Than secret Romans, that have spoke the Word,
And will not palter? And what other Oath
Than Honesty to Honesty engag'd,
That this shall be, or we will fall for it.
Swear Priests and Cowards, and Men Cautelous,
Old feeble Carrions, and such Suffering Souls
That welcome Wrongs; unto Bad Causes swear
Such Creatures as men doubt; but do not stain
The even Virtue of our Enterprise,
Nor th' unsuppressive Mettle of our Spirits,
To think that or our Cause or our Performance
Did need an Oath; when every drop of Blood
That every Roman bears, and nobly bears,
Is guilty of a several Bastardy
If he do break the smallest Particle
Of any Promise that hath pass'd from him.

CASSIUS But what of Cicero? Shall we sound him?
I think he will stand very strong with us.

CASCA Let us not leave him out.

CINNA No, by no means.

METELLUS O let us have him, for his Silver Hairs
Will purchase us a Good Opinion,
And buy men's Voices to commend our Deeds.
It shall be said his Judgement rul'd our Hands;
Our Youths and Wildness shall no whit appear,
But all be buried in his Gravity.

BRUTUS O name him not; let us not break with him,
For he will never follow any thing
That other men begin.

CASSIUS Then leave him out.

151 **fit** suitable. Notwithstanding Brutus' remarks in lines 148–50, Cicero had opposed Caesar much longer than had Brutus.

152 **touch'd** killed (one of many euphemisms in this scene). Here, as in I.ii.154, *onely* hints at wordplay on 'oneliness'; see the quotation from North's Plutarch in the note to I.ii.304, and observe how Caesar depicts himself in III.i.60–75.

153 **urg'd** suggested, recommended.
meet appropriate [that].

156 **shrew'd** both (a) beshrewed, cursed, uncooperative (as in the related word 'shrewish'), and (b) shrewd, cunning.

157 **improve** turn to his advantage. Here the word has many of the implications of 'improvise'.

158 **annoy** do injury to (a much stronger word in Shakespeare's time than it is today).

160 **Course** proceeding. Here as in III.i.293, *Course* puns on 'corse' (corpse). Brutus wishes to minimize the injury to the Body Politic of Rome.

162 **Wrath in Death** judicial execution. Brutus is probably thinking of 'Wrath' in the sense that applies to divine justice. By line 170 he decides that even the emotion attached to that kind of slaying would be wrong.
Envy malice.

166 **Blood** both (a) physical blood, and (b) passion (here the excess Brutus identifies with malicious 'Envy').

169 **gentle** both (a) civilized, noble (as in *gentleman*), and (b) tender, compassionate. Either meaning is difficult to reconcile with the context in which Brutus is using the word.

170 **Boldly** forthrightly.

172 **hew** chop. Brutus is drawing a contrast between the crude hatchet work of a butcher or woodsman and the delicate carving of a priest preparing a sacrificial offering.

173 **subtle** crafty. Shakespeare depicts such a 'Master' in *Richard II*, where the newly installed Henry IV hints to Exton that he should assassinate the imprisoned Richard and then chides the 'Murtherer' for his deed (see V.vi.34–52).

176 **Envious** malicious, deriving from personal jealousy and rivalry. Compare line 162.

CASCA Indeed, he is not fit.
DECIUS Shall no man else be touch'd but onely Caesar?
CASSIUS Decius, well urg'd. I think it is not meet,
Mark Antony, so well belov'd of Caesar,
Should outlive Caesar: we shall find of him
A shrew'd Contriver. And you know, his Means,
If he improve them, may well stretch so far
As to annoy us all: which to prevent,
Let Antony and Caesar fall together.
BRUTUS Our Course will seem too Bloody, Caius
Cassius,
To cut the Head off and then hack the Limbs
(Like Wrath in Death, and Envy afterwards),
For Antony is but a Limb of Caesar.
Let's be Sacrificers but not Butchers, Caius.
We all stand up against the Spirit of Caesar,
And in the Spirit of Men there is no Blood.
O that we then could come by Caesar's Spirit
And not dismember Caesar! But alas,
Caesar must bleed for it. And gentle Friends,
Let's kill him Boldly, but not Wrathfully:
Let's carve him as a Dish fit for the Gods,
Not hew him as a Carcass fit for Hounds.
And let our Hearts, as subtle Masters do,
Stir up their Servants to an act of Rage
And after seem to chide 'em. This shall make
Our purpose Necessary, and not Envious;
Which, so appearing to the Common Eyes,

178 **Purgers** purifiers, those who minister to the health of a body (in this case the Body Politic) by ridding it of any impurities or members that afflict it with disease. As 'Sacrificers' (priests) and 'Purgers', these caring physicians will only be doing what is 'Necessary' to 'mend' and 'recover' a State that is 'in great Danger' without a 'Surgeon' to minister to it (I.i.19–29).

182 **ingrafted** implanted, incorporated into another organism.

188 **no Fear in him** nothing in him to cause fear.

190 **count the Clock** count the number of strokes on the clock. Mechanical clocks were not invented until the thirteenth century, so this is an anachronism. So is the method of calculating the hours, which is here based on the modern system. The Romans measured time in terms of divisions of the hours of actual daylight.

192 **Whether** often, as here, to be pronounced as an unaccented word with the metrical value of a single syllable. Here the Folio form *to day* has an ambiguity that becomes obscured when the spelling is modernized. Compare I.ii.178, and see line 199. After the assassination of Duncan, Macduff asks 'Goes the King hence to day?' (*Macbeth*, II.iii.59).

194 **Quite from** a long way from.
main prevailing. Here *Opinion* means 'viewpoint'; compare lines 141–43.

196 **these apparent Prodigies** these extraordinary phenomena that have been appearing. See I.iii.28, 76–78.

198 **Augurers** prophets who read (augured) the future from natural and unnatural phenomena.

201 **o'ersway him** persuade him otherwise. See the note to I.iii.3.

202 **Unicorns . . . Trees** In Book II of *The Faerie Queene* (1590), Edmund Spenser describes how a lion, charged by a unicorn, steps aside at the last moment so that the attacker buries his horn in a tree.

203 **Glasses** mirrors. Bears were often depicted as vain. Compare I.ii.49–68.
Holes camouflaged pits into which they fell when 'betrayed' (led or driven by hunters).

204 **Toils** nets, snares.

We shall be call'd Purgers, not Murderers.
And for Mark Antony, think not of him:
For he can do no more than Caesar's Arm
When Caesar's Head is off.

CASSIUS Yet I fear him,
For in the ingrafted Love he bears to Caesar –

BRUTUS Alas, good Cassius, do not think of him.
If he love Caesar, all that he can do
Is to himself: take thought, and die for Caesar,
And that were much he should, for he is given
To Sports, to Wildness, and much Company.

TREBONIUS There is no Fear in him; let him not die,
For he will live, and laugh at this hereafter.

Clock strikes.

BRUTUS Peace, count the Clock.

CASSIUS The Clock hath stricken three.

TREBONIUS 'Tis time to part.

CASSIUS But it is doubtful yet
Whether Caesar will come forth to day, or no:
For he is Superstitious grown of late,
Quite from the main Opinion he held once
Of Fantasy, of Dreams and Ceremonies.
It may be these apparent Prodigies,
The unaccustom'd Terror of this Night,
And the persuasion of his Augurers
May hold him from the Capitol to day.

DECIUS Never fear that: if he be so resolv'd,
I can o'ersway him. For he loves to hear
That Unicorns may be betray'd with Trees,
And Bears with Glasses, Elephants with Holes,
Lions with Toils, and Men with Flatterers;
But when I tell him he hates Flatterers,
He says he does, being then most flattered.
Let me work:

208 **give . . . Bent** take his disposition and turn it in the proper direction. Caesar's 'Humour' is here depicted as a debility. *Humour* recalls I.ii.318–19, where Cassius congratulates himself on his ability to give Brutus' 'Humour the true Bent'. *Bent* echoes I.ii.114–16, 120–22.

212 **uttermost** latest, most extreme. By this hour Decius will have uttered the uttermost mendacity, to make sure that the reluctant Caesar is 'then most flattered' (line 206). See the note to II.ii.104.

213 **bear Caesar hard** bear hard feelings toward Caesar. Compare I.ii.30–34, 317.

214 **rated** berated, scolded. But *rated* can also mean 'evaluated' (here devalued).

216 **go along by him** stop by his house.

218 **fashion him** mould him to our purposes. Compare line 30.

223 **put on** display, wear (as a costume).

225 **untir'd Spirits** spirits that do not show any of the weariness they may feel. Compare lines 222–25 with *Macbeth*, I.v.64–68, 73–75, I.vii.81–82. Ironically, a Caesar who distrusts men 'who love no plays' (I.ii.199) will fall victim to 'Players in the Theatre' (I.ii.260). The Greek term for 'Actors' (line 224) was the root of our word *hypocrite*.
formal maintaining form, decorum, self-control.

228 **honey-heavy Dew of Slumber** This image conveys the idea that the sleep Lucius enjoys is sweet, natural, nourishing, peaceful, and deeply settled. Compare I.ii.188–89, 204–5; I.iii.161–64; II.i.4, 45, 60–61, 87–88, 97–98, 224–25.

229 **Figures** figments of imagination, images created by a mind troubled with cares. *Care* echoes lines 97–98.

231 **sound** both (a) soundly, deeply, and (b) healthily. *Sound* echoes line 139. Here as elsewhere, the careworn, troubled Brutus can only look on wistfully as he sees young Lucius enjoy a restorative slumber. Sleeplessness is regularly associated with tragic figures in Shakespeare, and it usually betokens a conscience as well as a consciousness (the two meanings were both conveyed by the word *conscience* at this time) that is not at ease with itself.

232 **mean** intend, think.

For I can give his Humour the true Bent,
And I will bring him to the Capitol.
CASSIUS Nay, we will all of us be there to fetch him.
BRUTUS By the eight hour, is that the uttermost?
CINNA Be that the uttermost, and fail not then.
METELLUS Caius Ligarius doth bear Caesar hard,
Who rated him for speaking well of Pompey;
I wonder none of you have thought of him.
BRUTUS Now, good Metellus, go along by him:
He loves me well, and I have given him Reasons;
Send him but hither, and I'll fashion him.
CASSIUS The Morning comes upon's: we'll leave you, Brutus.
– And Friends, disperse your selves; but all remember
What you have said, and shew your selves true Romans.
BRUTUS Good Gentlemen, look fresh and merrily;
Let not our Looks put on our Purposes,
But bear it as our Roman Actors do,
With untir'd Spirits and formal Constancy.
And so good morrow to you every one.
Exeunt. Manet Brutus.
– Boy, Lucius: fast asleep? It is no matter,
Enjoy the honey-heavy Dew of Slumber.
Thou hast no Figures, nor no Fantasies,
Which busy Care draws in the Brains of Men:
Therefore thou sleep'st so sound.

Enter Portia.

PORTIA Brutus, my Lord.
BRUTUS Portia: what mean you? Wherefore rise you now?
It is not for your Health thus to commit

234 **Condition** constitution, state of health.

235 **ungently** in a manner not in keeping with the courtesy a noble, civilized husband owes to his devoted wife. Portia's phrasing recalls what Cassius has said to Brutus in I.ii.30–34. It also echoes line 169 and anticipates line 240.

238 **Arms-a-cross** a posture conventionally associated with a person in the throes of melancholy.

244 **wafter** wafture, a waving gesture of dismissal.

247 **withal** with all, in the meantime.

248 **Humour** Here Portia refers to an imbalance of a psychological makeup in which one of the four humours becomes so dominant as to gain control over the mind and emotions. In Brutus' case, black bile (a cold, dry humour derived from the element Earth) has effected this kind of psychological usurpation, causing Brutus to become a melancholic. Compare lines 208, 260.

251 **Shape** physical makeup, bodily appearance.

253 **know you Brutus** Because the First Folio does not place a comma before *Brutus*, it is possible to interpret Portia's meaning as 'know you to be Brutus'. But in fact it is unusual for the Folio to place a comma before the name of a person addressed, so 'know you, Brutus' is equally likely. In either case *know* means 'recognize'. Compare I.ii.56–60, II.i.45. The words Shakespeare gives Portia here may have been influenced by North's Plutarch, where Ligarius tells Brutus he will join the conspiracy provided that 'thou wilt show thyself to be the man thou art taken for, and that they hope thou art'.

259 **Physical** healthful, in keeping with a physician's counsel.

260 **unbraced** with one's doublet unfastened or unlaced. This word echoes I.iii.48, where Cassius employs it with the bravado of a Roman who refuses to acknowledge that 'It is the part of Men to fear and tremble' in the presence of forces beyond human reckoning (I.iii.54–55).

Humours the damp night air, then considered unhealthy.

264 **rheumy and unpurged Air** Portia refers to air that is still damp because it has not yet been dried out by the sun's rays. Exposure to such air was thought to cause rheum (a term that could refer to any buildup of body fluids, from the common cold to pneumonia and tuberculosis). Compare I.ii.247–49.

Your weak Condition to the raw cold Morning.
PORTIA Nor for yours neither. Y' have ungently, Brutus,
Stole from my Bed. And yesternight at Supper
You suddenly arose, and walk'd about,
Musing, and Sighing, with your Arms a-cross;
And when I ask'd you what the Matter was,
You star'd upon me with ungentle Looks.
I urg'd you further, then you scratch'd your Head,
And too impatiently stamp'd with your Foot;
Yet I insisted, yet you answer'd not,
But with an angry wafter of your Hand
Gave sign for me to leave you. So I did,
Fearing to strengthen that Impatience
Which seem'd too much enkindled, and withal
Hoping it was but an effect of Humour,
Which sometime hath his Hour with every Man.
It will not let you eat, nor talk, nor sleep;
And could it work so much upon your Shape
As it hath much prevail'd on your Condition,
I should not know you Brutus. Dear my Lord,
Make me acquainted with your cause of Grief.
BRUTUS I am not well in Health, and that is all.
PORTIA Brutus is wise, and were he not in Health
He would embrace the Means to come by it.
BRUTUS Why so I do: good Portia, go to Bed.
PORTIA Is Brutus sick? And is it Physical
To walk unbraced and suck up the Humours
Of the dank Morning? What, is Brutus sick?
And will he steal out of his wholesome Bed
To dare the vile Contagion of the Night?
And tempt the rheumy and unpurged Air
To add unto his Sickness? No, my Brutus,

266 **Sick Offence** offensive (harmful) sickness.

269 **charm** conjure; attempt to sway, as if by the magic of a spell or ritual incantation.

271 **incorporate** literally, 'make us One' in *corpus* (Latin for 'body'). Elizabethans would have recognized the commonplace that a husband and wife are 'one flesh' (Genesis 2:24, Ephesians 5:30–32).

272 **unfold** open up, reveal.
your Half your half of the 'One' we have become through marriage.

273 **Heavy** despondent.
to night tonight. But *to night* can also mean 'to lead you to night [and, to all the evils associated with it]'. See the note to line 192, and compare the imagery of I.iii.42–45, 72–78, 137–38, 162–64, II.i.97–98.

274 **Have had resort to you** have come to see you.

281 **in Sort** in part, to a limited degree.

283 **Suburbs** Portia is invoking the same sense of 'Romanness' that Brutus referred to earlier. She is saying that if she cannot live in the 'city' that constitutes Brutus' 'State of a Man' (line 66), she cannot be the true wife of the man Antony will later call 'the Noblest Roman of them all' (V.v.67).

287 **ruddy Drops** red drops, blood.

290 **withal** for all that, notwithstanding.

293 **Cato's Daughter** Portia was the daughter of Marcus Porcius Cato, an orator and statesman renowned for his integrity. Cato had opposed Caesar, fighting as an ally of Pompey until his fall at the battle of Pharsalia and then moving on to Africa, where he fought with Metellus Scipio. Once Africa too fell into Caesar's hands, Cato killed himself at Utica rather than surrender to his conqueror. This phrase also occurs in *The Merchant of Venice*, I.i.166.

297 **Proof of my Constancy** demonstration of my resolve. North's Plutarch was Shakespeare's source for this incident, as well as for much of the phrasing in this conversation.

299 **Here, in the Thigh** At this moment Portia probably bares her wound to show Brutus the proof of her resolution.

You have some Sick Offence within your Mind,
Which by the Right and Virtue of my Place
I ought to know of. And upon my Knees,
I charm you, by my once commended Beauty,
By all your vows of Love, and that great Vow
Which did incorporate and make us One,
That you unfold to me your Self, your Half,
Why you are Heavy, and what men to night
Have had resort to you: for here have been
Some six or seven who did hide their Faces
Even from Darkness.

BRUTUS Kneel not, gentle Portia.

PORTIA I should not need, if you were gentle Brutus.
Within the Bond of Marriage, tell me, Brutus,
Is it excepted, I should know no Secrets
That appertain to you? Am I your Self
But as it were in Sort, or Limitation?
To keep with you at Meals, comfort your Bed,
And talk to you sometimes? Dwell I but in the Suburbs
Of your good Pleasure? If it be no more,
Portia is Brutus' Harlot, not his Wife.

BRUTUS You are my True and Honourable Wife,
As dear to me as are the ruddy Drops
That visit my sad Heart.

PORTIA If this were true, then should I know this Secret.
I graunt I am a Woman; but withal
A Woman that Lord Brutus took to Wife.
I graunt I am a Woman; but withal
A Woman well reputed: Cato's Daughter.
Think you I am no stronger than my Sex
Being so Father'd and so Husbanded?
Tell me your Counsels, I will not disclose 'em:
I have made strong Proof of my Constancy,
Giving my self a voluntary Wound
Here, in the Thigh. Can I bear that with Patience,
And not my Husband's Secrets?

305 **construe** explain. Compare I.iii.34–35.

306 **the Charactery of my sad Brows** the handwriting on my sober forehead (that is, the meaning of the lines that furrow my brow).

308 **Sick Man** As the dialogue will shortly make clear, Caius Ligarius is wearing a kerchief (a linen headcloth to protect a sick person against harmful draughts).

309 **that** whom.

310 **how?** how are you? Whether Lucius exits or merely stands 'aside' while Brutus and Caius Ligarius speak is not clear.

311 **Vouchsafe** be so kind as to accept. *Feeble* recalls I.i.126–29.

319 **discard my Sickness** At this moment, Caius Ligarius probably removes his kerchief. See the note to line 322.

320 **from Honourable Loins** another reference to the earlier Brutus. Compare lines 45–57, 130–38.

321 **Exorcist** one who summons spirits by exhorting or conjuring them. In this speech Brutus is depicted as a priestly physican to the sick spirits of other Romans, 'a Mender of bad Souls' (I.i.15–16). What has yet to be demonstrated, however, is that the healer has the power to cure his own unhealthy spirit. An attentive theatregoer in Shakespeare's audience might have been reminded of such New Testament passages as 'Physician, heal thyself' (Luke 4:23).

322 **mortified** deadened, near death. Lines 322–25 suggest ironic analogies between Brutus and another miracle-worker. See Mark 2:1–17, where Jesus rewards the 'faith' of those who bring him the sick and says, 'Arise and take up thy bed and walk.' He then responds to the criticism of 'the scribes and Pharisees' with the words 'They that are whole have no need of the physician, but they that are sick: I come not to call the righteous, but sinners to repentance.'

323 **with** against. The word *impossible* echoes such Gospel passages as Luke 18:27, where Jesus says that 'The things which are impossible with men are possible with God.' It also recalls Mark 9:23–24, where Jesus tells the father of a sick child, 'If thou canst believe, all things are possible,' and the father replies, 'Lord, I believe; help thou mine unbelief.'

BRUTUS — O ye Gods!
Render me worthy of this Noble Wife. *Knock.*
– Hark, hark, one knocks: Portia, go in a while,
And by and by thy Bosom shall partake
The Secrets of my Heart.
All my Engagements I will construe to thee,
All the Charactery of my sad Brows:
Leave me with haste. *Exit Portia.*

Enter Lucius and Caius Ligarius.

– Lucius, who's that knocks?
LUCIUS Here is a Sick Man that would speak with you.
BRUTUS Caius Ligarius, that Metellus spake of.
– Boy, stand aside. – Caius Ligarius, how?
CAIUS Vouchsafe good morrow from a feeble Tongue.
BRUTUS O what a Time have you chose out, brave Caius,
To wear a Kerchief? Would you were not Sick.
CAIUS I am not Sick, if Brutus have in hand
Any Exploit worthy the name of Honour.
BRUTUS Such an Exploit have I in hand, Ligarius,
Had you a healthful Ear to hear of it.
CAIUS By all the Gods that Romans bow before,
I here discard my Sickness. Soul of Rome,
Brave Son, deriv'd from Honourable Loins,
Thou like an Exorcist hast conjur'd up
My mortified Spirit. Now bid me run,
And I will strive with things impossible,
Yea, get the better of them. What's to do?
BRUTUS A pretty piece of Work, that will make Sick Men whole.

326 **Whole** healthy. Lines 325–26 echo North's Plutarch, where Ligarius tells Brutus 'if thou hast any enterprise in hand worthy of thyself, I am whole.'

328 **unfold** reveal, disclose. Compare line 272.

329 **Set on your Foot** take the first step.

330 **new-fir'd** reinvigorated. See the note to line 127.

332 **Brutus . . . on** The modern sense of 'leads me on' (misleads me) is not irrelevant here. Caius Ligarius regards Brutus as a healer who has, in effect, raised him from the dead (compare lines 318–22 with John 11:1–44), and he will now follow Brutus as his 'Lord' (line 232, anticipating IV.ii.279–80, 287). See Matthew 8:22, where Jesus says, 'Follow me; and let the dead bury their dead.'

S.D. **Thunder** This is a stage direction instructing a person backstage to rattle a sheet of metal to indicate the sound of thunder.

II.ii The setting shifts to Caesar's house, which has also had an unquiet night.

5 **present** immediate.

6 **their Opinions of Success** their opinions about what the future holds.

8 **mean** intend. Compare II.i.232. Calphurnia's wifely concerns echo the conversation between Brutus and Portia in the preceding scene (II.i.232–65).

9 **to day** Here as in II.i.192, 273, the original spelling suggests more than one implication. Compare lines 38, 43, 50, 53, 62, 64, 76, 82, 122.

10 **shall forth** an elliptical way of saying 'shall walk forth'.

CAIUS But are not some Whole that we must make Sick?
BRUTUS That must we also. What it is, my Caius,
I shall unfold to thee, as we are going,
To whom it must be done.
CAIUS Set on your Foot,
And with a Heart new-fir'd I follow you
To do I know not what; but it sufficeth
That Brutus leads me on. *Thunder.*
BRUTUS Follow me then. *Exeunt.*

Scene 2

Thunder and Lightning. Enter Julius Caesar in his Night-gown.

CAESAR Nor Heaven nor Earth have been at Peace to night:
Thrice hath Calphurnia in her Sleep cried out
'Help, ho: they murther Caesar.' – Who's within?

Enter a Servant.

SERVANT My Lord.
CAESAR Go bid the Priests do present Sacrifice,
And bring me their Opinions of Success.
SERVANT I will, my Lord. *Exit.*

Enter Calphurnia.

CALPHURNIA What mean you, Caesar? Think you to walk forth?
You shall not stir out of your House to day.
CAESAR Caesar shall forth. The things that threaten'd me
Ne'er look'd but on my Back: when they shall see

13 **stood on Ceremonies** put reliance in rituals, paid heed to omens and used them as the basis for determining a course of action. Compare *Macbeth*, III.iv.117–18.

16 **Recounts** an implied 'who' is understood to precede this verb.

17 **whelped** given birth to cubs; here pronounced as a two-syllable word.

18 **yawn'd** opened up.

19 **Fierce . . . Clouds** Portia refers to the lightning.

20 **and right form of War** as if going through all the actions of soldiers at war.

25 **beyond all Use** completely abnormal; here *Use* means custom, ordinary experience.

28 **Yet** still, notwithstanding all these things. Shakespeare's Caesar is much more confident than Plutarch's. Only in Shakespeare does Caesar harbour illusions of divinity and invincibility. In Plutarch Caesar expresses his fear of Cassius (I.ii.188–91) without the disclaimer that he only describes what any man other than Caesar would fear (I.ii.194–208). And in Plutarch it is Caesar, rather than Calphurnia, who concludes that he should not go to the Capitol on the Ides of March.

Predictions phenomena that are thought to portend disaster.

29 **as** as much as. *General* recalls II.i.11–12.

31 **blaze forth** proclaim, blazon (a term from heraldry). But here *blaze* serves as a reminder of the blazes the Heavens have displayed. Compare II.i.330.

32–37 **Cowards . . . come** These words echo North's Plutarch: 'And when some of his friends did counsel him to have a guard for the safety of his person, and some also did offer themselves to serve him, he would never consent to it, but said: "It was better to die once, than always to be afraid of death." ' On the day before his assassination, according to Plutarch, in response to a question about what death was best, Caesar 'cried out aloud, "Death unlook'd for." '

The Face of Caesar, they are vanished.
CALPHURNIA Caesar, I never stood on Ceremonies,
Yet now they fright me. There is one within,
Besides the things that we have heard and seen,
Recounts most horrid Sights seen by the Watch.
A Lioness hath whelped in the Streets,
And Graves have yawn'd, and yielded up their Dead;
Fierce fiery Warriors fight upon the Clouds
In Ranks and Squadrons, and right form of War,
Which drizzl'd Blood upon the Capitol;
The noise of Battle hurtled in the Air;
Horses do neigh, and Dying Men did groan,
And Ghosts did shriek and squeal about the Streets.
O Caesar, these things are beyond all Use,
And I do fear them.
CAESAR What can be avoided
Whose end is purpos'd by the mighty Gods?
Yet Caesar shall go forth: for these Predictions
Are to the World in general, as to Caesar.
CALPHURNIA When Beggars die, there are no Comets seen;
The Heavens themselves blaze forth the Death of Princes.
CAESAR Cowards die many Times before their Deaths,
The Valiant never taste of Death but once:
Of all the Wonders that I yet have heard,
It seems to me most strange that men should fear,
Seeing that Death, a necessary End,
Will come when it will come.

Enter a Servant.

What say the Augurers?
SERVANT They would not have you to stir forth to day.

39 **Offering** an animal to be sacrificed. In Plutarch, it is Caesar himself who performs the sacrifice and discovers the beast without a heart. Shakespeare's Caesar orders the sacrifice performed, and then he disregards the advice of the priests whose counsel he has commissioned.

44 **Danger** threat, menace. Lines 44–45 echo I.ii.61, 84–85, 190–91, 204–6; II.i.114–15, 121–24; II.i.15–17, 76–78.

46 **We . . . Day** We hear of two lions born in the same litter. Here Caesar is referring to himself and 'Danger' (line 44) as twins. Because he is the 'elder' (line 47) of the two, he says, he is the more powerful. In this line most modern editions alter *We hear* to *We are*, but the Folio reading does not require emendation.

47 **terrible** terrifying, fearsome; intimidating.

48 **foorth** forth.

49 **Your . . . Confidence** Your reasoning powers are overcome by your complacency, your misplaced sense of invulnerability. The Greek term for Caesar's condition is *pleonexia*, 'Security' (III.i.9); it leads to *atê*, a blindness to danger, and often to *hubris*, an intolerable violation of cosmic limits that results in self-destruction. See the note to I.iii.53.

54 **my Knee** Here the audience would be reminded of Portia's kneeling to Brutus in the preceding scene (II.i.265–76). Once again a pleading wife obtains a concession from her husband. In this case, however, it will be short-lived.

56 **thy Humour** Caesar grudgingly yields to what he regards as an irrational fear on the part of Calphurnia. And for now he agrees to the pretence that he is 'not well'. Compare II.i.248.

57 **Decius Brutus** According to North's Plutarch, this conspirator was 'surnamed Albinus, in whom Caesar put such confidence that in his last will and testament he had appointed him to be his next heir'.

65 **Shall Caesar send a Lie?** The unexpected entry of Decius Brutus has made it impossible for Caesar to commission Mark Antony to carry to the Senate the message that he is ill. And now that Calphurnia has spoken for him, and in such a way as to weaken the force of his initial assertion that he simply 'will not' go to the Senate, Caesar feels constrained to save face by spurning the pretext to which he had agreed only a moment before.

Plucking the Entrails of an Offering forth,
They could not find a Heart within the Beast.

CAESAR The Gods do this in shame of Cowardice:
Caesar should be a Beast without a Heart
If he should stay at Home to day for Fear.
No, Caesar shall not; Danger knows full well
That Caesar is more dangerous than he.
We hear two Lions litter'd in one Day,
And I the elder and more terrible,
And Caesar shall go foorth.

CALPHURNIA Alas, my Lord,
Your Wisdom is consum'd in Confidence:
Do not go forth to day. Call it my Fear
That keeps you in the House, and not your own.
We'll send Mark Antony to the Senate-house,
And he shall say you are not well to day.
Let me upon my Knee prevail in this.

CAESAR Mark Antony shall say I am not well,
And for thy Humour I will stay at Home.

Enter Decius.

Here's Decius Brutus, he shall tell them so.

DECIUS Caesar, all hail: good morrow, worthy Caesar,
I come to fetch you to the Senate-house.

CAESAR And you are come in very happy time
To bear my Greeting to the Senators,
And tell them that I will not come to day.
'Cannot' is false, and that I dare not falser;
I will not come to day, tell them so, Decius.

CALPHURNIA Say he is Sick.

CAESAR Shall Caesar send a Lie?
Have I in Conquest stretch'd mine Arm so far,

67 **afear'd** afraid.
Greybeards Caesar's dismissive epithet derives from the Latin meaning of *Senator*: old man.

69 **let me know some Cause** Decius refuses to let Caesar off so easily. Knowing that Caesar's vanity will not allow him to admit to any weakness, he thinks that he will eventually be able to divest Caesar of any excuses he is willing to have Decius carry back with him to the Senate. *Cause* recalls II.i.11, 121, 133, 254.

75 **stays** keeps, detains.

76 **Statue** Here the metrical position of the word may well have dictated that *Statue* be pronounced as a three-syllable word (stát-you-ày). In line 85, on the other hand, the word is to be pronounced in the normal fashion.

80 **Portents** here accented on the second syllable. This line is an alexandrine (iambic hexameter, rather than pentameter).

83 **amiss** incorrectly, in such a way as to miss its true meaning.

84 **Vision** This word was normally reserved for 'good dreams' that foretold happy fortunes or offered recipients warnings that would enable them to escape impending dangers. North's Plutarch says that Decius, 'fearing that if Caesar did adjourn the session that day the conspiracy would out, laughed the soothsayers to scorn; and reproved Caesar, saying that he gave the Senate occasion to mislike with him, and that they might think he mocked them, considering that by his commandment they were assembled'. Compare Shakespeare's variation on Plutarch in lines 95–99.

85–88 **Your . . . Blood** Although Plutarch mentions that Calphurnia had a dream in which 'Caesar was slain', he says nothing about a statuary fountain flowing with blood. These details are thus Shakespeare's invention, and they are undoubtedly meant to relate to the imagery of priestly sacrifice in Brutus' remarks about carving Caesar as 'a Dish fit for the Gods' (II.i.164–72). Those remarks, too, were supplied by Shakespeare; they do not derive from Plutarch, and the playwright probably added them to suggest unintended, ironic parallels with sacrificial rituals in the Old and New Testaments. *Blood* recalls II.i.166. Compare these lines with I.i.12–31.

To be afear'd to tell Greybeards the Truth?
– Decius, go tell them Caesar will not come.

DECIUS Most mighty Caesar, let me know some Cause,
Lest I be laugh'd at when I tell them so.

CAESAR The Cause is in my Will, I will not come,
That is enough to satisfy the Senate.
But for your private Satisfaction,
Because I love you, I will let you know.
Calphurnia here, my Wife, stays me at Home.
She dreamt to night she saw my Statue,
Which, like a Fountain, with an hundred Spouts
Did run pure Blood; and many lusty Romans
Came smiling, and did bathe their Hands in it;
And these does she apply for Warnings and Portents,
And Evils imminent; and on her Knee
Hath begg'd that I will stay at home to day.

DECIUS This Dream is all amiss interpreted,
It was a Vision, fair and fortunate:
Your Statue spouting Blood in many Pipes,
In which so many smiling Romans bath'd,
Signifies that from you great Rome shall suck
Reviving Blood, and that Great Men shall press

88–89 **Great . . . Cognizance** Decius is implying that Caesar will be revered as a saint, and one for whom 'Great Men' (those who wish to partake of Caesar's greatness) will 'press' (crowd around) his memorial fountain to obtain 'Tinctures' (handkerchiefs dipped in blood) and other relics that will gain them 'Cognizance' (recognition) as leaders identified with him. (Here *Reliques* – relics, objects of veneration – is to be accented on the second syllable.) We should note that Decius' interpretation of Calphurnia's dream is fully compatible with the one that Caesar has just described. Nowhere does Decius say that Calphurnia's fears are unfounded. Lines 85–90 anticipate III.i.106–10.

96–97 **it . . . render'd** it would not be surprising if someone offered a mocking remark. In Plutarch, Decius says that 'if any man should tell' the Senate 'that they should depart for the present time, and return again when Calpurnia should have better dreams – what would his enemies and ill-willers say, and how could they like of his friends' words? And who could persuade them otherwise, but that they would think his dominion a slavery unto them, and tyrannical in himself?' See the note to line 84.

102–3 **my . . . Proceeding** my genuine desire to see your cause advanced. Decius has done what he promised in II.i.200–9.

104 **And . . . liable** and my reason is subservient to my love. *Liable* puns cleverly on *lie*.

105 **How . . . Calphurnia?** The Folio question mark (replaced by an exclamation mark in most of today's editions) gives this line an ambiguity that will soon prove to the point.

112 **your Enemy** Here Caesar alludes to the same conflict that Metellus Cimber refers to in II.i.213–14. Caius Ligarius had fought on Pompey's side in the civil war, and Caesar had only recently restored his civil rights. According to Plutarch, 'Ligarius thanked not Caesar so much for his discharge, as he was offended with him for that he was brought into danger by his tyrannical power. And therefore in his heart he was alway his mortal enemy.'

For Tinctures, Stains, Reliques, and Cognizance.
This by Calphurnia's Dream is signified.
CAESAR And this way have you well expounded it.
DECIUS I have, when you have heard what I can say:
And know it now, the Senate have concluded
To give this Day a Crown to mighty Caesar.
If you shall send them word you will not come,
Their Minds may change. Besides, it were a Mock
Apt to be render'd, for some one to say,
'Break up the Senate till another Time:
When Caesar's Wife shall meet with better Dreams.'
If Caesar hide himself, shall they not whisper
'Lo Caesar is afraid'?
Pardon me, Caesar, for my dear dear Love
To your Proceeding bids me tell you this:
And Reason to my Love is liable.
CAESAR – How foolish do your Fears seem now,
Calphurnia?
I am ashamed I did yield to them.
Give me my Robe, for I will go.

Enter Brutus, Ligarius, Metellus, Casca, Trebonius, Cinna, and Publius.

And look where Publius is come to fetch me.
PUBLIUS Good morrow, Caesar.
CEASAR Welcome, Publius.
– What, Brutus, are you stirr'd so early too?
– Good morrow, Casca. – Caius Ligarius,
Caesar was ne'er so much your Enemy

113 **Ague** a fever causing intense chills and shaking (pronounced aý-gue). In this line Caesar refers to the same sickness that has been the subject of conversation with Caius Ligarius in the preceding scene at Brutus' house. See II.i.308–32. *Lean* echoes I.ii.188–208.

118 **Bid them prepare within** Caesar may address this line to Calphurnia (who has had nothing to say since Caesar put her to silence by his decision to overrule her in favour of the counsel of Decius Brutus). Otherwise it is probably spoken to a servant, who is presumably being reminded to pour some wine for Caesar's guests (see line 126).

119 **too blame** too blameworthy.

121 **hour's** Here, as is often the case, *hour* is to be pronounced as a two-syllable word.

124–25 **and . . . further** Most editions mark these words as an aside. But it is equally plausible that Trebonius speaks them to Caesar with a jocular tone. If so 'Friends' in line 126 can be read as Caesar's reply to what his colleague has just said.

126 **Good . . . me** Caesar's final gesture of hospitality is another detail of Shakespeare's own invention (there is no mention of it in Plutarch, where it was Decius alone who went and 'took Caesar by the hand and brought him out of his house'), and it would probably have reminded the original audience of the wine another 'King' was to offer his friends on the eve of his sacrifice (see Mark 14:22–25). If Shakespeare was implicitly associating the assassination of Caesar with the crucifixion of Christ, he would not have been the first to do so. Dante had placed Cassius and Brutus with Judas in the lowest circle of Hell in Canto XXXIV of his *Inferno* in 1321.

128–29 **That . . . upon** Brutus picks up on Caesar's 'like Friends' and alludes to a Latin proverb, *Omne simile non est idem*, 'Every similitude is not identical.' His meaning is that not everyone who appears to be a friend is one in reality. Brutus probably lingers to speak these lines behind Caesar's back as he exits. But again it would be possible for him to speak them proverbially and openly. Compare lines 104, 124–25. Shakespeare may have found a hint for his portrayal of Brutus as a Judas in Plutarch's statement that just before the assassination the conspirators took Caesar 'by the hands and kissed his head and breast'. Compare III.i.52, and see Matthew 26:46–56. *Like* recalls I.ii.312–15.

As that same Ague which hath made you Lean.
– What is't a'clock?

BRUTUS Caesar, 'tis strucken eight.

CAESAR I thank you for your Pains and Curtesy.

Enter Antony.

See, Antony, that revels long a-nights,
Is notwithstanding up. – Good morrow, Antony.

ANTONY So to most Noble Caesar.

CAESAR Bid them prepare within:
I am too blame to be thus waited for.
– Now Cinna. – Now Metellus. – What, Trebonius,
I have an hour's Talk in store for you:
Remember that you call on me to day;
Be near me, that I may remember you.

TREBONIUS Caesar, I will; and so near will I be
That your best Friends shall wish I had been further.

CAESAR Good Friends, go in, and taste some Wine with me,
And we, like Friends, will straightway go together.

BRUTUS That every Like is not the same, O Caesar,

129 **earns** grieves; a variant of *yearns*. After the assassination, according to Plutarch, Antony 'framed his eloquence' in his oration to the Roman people 'to make their hearts yearn the more'.

II.iii This scene occurs on a street near the Capitol in Rome.

1 **Artemidorus** In Plutarch, Artemidorus is 'a doctor of rhetoric in the Greek tongue'.

9 **Security** Here, as often in Shakespeare, the word means 'free from concerns'; it thus refers to a lack of prudence that stems from overconfidence. In Homer's *Iliad* there are several instances in which a character who becomes too sure of himself (too filled with *pleonexia* and *hubris*, a pride that stems from not recognizing one's limitations or the boundaries imposed by Nature or the Gods) is afflicted with *atê* (an infatuation that clouds his reason and blinds him to perils he should heed). Thus debilitated, he stumbles into a situation that destroys him. Subsequent writers built on this tradition (Chaunticleer recapitulates the pattern, for example, in Chaucer's 'Nun's Priest's Tale'), and Shakespeare draws on it in his depiction of Caesar's fall. What Artemidorus says here echoes Calphurnia's warning in II.ii.49.
gives way to yields to, is defeated by.

16 **Out . . . Emulation** apart from the threat of destruction by envious rivals.

18 **contrive** cooperate.

II.iv The setting shifts to a street in front of the house of Brutus and Portia.

2 **Stay** delay.

The Heart of Brutus earns to think upon. *Exeunt.*

Scene 3

Enter Artemidorus.

[ARTEMIDORUS] 'Caesar, beware of Brutus; take heed of Cassius; come not near Casca; have an eye to Cinna; trust not Trebonius; mark well Metellus Cimber; Decius Brutus loves thee not; thou hast wrong'd Caius Ligarius. There is but one Mind in all these Men, and it is bent against Caesar. If thou beest not Immortal, look about you: Security gives way to Conspiracy. The mighty Gods defend thee.

Thy Lover,
Artemidorus.'

Here will I stand till Caesar pass along,
And as a Suitor will I give him this.
My Heart laments, that Virtue cannot live
Out of the Teeth of Emulation.
– If thou read this, O Caesar, thou mayest live;
If not, the Fates with Traitors do contrive.
Exit.

Scene 4

Enter Portia and Lucius.

PORTIA I prythee, Boy, run to the Senate-house,
Stay not to answer me, but get thee gone.

6 **Constancy** self-control, steadiness. Compare II.i.290–300.

8 **Woman's Might** Portia means a woman's weakness.

9 **keep Counsel** keep a secret. According to North's Plutarch, while the conspirators anxiously awaited the dilatory Caesar's arrival at Pompey's Theatre for the Senate Session, 'there came one of Brutus' men post-haste unto him and told him his wife was a-dying. For Portia being very careful and pensive for that which was to come and being too weak to away with so great and inward grief of mind, she could hardly keep within, but was frighted with every little noise and cry she heard, . . . asking every man that came from the market-place what Brutus did, and still sent messenger after messenger, to know what news. At length, Caesar's coming being prolonged . . ., Portia's weakness was not able to hold out any longer, and thereupon she suddenly swounded, that she had no leisure to go to her chamber, but was taken in the midst of her house, where her speech and senses failed her. Howbeit she soon came to herself again. . . . When Brutus heard these news, it grieved him, as it is to be presupposed. Yet he left not off the care of his country and commonwealth; neither went home to his house for any news he heard.'

18 **a bussling Rumour** an indistinct hint of tumult. Here a *bustling* disturbance being carried on the wind is depicted as what the First Quarto of *King Lear* calls an 'ear-bussing' argument (II.i.9); the Folio text emends the phrase to 'Ear-kissing'.

20 **Sooth** truly.

23 **ninth hour** Plutarch says nothing about the time of Caesar's assassination. Shakespeare probably chose this particular hour to echo a passage from the account of the Crucifixion in the synoptic Gospels: 'Now from the sixth hour there was darkness over all the land unto the ninth hour. And about the ninth hour Jesus cried with a loud voice, saying, Eli, Eli, lama sabachthani? That is to say, My God, my God, why hast thou forsaken me?' (Matthew 27:45–46; parallelled by Mark 15:33–34 and Luke 23:44–45). The sense of betrayal Caesar feels is quite different from that of Christ, of course, but it is just as poignantly conveyed in his cry from the heart (which is not to be found in Plutarch) in III.i.78. Portia's uncertainty about the time suggests disorientation. Her question recalls such previous passages as I.ii.1–2; I.iii.33, 42, 137; II.i.2–3, 40, 99–109, 211–12, 312–13; II.ii.32–37, 114.

Why doest thou stay?
LUCIUS To know my Errand, Madam.
PORTIA I would have had thee there and here again
Ere I can tell thee what thou shouldst do there.
– O Constancy, be strong upon my side,
Set a huge Mountain 'tween my Heart and Tongue.
I have a Man's Mind, but a Woman's Might:
How hard it is for Women to keep Counsel.
– Art thou here yet?
LUCIUS Madam, what should I do?
Run to the Capitol, and nothing else?
And so return to you, and nothing else?
PORTIA Yes, bring me word, Boy, if thy Lord look well,
For he went sickly forth: and take good note
What Caesar doth, what Suitors press to him.
Hark, Boy, what Noise is that?
LUCIUS I hear none, Madam.
PORTIA Prythee listen well:
I heard a bussling Rumour like a Fray,
And the Wind brings it from the Capitol.
LUCIUS Sooth, Madam, I hear nothing.

Enter the Soothsayer.

PORTIA Come hither, Fellow, which way hast thou been?
SOOTHSAYER At mine own House, good Lady.
PORTIA What is't a' clock?
SOOTHSAYER About the ninth hour, Lady.
PORTIA Is Caesar yet gone to the Capitol?

25 **my stand** my position. Compare III.i.90, 101.

31 **towards** here pronounced as a one-syllable word.

36 **Praetors** justices.
common Suitors ordinary citizens with requests to bring before Caesar.

38 **void** empty. *Feeble* (line 37) recalls I.i.110–13, 126–29, II.i.223–25, 311.

42 **speed** prosper. But Portia's words are also a reminder that the 'Enterprise' must be executed immediately if the conspirators hope to avoid being detected. In John 13:27, Jesus says to Judas, 'That thou doest, do quickly.'

43 **Sure** surely.

43–44 – **Brutus . . . grant** Portia speaks this sentence to Lucius to camouflage the remark she fears he has overheard.

47 **Exeunt** The dialogue suggests that Lucius and Portia depart 'severally', in different directions.

SOOTHSAYER Madam, not yet. I go to take my stand,
To see him pass on to the Capitol.
PORTIA Thou hast some Suit to Caesar, hast thou not?
SOOTHSAYER That I have, Lady, if it will please Caesar
To be so good to Caesar as to hear me:
I shall beseech him to befriend himself.
PORTIA Why, know'st thou any Harm's intended
towards him?
SOOTHSAYER None that I know will be,
Much that I fear may chance.
Good morrow to you. Here the Street is narrow:
The Throng that follows Caesar at the Heels,
Of Senators, of Praetors, common Suitors,
Will crowd a feeble Man, almost, to death.
I'll get me to a place more void, and there
Speak to great Caesar as he comes along.
PORTIA I must go in. Ay me, how Weak a thing
The Heart of Woman is? – O Brutus,
The Heavens speed thee in thine Enterprise.
– Sure the Boy heard me. – Brutus hath a Suit
That Caesar will not grant. O I grow faint:
Run, Lucius, and commend me to my Lord,
Say I am merry. Come to me again,
And bring me word what he doth say to thee.

Exeunt.

III.i This scene begins on the street outside the Capitol in Rome. Then, presumably, it shifts inside.

3 **Schedule** document.

4 **o'er-read** read over.

7 **touches Caesar nearer** concerns Caesar more immediately. In view of Decius' earlier use of *touch* as a euphemism for kill (II.i.152), Artemidorus' choice of words (which Shakespeare takes almost verbatim from North's Plutarch) is ominously apt.

8 **What . . . serv'd** Caesar here presents himself as a selfless public servant for whom personal concerns are always to be thought of as subsidiary to the good of the commonwealth. Plutarch's image of him is quite different: 'Caesar took it of [Artemidorus], but could never read it, though he many times attempted it, for the number of people that did salute him; but holding it still in his hand, keeping it to himself, went on withal into the Senate-house.' Unlike Plutarch's Caesar, Shakespeare's remains so secure in his sense of invulnerability that he simply brushes aside the warnings thrust his way. In view of the other biblical allusions in the play, it seems likely that Shakespeare expects his audience to detect in Caesar's words an ironic echo of Matthew 19:30, 'many that are first shall be last; and the last shall be first'. See the notes to I.i.72; I.ii.23, 180, 208–9; II.i.97, 142, 321–23; II.ii.85–88, 126, 128–29; II.iv.23, 42; III.i.52, 117, 163, 233; III.ii.172, 177, 180–82, 184, 198, 226–27; IV.i.6; IV.ii.130; V.i.32, 52; V.iii.68–70; V.v.20.

11–12 **What . . . Capitol** After this speech most editions insert a stage direction to indicate that Caesar and his train enter the Capitol. Precisely what this would mean in staging terms is not clear.

13 **I . . . thrive** In Plutarch, Popilius Lena wishes the conspirators success in their undertaking and urges them to proceed rapidly because their enterprise is 'bewrayed' (revealed). But when they see him talking to Caesar, they fear that there should be no 'tarrying' lest they be 'apprehended'.

21 **Cassius . . . back** Cassius seems to be saying that neither he nor Caesar will survive. His implication is that he will first try to kill Caesar; if that is not possible, he will slay himself. Compare I.iii.85–102.

ACT III

Scene 1

Flourish. Enter Caesar, Brutus, Cassius, Casca, Decius, Metellus, Trebonius, Cinna, Antony, Lepidus, Artemidorus, Publius, [*Popilius,*] *and the Soothsayer.*

CAESAR The Ides of March are come.
SOOTHSAYER Ay, Caesar, but not gone.
ARTEMIDORUS Hail, Caesar: read this Schedule.
DECIUS Trebonius doth desire you to o'er-read,
At your best leisure, this his humble Suit.
ARTEMIDORUS O Caesar, read mine first: for mine's a Suit
That touches Caesar nearer. Read it, great Caesar.
CAESAR What touches us our self shall be last serv'd.
ARTEMIDORUS Delay not, Caesar, read it instantly.
CAESAR What, is this Fellow mad?
PUBLIUS Sirrah, give place.
CASSIUS What, urge you your Petitions in the Street?
Come to the Capitol.
POPILIUS I wish your Enterprise to day may thrive.
CASSIUS What Enterprise, Popilius?
POPILIUS Fare you well.
BRUTUS What said Popilius Lena?
CASSIUS He wish'd to day our Enterprise might thrive.
I fear our Purpose is discovered.
BRUTUS Look how he makes to Caesar: mark him.
CASSIUS – Casca, be sudden, for we fear Prevention.
– Brutus, what shall be done? If this be known,
Cassius or Caesar never shall turn back,
For I will slay my self.

22 **constant** steady, unchanging in aspect.

26 **He . . . way** Whether Trebonius completely leaves the stage with Mark Antony, as most editions indicate, is uncertain. North's Plutarch says that after the Senate party entered the council chamber and Caesar sat in his chair, 'Cassius, casting his eyes upon Pompey's image, made his prayer unto it, as if it had been alive. Trebonius on the other side, drew Antonius aside as he came into the house where the Senate sat, and held him with a long talk without.'

28 **presently prefer** immediately present.

30 **rears** raises. In line 77 Casca addresses his hands when he raises them to 'speak' for him.

31–32 **Are . . . redress?** Caesar is calling the Senate into session to consider all the petitions and complaints to be brought before it. The word *redress* recalls II.i.54–57.

33 **puissant** powerful.

36 **Couchings** bowings.

37 **fire the Blood** heat the blood, warm the heart. *Fire* recalls II.i.330.

38–39 **And . . . Children** and shunt first principles and legal precedents into the kind of courtroom where children rather than mature men preside over the laws of the State.

39 **fond** foolish.

41 **true Quality** the quality of blood that is properly cool and dispassionate, not 'thaw'd' (dissolved) by the kinds of emotional appeal that would cause fools and children to melt. Caesar is here presenting himself as a man of objectivity and self-control. Unlike that which Brutus described in II.i.62–68, Caesar's 'State of a Man', he maintains, is lacking in the kind of 'Rebel Blood' (passion) that could bring about an insurrection and usurp Reason's role, either in Caesar's personal life or in his administration of the affairs of the Roman State. Caesar's phrasing is another variation on the 'Mettle' imagery of II.ii.117–21 and the fire imagery of II.ii.31 and previous passages.

43 **Spaniel** Spaniels were proverbial for displays of affection. *Curtsies* plays on *cur*; compare *The Merchant of Venice*, I.iii.112–30.

BRUTUS Cassius, be constant:
Popilius Lena speaks not of our Purposes,
For look, he smiles, and Caesar doth not change.
CASSIUS Trebonius knows his Time: for look you, Brutus,
He draws Mark Antony out of the way.
DECIUS Where is Metellus Cimber, let him go,
And presently prefer his Suit to Caesar.
BRUTUS He is address'd: press near, and second him.
CINNA Casca, you are the first that rears your Hand.
CAESAR Are we all ready? What is now amiss
That Caesar and his Senate must redress?
METELLUS Most high, most mighty, and most puissant Caesar,
Metellus Cimber throws before thy Seat
An humble Heart.
CAESAR I must prevent thee, Cimber:
These Couchings, and these lowly Courtesies
Might fire the Blood of ordinary Men,
And turn pre-Ordinance and first Decree
Into the Lane of Children. Be not fond,
To think that Caesar bears such Rebel Blood
That will be thaw'd from the true Quality
With that which melteth Fools: I mean sweet Words,
Low-crooked Curtsies, and base Spaniel Fawning.
Thy Brother by Decree is banished:
If thou doest bend, and pray, and fawn for him,

46 **spurn** kick. Brutus has used this verb in II.i.11. *Cause* (line 47) recalls II.ii.69, 71.

48 **Satisfied** contented. Caesar means that because he always acts on rational principles, he always bases his decisions on the satisfactory establishment of a just cause. *Sound* echoes II.i.231.

51 **repealing** recalling from exile.

52 **kiss** Brutus' gesture occurs in Plutarch; in North's words, 'the conspirators flocked about' Caesar, and 'all made as though they were intercessors' for Cimber, and took Caesar 'by the hands and kissed his head and breast'. But of course an Elizabethan audience would have been reminded of Matthew 26:46–56, where Judas 'betrayed' Jesus to the 'chief priests and elders of the people', when he came up to him in the Garden of Gethsemane 'and said, Hail, master; and kissed him'.

58 **Enfranchisement** return from banishment, and restoration of the rights of citizenship.

62 **resting** unmoving. If the Elizabethan staging followed Plutarch, Caesar would be sitting in his chair as he speaks this word.

63 **Fellow** peer, equal.

66 **But . . . Place** Caesar's phrasing echoes what Cassius has said about this 'Great' and 'onely' man in I.ii.145–54. As Caesar speaks, he alone is upright, like the 'Constant', omnipotent 'One' he describes, ironically, as possessing a higher order of 'Flesh and Blood'.

I spurn thee like a Cur out of my way.
Know, Caesar doth not Wrong, nor without Cause
Will he be Satisfied.

METELLUS Is there no Voice more worthy than my own,
To sound more sweetly in great Caesar's Ear
For the repealing of my banish'd Brother?

BRUTUS I kiss thy Hand, but not in Flattery, Caesar,
Desiring thee that Publius Cimber may
Have an immediate freedom of Repeal.

CAESAR What, Brutus?

CASSIUS Pardon, Caesar; Caesar, pardon;
As low as to thy Foot doth Cassius fall,
To beg Enfranchisement for Publius Cimber.

CAESAR I could be well mov'd, if I were as you;
If I could pray to move, Prayers would move me;
But I am Constant as the Northern Star,
Of whose true fix'd and resting Quality
There is no Fellow in the Firmament.
The Skies are painted with Unnumb'red Sparks,
They are all Fire, and every one doth shine;
But there's but one in all doth hold his Place.
So in the World: 'tis furnish'd well with Men,

68 **Men . . . Apprehensive** Here Caesar is alluding to the doctrine that each human being was made up of two basic parts: (a) a 'lower soul' comprised of 'Flesh and Blood' (the body and the emotions), and (b) a 'higher soul' where Reason dwelled (a person's 'Apprehensive' capacity). Ideally, the higher soul presided, resisting any promptings of the emotions that went against the judgements of reason. This doctrine was taken to its fullest extreme in Roman Stoicism, for which Caesar is here a spokesman. Whereas Aristotelian and Christian philosophy allowed a place for the emotions so long as they were kept subordinate to the reason, Stoicism tended to the view that any influence by the emotions was a violation of the 'Constancy' that reason should maintain 'Unshak'd of Motion' (line 71). Christian philosophers such as St Augustine and, later, Erasmus regarded Roman Stoicism as a misguided system that futilely sought to turn men into gods by denying the lower soul its natural role in human life; in their view, Stoicism sought to transform a king (reason) into a tyrant, with disastrous consequences. What Caesar doesn't realize is that the 'Men' he addresses are moved by 'Blood' (passion, as noted in II.i.166) and are 'Apprehensive' (anxious) about being 'apprehended' (see the note to line 13).

69 **One** This word, which is capitalized in the Folio text, echoes the suggestions of erection and copulation in line 66; meanwhile it recalls such previous passages as I.ii.153–54, I.iii.157–60, II.i.116–17.

71 **Unshak'd** Caesar's verb echoes I.ii.325–26 and illustrates II.ii.49.

75 **Hence . . . Olympus?** Caesar's image suggests that he is now claiming deity. At this moment he towers over the kneeling conspirators, who appear to be trying to lift him higher.

76 **Doth . . . kneel?** Caesar's point is that if the esteemed Brutus' kneeling is 'bootless' (unavailing), that of the others is even more so.

78 **Et tu, Brutè?** Latin, with the implication 'Even thou, Brutus?' According to Plutarch, after calling the 'vile Casca' a traitor and struggling to defend himself, Caesar 'saw Brutus with his sword drawn in his hand, then he pulled his gown over his head and made no more resistance'.

88 **least** lest. Compare line 93, and II.i.28.

And Men are Flesh and Blood, and Apprehensive;
Yet in the Number, I do know but One
That unassailable holds on his Rank
Unshak'd of Motion; and that I am he
Let me a little shew it, even in this:
That I was constant Cimber should be banish'd,
And constant do remain to keep him so.

CINNA O Caesar.

CAESAR Hence: wilt thou lift up Olympus?

DECIUS Great Caesar.

CAESAR Doth not Brutus bootless kneel?

CASCA Speak Hands for me. *They stab Caesar.*

CAESAR *Et tu, Brutè?* – Then fall, Caesar. *Dies.*

CINNA Liberty, Freedom; Tyranny is dead,
Run hence, proclaim, cry it about the Streets.

CASSIUS Some to the common Pulpits, and cry out
Liberty, Freedom, and Enfranchisement.

BRUTUS People and Senators, be not affrighted.
Fly not, stand still: Ambition's Debt is paid.

CASCA Go to the Pulpit, Brutus.

DECIUS And Cassius too.

BRUTUS Where's Publius?

CINNA Here, quite confounded with this Mutiny.

METELLUS Stand fast together, least some Friend of Caesar's

90 **Talk not of standing** Brutus continues to insist that as noble Romans he and his companions need no oaths or exhortations to do what their honour and integrity prompt them to do. He also assumes that their fellow citizens will unquestioningly applaud their deed when it is explained to them, and that the assassins will therefore have no need to stand together in a display of solidarity. *Standing* echoes lines 60–75.

Publius a Roman Senator, to whom Brutus offers reassurance that all is well, despite the 'Mutiny' (insurrection) that has left him 'confounded' (line 87), astounded. *Harm* (line 91) recalls II.iv.31.

95 **abide** both (a) tarry after, and (b) take responsibility for. According to Plutarch, 'some followed' Brutus and his companions out of the Senate 'and went amongst them as if they had been of the conspiracy and falsely challenged part of the honour with them'.

97 **amaz'd** in a maze, bewildered.

98 **stare** gaze open-eyed in fear and wonder.

100 **the Time** the exact time when death will occur.

101 **drawing Days out** extending the waiting period, prolonging the inevitable. Brutus is attempting to lessen the severity of what he and his companions have done by suggesting that life is less important than death. See the note to II.ii.32–37.

stand upon attach significance to. Brutus' phrasing, which echoes lines 60–75, 88–90, recalls II.ii.13, where Calphurnia says that she 'never stood on Ceremonies'.

105 **abridg'd** abbreviated.

106 **Stoop, Romans, stoop** Brutus addresses these words to his fellow assassins. Having defined Death as a 'Benefit (line 104) and themselves as Caesar's 'Friends' (105), they will now link themselves to Caesar and to each other through communion with Caesar's 'Reviving Blood' (II.ii.88). In Plutarch, all the conspirators redden their swords by striking Caesar, and Brutus even catches 'a blow on his hand'; but there is no bathing ritual such as the one Shakespeare supplies here. After the assassination, Plutarch says, 'Brutus and his consorts, having their swords bloody in their hands, went straight to the Capitol, persuading the Romans as they went, to take their liberty again.'

Should chance –
BRUTUS Talk not of standing. – Publius, good cheer,
There is no Harm intended to your person,
Nor to no Roman else: so tell them Publius.
CASSIUS And leave us, Publius, least that the
People
Rushing on us should do your Age some Mischief.
BRUTUS Do so, and let no man abide this Deed
But we the Doers. *Exit Publius* [*Exit.*]

Enter Trebonius.

CASSIUS Where is Antony?
TREBONIUS Fled to his House amaz'd.
Men, Wives, and Children stare, cry out, and run,
As it were Doomsday.
BRUTUS Fates, we will know your pleasures:
That we shall die we know, 'tis but the Time
And drawing Days out that men stand upon.
CASCA Why he that cuts off twenty Years of Life
Cuts off so many Years of fearing Death.
BRUTUS Grant that, and then is Death a Benefit:
So are we Caesar's Friends, that have abridg'd
His time of fearing Death. Stoop, Romans, stoop,
And let us bathe our Hands in Caesar's Blood
Up to the Elbows, and besmear our Swords:
Then walk we forth, even to the Market-place,
And waving our red Weapons o'er our Heads,

111 **Peace, Freedom, and Liberty** These or similar words have rallied patriots and freedom fighters in dozens of countries over the centuries since they were first uttered. Lest we conclude too quickly that Shakespeare expected his first audience to endorse them uncritically, however, we should note the image the assassins project (lines 106–10) as they exclaim this line.

112–14 **How . . . unknown?** In writing these words for his theatre company, Shakespeare must have been acutely aware of the paradox of having them spoken for the first time by an Elizabethan actor who was himself an illustration of what he described. It is intriguing to ponder whether Shakespeare imagined how many times Cassius' prophecy would subsequently be spoken in states and accents 'yet unknown' to the playwright himself. Here *unborne* means both (a) unborne (unconceived and thus uncarried) and (b) unborn.

115 **in Sport** in re-enactments for the entertainment of playgoers.

116 **Pompey's Basis** the base (pedestal) upon which Pompey's statue was erected. Ironically, Caesar died at the foot of the monument to a Roman whose defeat he had himself engineered. According to North's Plutarch, Caesar 'was driven, either casually or purposedly by the conspirators against the base whereon Pompey's image stood, which ran all of a gore blood till he was slain. Thus it seemed that the image took just revenge of Pompey's enemy.' See the note to line 26.

117 **No worthier than the Dust** Elizabethan audiences would have been reminded of Genesis 3:19, 'dust thou art, and unto dust shalt thou return'. Without realizing the full import of his words, Brutus is drawing attention to an ethical principle central to the Western tradition: the fall that comes in the wake of any display of overweening pride. See Proverbs 16:18 ('Pride goeth before destruction, and an haughty spirit before a fall') and Matthew 7:24–27, and compare *Hamlet*, II.ii.324–30, IV.iii.16–31, V.i.102–18, 215–31, V.ii.83–89.

118 **Knot** group, cluster.

122 **the . . . Rome** Cassius' words echo North's Plutarch, which calls Brutus and his companions 'the noblest men of the city'. Compare lines 127, 134–36, 154–57.

131 **vouchsafe** condescend to permit.

Let's all cry Peace, Freedom, and Liberty.
CASSIUS Stoop then and wash. How many Ages hence
Shall this our lofty Scene be acted over,
In States unborne, and Accents yet unknown?
BRUTUS How many Times shall Caesar bleed in Sport,
That now on Pompey's Basis lies along,
No worthier than the Dust?
CASSIUS So oft as that shall be,
So often shall the Knot of us be call'd
The Men that gave their Country Liberty.
DECIUS What, shall we forth?
CASSIUS Ay, every man away.
Brutus shall lead, and we will grace his Heels
With the most boldest and best Hearts of Rome.

Enter a Servant.

BRUTUS Soft, who comes here? A Friend of Antony's.
SERVANT Thus, Brutus, did my Master bid me kneel;
Thus did Mark Antony bid me fall down;
And, being prostrate, thus he bad me say:
'Brutus is Noble, Wise, Valiant, and Honest;
Caesar was Mighty, Bold, Royal, and Loving.'
Say 'I love Brutus, and I honour him';
Say 'I fear'd Caesar, honour'd him, and lov'd him.
If Brutus will vouchsafe that Antony
May safely come to him, and be resolv'd
How Caesar hath deserv'd to lie in Death,
Mark Antony shall not love Caesar dead
So well as Brutus living, but will follow
The Fortunes and Affairs of Noble Brutus,

137 **Thorough** through
untrod State Here *State* probably refers both to the Roman state and to the new state of affairs created by the death of Caesar; both are 'untrod' (unexplored, unknown). *Untrod* hints at *untoward*, unruly, refractory.

141 **so please him** if he will be so pleased as to.

142 **He shall be satisfied** he shall be given reasons that will satisfy his curiosity. *Satisfied* echoes lines 47–48; it also recalls II.ii.71–72.

143 **presently** immediately. In North's Plutarch, Shakespeare would have read that 'Antonius, being put in a fear withal, cast a slave's gown upon him and hid himself. But afterwards, when it was told him that the murderers slew no man else and that they went only into the Capitol, he sent his son unto them for a pledge and bade them boldly come down upon his word. The selfsame day he did bid Cassius to supper, and Lepidus also bade Brutus. The next morning the Senate was assembled; and Antonius himself preferred a law that all things past should be forgotten, and that they should appoint provinces unto Brutus and Cassius.'

144 **have him well to Friend** find him to be a good friend.

146–47 **my . . . Purpose** my misgivings always prove shrewd. *Shrewdly* recalls II.i.153–59; *Fear* echoes II.i.188–89.

149 **– O mighty Caesar!** Antony ignores Brutus' greeting and speaks directly to Caesar's corpse. See the note to line 117.

153 **be let Blood . . . Rank** Antony's imagery derives from the medical practice of the day, when those who were 'rank' (swollen) with disease were bled to rid their bodies of infection. He continues the medical metaphor with the word *Instrument* in line 155. In both cases he sardonically depicts Brutus and Cassius as physicians who have taken upon themselves the responsibility of curing Rome of its sickness. In II.i.178 Brutus has predicted that 'We shall be call'd Purgers, not Murderers'; what he has not foreseen is that the one person who does refer to them thus will do so with devastating irony. See the notes to II.i.166, 321, 322, III.i.66, 68, 106.

158 **bear me hard** bear me ill will. Compare II.i.213.

159 **purpled** bloodied. Shakespeare frequently associates blood with the colour purple, which meant 'crimson' in his time.
reek and smoke steam from the warm blood on them.

Thorough the Hazards of this untrod State,
With all true Faith.' So says my Master Antony.

BRUTUS Thy Master is a Wise and Valiant Roman,
I never thought him worse.
Tell him, so please him come unto this place,
He shall be satisfied: and by my Honour
Depart untouch'd.

SERVANT I'll fetch him presently. *Exit.*

BRUTUS I know that we shall have him well to Friend.

CASSIUS I wish we may; but yet have I a Mind
That fears him much; and my Misgiving still
Falls shrewdly to the Purpose.

Enter Antony.

BRUTUS But here comes Antony. – Welcome, Mark Antony.

ANTONY – O mighty Caesar! Dost thou lie so low?
Are all thy Conquests, Glories, Triumphs, Spoils,
Shrunk to this little Measure? Fare thee well.
– I know not, Gentlemen, what you intend,
Who else must be let Blood, who else is Rank:
If I my self, there is no Hour so fit
As Caesar's Death's Hour, nor no Instrument
Of half that Worth as those your Swords, made rich
With the most Noble Blood of all this World.
I do beseech ye, if you bear me hard,
Now, whilst your purpled Hands do reek and smoke,

160 **Live** if I should live.

161 **apt** prepared, disposed.

163 **cut off** clipped short. See the note to *King Lear*, I.v.55, with its comment on Luke 12:42–48, where the unjust, unwise, irresponsible 'servant' is warned that his master 'will come in a day when he thinketh not, and at hour when he is not ware of, and will cut him off'.

170 **Our Hearts you see not** It doesn't occur to Brutus that his words can be interpreted in a way that differs from the meaning he intends. To Antony at this moment Brutus comes across as 'a Beast without a Heart' (II.ii.42).
Pitiful filled with pity.

172 **Pity Pity** Brutus is saying that their pity for Rome drove out their pity for Caesar. He alludes to the belief that 'like cures like', later the basis of homeopathy; compare *Romeo and Juliet*, I.i.172–240, I.ii.47–60, I.iv.25–28. *General* recalls II.ii.28–29.

174 **leaden Points** 'points' that will do no harm because they cover the sharp points of our blades.

175 **in strength of Malice** with the strength they have shown in doing malice.

176 **Of Brothers' Temper** with the strength of love that links brothers. *Temper* recalls I.ii.127. Compare II.i.330–31.

179 **disposing of new Dignities** determination of new titles and responsibilities. See the note to line 143. According to Plutarch Antony persuaded the Senate to give 'certain provinces also and convenient honours unto Brutus and his confederates, whereby every man thought all things were brought to good peace and quietness again'.

180 **appeas'd** pacified, quieted.

182 **Cause** both (a) reason, and (b) case (as in II.i.11); compare III.i.47, 182.

183 **strook** struck. The phrasing in this line recalls line 52. In this sentence Brutus switches from *we* to *I*.

Fulfil your Pleasure. Live a thousand Years,
I shall not find my self so apt to die.
No Place shall please me so, no Mean of Death,
As here by Caesar, and by you cut off,
The Choice and Master Spirits of this Age.

BRUTUS O Antony! Beg not your Death of us:
Though now we must appear Bloody and Cruel,
As by our Hands and this our present Act
You see we do. Yet see you but our Hands,
And this, the bleeding Business they have done:
Our Hearts you see not, they are Pitiful.
And Pity to the general Wrong of Rome
(As Fire drives out Fire, so Pity Pity)
Hath done this Deed on Caesar. For your part,
To you our Swords have leaden Points, Mark Antony:
Our Arms in strength of Malice, and our Hearts
Of Brothers' Temper, do receive you in
With all kind Love, good Thoughts, and Reverence.

CASSIUS Your Voice shall be as strong as any Man's
In the disposing of new Dignities.

BRUTUS Onely be Patient till we have appeas'd
The Multitude, beside themselves with Fear,
And then we will deliver you the Cause
Why I, that did love Caesar when I strook him,
Have thus proceeded.

ANTONY I doubt not of your Wisdom:

185 **bloody** Here, as in line 199, Antony hints at the sense that means 'murderous', 'violent'. According to North's Plutarch, 'Caesar turned him nowhere but he was stricken at by some, and still had naked swords in his face, and was hacked and mangled among them as a wild beast taken of hunters. And then Brutus himself gave him one wound about his privities.' See the notes to lines 106, 163.

186 **shake** This word echoes lines 69–71.

192 **My Credit** my reputation. *Stands* echoes lines 60–75, 101.
Slippery Ground uncertain basis. It may be that Antony is being literal here as he looks down at a pool of Caesar's blood. It may also be that he feels that he will have stained his credit by shaking the bloody hands of Caesar's assassins.

193 **conceit me** conceive of me, think of me.

200 **Corse** corpse. See the note to II.i.160.

203 **then** both (a) then, and (b) than, compare *Macbeth*, III.ii.6–7.
close agree, form a compact.

205 **bay'd** hunted down by baying (barking) dogs.
Hart stag deer, with a pun on *heart*. Compare lines 121–22, 170, 175–76, 208–9.

207 **Sign'd in thy Spoil** bearing the signs or marks of the animal they have hunted down. The word *spoil* normally refers to the prize to be divided among the hunters. See the note to line 185.
crimson'd in thy Lethe their hands made crimson by bathing in the river of your blood. *Lethe* is the River of Forgetfulness in the Hades of Greek mythology; here, then, it is a symbol of death and oblivion. *Lethe* also appears in *Hamlet*, I.v.30–33, *Antony and Cleopatra*, II.vii.108–9, *Twelfth Night*, IV.i.65–66, 2 *Henry IV*, V.ii.71, and *Richard III*, IV.iv.251–53.

210 **stroken** stricken. Compare V.i.29–32.

214 **Then** thus, therefore.
cold Modesty a dispassionate and moderate appraisal. *Modesty* recalls I.ii.66–68.

217 **prick'd in number** counted among the number. A prick is a tiny mark to indicate an item on a list. Compare II.i.121–22, IV.i.1.

Let each Man render me his bloody Hand.
First, Marcus Brutus, will I shake with you;
Next, Caius Cassius, do I take your Hand;
Now, Decius Brutus, yours; now yours, Metellus;
Yours, Cinna; and my valiant Casca, yours;
Though last, not least in Love, yours, good Trebonius.
Gentlemen all: alas, what shall I say?
My Credit now stands on such Slippery Ground
That one of two bad ways you must conceit me,
Either a Coward or a Flatterer.
– That I did love thee, Caesar, O 'tis true:
If then thy Spirit look upon us now,
Shall it not grieve thee dearer than thy Death
To see thy Antony making his Peace,
Shaking the bloody Fingers of thy Foes?
Most Noble, in the presence of thy Corse,
Had I as many Eyes as thou hast Wounds,
Weeping as fast as they stream forth thy Blood,
It would become me better then to close
In terms of Friendship with thine Enemies.
Pardon me, Julius, here wast thou bay'd, brave Hart,
Here didst thou fall, and here thy Hunters stand
Sign'd in thy Spoil, and crimson'd in thy Lethe.
– O World! thou wast the Forest to this Hart,
And this indeed, O World, the Hart of thee.
– How like a Deer, stroken by many Princes,
Dost thou here lie?

CASSIUS Mark Antony.

ANTONY Pardon me, Caius Cassius.
The Enemies of Caesar shall say this:
Then in a Friend, it is cold Modesty.

CASSIUS I blame you not for praising Caesar so,
But what Compact mean you to have with us?
Will you be prick'd in number of our Friends,

218 **Or shall we on** or shall we proceed.

220 **sway'd** diverted. See the notes to I.iii.3, II.i.20.
Point both (a) subject, and (b) 'true fix'd and resting' position (III.i.62).

223 **wherein** in what specific ways. *Reasons* echoes North's Plutarch, where Shakespeare would have read that once the conspirators went to the Capitol and assembled an audience, 'Brutus made an oration unto them to win the favour of the people and to justify what they had done'.

224 **Or . . . Spectacle** Brutus says that otherwise this would be a display of savagery. That, of course, is precisely what Antony has just been implying with his hunting metaphors: that the assassins have proceeded, not like 'Sacrificers', but like 'Butchers' (II.i.164). See the notes to lines 116, 163, 185.

226 **Son of Caesar** Plutarch alludes to Suetonius' story that Brutus was an illegitimate son of Caesar, conceived during a time when Brutus' mother, Servilia, 'was extremely in love' with Caesar. According to Suetonius, just before Caesar died he said in Greek to Brutus, 'And you, son'; compare line 78.

229 **Produce** bring forward. *Satisfied* (line 227) echoes line 142.

230 **Pulpit** a speaker's platform or rostrum in the Forum. For an Elizabethan audience it would also have been associated with the orations of a priestly elite.

231 **Order** ceremony.

233 **You know not what you do** Speaking confidentially, Cassius refers to Brutus' pledge to allow Mark Antony a role in Caesar's funeral. His words have an unintended pertinence to virtually everything Brutus does in the play. For Shakespeare's audience, moreover, they would have echoed Luke 23:34. See the notes to lines 8, 52, 117, 163.

235 **mov'd** stirred, persuaded. Compare line 60 and I.iii.3. Cassius echoes what Brutus himself has said in lines 180–81.

236 **utter** literally, speak out. Cassius' verb echoes II.i.211–12; as he fears, the 'uttermost' speaker at Caesar's funeral will utter the most moving words.

238 **Reason of** justification for. See lines 180–84, 221–27. Lines 239–50 recall the reasoning in II.i.152–81.

Or shall we on, and not depend on you?

ANTONY Therefore I took your Hands, but was indeed
Sway'd from the Point by looking down on Caesar.
Friends am I with you all, and love you all,
Upon this Hope, that you shall give me Reasons,
Why, and wherein, Caesar was Dangerous.

BRUTUS Or else were this a Savage Spectacle.
Our Reasons are so full of good Regard
That were you, Antony, the Son of Caesar,
You should be Satisfied.

ANTONY That's all I seek,
And am moreover Suitor, that I may
Produce his Body to the Market-place,
And in the Pulpit, as becomes a Friend,
Speak in the Order of his Funeral.

BRUTUS You shall, Mark Antony.

CASSIUS Brutus, a word with you.
You know not what you do; do not consent
That Antony speak in his Funeral.
Know you how much the People may be mov'd
By that which he will utter.

BRUTUS By your pardon:
I will my self into the Pulpit first,
And shew the Reason of our Caesar's Death.

239 **protest** proclaim.

242 **true** proper, legitimate. *Rites* can mean both (a) rites, rituals, and (b) rights.

255 The speech heading included here does not appear in the Folio.

257 **Ruins** remains. Antony's image associates Caesar with architectural ruins and thus suggests that he will endure as a monument to the glory that was Rome.

258 **Tide of Times** course of history. *Tide* anticipates IV.ii.260–63.

259 **costly** Antony probably means both (a) precious, of inestimable value, and (b) costly to those who perpetrated the crime.

261 **dumb** unspeaking, quiet.
Ruby Lips This image links Caesar's blood to precious gems.

262 **Voice** both (a) sound, and (b) vote (as in line 179).

265 **cumber** burden, encumber.
parts Antony probably means both (a) regions, and (b) bodily parts (treating Italy as an extended Body Politic). Compare II.i.160–81.

268 **but** only.

270 **chok'd with custom of Fell Deeds** throttled, owing to the commonness of terrible deeds. *Pity* echoes lines 165–77.

272 **Atê** the Greek Goddess of Retribution, a personification of the consequences of a seizure of *atê*, the delusion that results from *hubris*. See the notes to II.ii.49, II.iii.9.

What Antony shall speak, I will protest
He speaks by Leave, and by Permission:
And that we are contented Caesar shall
Have all true Rites, and lawful Ceremonies,
It shall advantage more than do us wrong.

CASSIUS I know not what may fall, I like it not.

BRUTUS Mark Antony, here take you Caesar's Body.
You shall not in your Funeral Speech blame us,
But speak all good you can devise of Caesar,
And say you do't by our Permission;
Else shall you not have any hand at all
About his Funeral. And you shall speak
In the same Pulpit whereto I am going,
After my Speech is ended.

ANTONY Be it so:
I do desire no more.

BRUTUS Prepare the Body then, and follow us.

Exeunt. Manet Antony.

[ANTONY] O pardon me, thou bleeding Piece of Earth:
That I am meek and gentle with these Butchers.
Thou art the Ruins of the Noblest Man
That ever lived in the Tide of Times.
Woe to the Hand that shed this costly Blood.
Over thy Wounds now do I prophesy
(Which like dumb Mouths do ope their Ruby Lips
To beg the Voice and Utterance of my Tongue)
A Curse shall light upon the Limbs of Men;
Domestic Fury and fierce Civil Strife
Shall cumber all the parts of Italy;
Blood and Destruction shall be so in use,
And Dreadful Objects so familiar,
That Mothers shall but smile when they behold
Their Infants quartered with the Hands of War;
All Pity chok'd with custom of Fell Deeds;
And Caesar's Spirit ranging for Revenge,
With Atê by his side, come hot from Hell,

273 **Confines** regions.

274 **Havoc** a war cry meaning 'No quarter!' or 'No mercy!'
let slip turn loose. Compare *Measure for Measure*, I.iv.20–21.

276 **Carrion Men** men who will be so accustomed to seeing death all around them that they will be little more than walking corpses themselves.

282 **– O Caesar!** At this moment the Servant's eyes fall upon the corpse.

283 **big** swelled to the bursting point. *Heart* echoes lines 208–9.

284 **catching from mine Eyes** contagious, from the tears in my eyes. Most modern editions alter *from* to *for* and add a comma or a semicolon before *for*. Since the Folio reading makes good sense, no emendation is necessary.

287 **lies** lodges.
seven Leagues twenty-one miles (a league being three miles in length). Here *seven* is an unstressed word with the metrical value of a single syllable. Compare the use of *to night* here with that of *to day* in II.ii.38.

288 **Post** hasten.

289–90 **Rome** Antony plays on *room*; compare I.ii.153–54.

291 **Hie** make haste.

291–93 **Yet . . . Market-place** This sentence is a reminder of one of the practical considerations that affected Shakespeare's work as a playwright. With no curtain to drop as a way of indicating the end of a scene, the playwright was forced to devise other means of removing corpses from the stage. The entry of Octavius' servant at the end of this scene is important, then, not only for the information it conveys to the audience but also for the help it supplies an Antony who would otherwise be left to drag Caesar's body unceremoniously from its resting place. We should note that as this scene ends, the battle lines are being drawn for the civil war that will be the consequence of the assassination. *Course* echoes line 200.

293 **try** test, examine.

Shall in these Confines, with a Monarch's Voice,
Cry Havoc, and let slip the Dogs of War,
That this Foul Deed shall smell above the Earth
With Carrion Men, groaning for Burial.

Enter Octavio's Servant.

– You serve Octavius Caesar, do you not?
SERVANT I do, Mark Antony.
ANTONY Caesar did write for him to come to Rome.
SERVANT He did receive his Letters, and is coming,
And bid me say to you by word of mouth –
– O Caesar!
ANTONY Thy Heart is big: get thee apart and weep.
Passion I see is catching from mine Eyes,
Seeing those beads of Sorrow stand in thine,
Began to water. Is thy Master coming?
SERVANT He lies to night within seven Leagues of
Rome.
ANTONY Post back with speed, and tell him what hath
chanc'd:
Here is a mourning Rome, a dangerous Rome,
No Rome of Safety for Octavius yet.
Hie hence and tell him so. Yet stay awhile:
Thou shall not back till I have borne this
Course
Into the Market-place. There shall I try,
In my Oration, how the People take
The cruel Issue of these Bloody Men,
According to the which thou shalt discourse
To young Octavius of the state of things.
Lend me your Hand. *Exeunt* [*with Caesar's Body*].

III.ii Now the setting shifts to the Forum in Rome. Plutarch indicates that the eulogies over Caesar's body took place the day after the assassination, and following the Senate session noted at III.i.143, 179.

1 **We will be Satisfied** We demand that you give us satisfactory reasons for what you have done. Compare III.i.142, 227.

2 **Audience** literally, a group of people who *hear* what a speaker has to say.

4 **part the Numbers** divide the crowd into two groups. Soon 'the Numbers' will be 'parted' from Brutus and Cassius both. *Part* echoes I.ii.26–27, 247–49, 286–87, I.iii.46–56, 98–100, II.i.10–11, 191, III.i.173, and anticipates line 56. See the note to line 198.

7 **rend'red** submitted for your approval. Brutus' phrasing recalls III.i.79–96, 106–22, 125–38, 166–77, 180–84, 237–52.

10 **severally** separately.

13 **Lovers** devoted friends.

13–14 **for my Cause** Brutus probably means 'because of the nobility of my cause', but the phrase can also mean 'to learn what caused me to commit the deed in question'. There may also be a suggestion that *Cause* means 'case' in the legal sense. In effect, this scene will turn out to be Brutus' trial. See the note to III.i.11, and compare III.i.182.

15 **for** both (a) because of, and (b) out of respect for.
to for.

16 **Censure** Brutus means 'judge me', but subsequent events will ironically give this verb the more usual modern meaning.

17 **awake your Senses** Brutus probably means 'be alert, attend carefully, so that your reason will lead you to the proper conclusion'. Naively, he does not see any need to appeal to the audience's senses in the other sense (their feelings and passions), and his failure to 'awake their senses' adequately is what eventually undoes him.

Scene 2

Enter Brutus, and goes into the Pulpit, and Cassius, with the Plebeians.

PLEBEIANS We will be Satisfied: let us be Satisfied.
BRUTUS Then follow me, and give me Audience, Friends.
– Cassius, go you into the other Street,
And part the Numbers.
Those that will hear me speak, let 'em stay here;
Those that will follow Cassius, go with him,
And public Reasons shall be rend'red
Of Caesar's Death.
FIRST PLEBEIAN I will hear Brutus speak.
SECOND I will hear Cassius, and compare their Reasons
When severally we hear them rend'red.
[*Exit Cassius and some of the Plebeians.*]
THIRD The Noble Brutus is ascended: Silence.
BRUTUS Be patient till the last.
Romans, Countrymen, and Lovers, hear me for my Cause, and be silent, that you may hear. Believe me for mine Honour, and have respect to mine Honour, that you may believe. Censure me in your Wisdom, and awake your Senses, that you may the better judge. If there be any in this Assembly, any dear Friend of Caesar's, to him I say that Brutus' love to Caesar was no less than his. If then that Friend demand why Brutus rose against Caesar, this is my Answer:

23–24 **not . . . more** This statement epitomizes Brutus' position. It is a straightforward, clear expression of the principles that undergirded his participation in the assassination. Like the rest of Brutus' account of his reasons, it is presented in unadorned, balanced clauses that lay out simple alternatives and offer rationales for the difficult choices that had to be made. What we should also notice is that this speech is spoken in prose and has little of the figurative language Brutus uses elsewhere in the play. According to North's Plutarch, Brutus was known for 'that brief compendious manner of speech of the Lacedaemonians'. By contrast, Antony 'used a manner of phrase in his speech called Asiatic, which carried the best grace and estimation at that time, and was much like to his manners and life; for it was full of ostentation, foolish bravery, and vain ambition'.

25 **then** Brutus means 'than'; but 'then' is ironically pertinent too. Compare line 40 and III.i.203.

32 **Base** low-minded, lacking in human dignity. Throughout this speech the Everyman edition follows the heavy punctuation of the Folio text.

Bondman slave or captive, one who is bound over to another.

34 **Rude** uncivilized, barbarous. The Greeks and Romans considered most other people to be barbarians, a word that was coined in imitation of the sheep-like 'baa-baa' sounds some of them seemed to make as they spoke their native languages. Compare I.ii.299–306.

40 **then** both (a) than (Brutus' meaning), and (b) then (an ironic sense that subsequent developments will impart).

41–42 **The . . . Capitol** Here Brutus seems to be saying that the issues that led to Caesar's 'execution' have been 'enroll'd' (written out and deposited) in the Capitol for the consideration of Rome's designated legal authorities. His words can also be taken as an allusion to the Senate's exoneration of Caesar's assassins; see the notes to III.i.143, 179, 223.

42 **extenuated** diminished. According to Plutarch, it was 'ordained that they should cancel none of Caesar's laws' and that 'Caesar's funerals should be honoured as a god'.

43 **enforc'd** unnecessarily emphasized.

45–48 **Here . . . not** Brutus' words will prove true in ways he is incapable of imagining. See the note to III.i.233. *Benefit* echoes III.i.104–6.

not that I lov'd Caesar less, but that I lov'd Rome more. Had you rather Caesar were living, and die all Slaves, then that Caesar were dead, to live all Freemen? As Caesar lov'd me, I weep for him; as he was Fortunate, I rejoice at it; as he was Valiant, I honour him; but, as he was Ambitious, I slew him. There is Tears, for his Love; Joy, for his Fortune; Honour, for his Valour; and Death, for his Ambition. Who is here so Base, that would be a Bondman? If any, speak, for him have I offended. Who is here so Rude, that would not be a Roman? If any, speak, for him have I offended. Who is here so Vile, that will not love his Country? If any, speak, for him have I offended. I pause for a Reply.

ALL None, Brutus, none.

BRUTUS Then none have I offended. I have done no more to Caesar, then you shall do to Brutus. The Question of his Death is enroll'd in the Capitol: his Glory not extenuated, wherein he was Worthy; nor his Offences enforc'd, for which he suffered Death.

Enter Mark Antony, with Caesar's Body.

Here comes his Body, mourn'd by Mark Antony, who, though he had no Hand in his Death, shall receive the Benefit of his Dying, a Place in the Commonwealth, as which of you shall not.

49–50 **best Lover** dearest friend. As Caesar's last words demonstrated, he felt a special affinity for Brutus.

52 **need** require, call for.

55 **Ancestors** This word can mean (a) ancestors, (b) ancestor's, and (c) ancestors'. See the notes to I.iii.146, II.i.53.

56 **Let him be Caesar** Despite what Brutus has done in an effort to forestall 'Caesarism', it is clear that many Romans feel the need for a head to the Body Politic. See the notes to I.ii.154, 160, 304, 313, II.i.148, 321.
parts attributes. Compare line 4, and see I.iii.154–56, III.i.264–65.

62 **for my sake** out of respect for my honour (line 15).

63 **grace** respect, courtesy.

64 **Tending to** Brutus probably means 'pertaining to', but it seems evident that he also views Mark Antony's role as a kind of chore or duty that someone has to carry out. Now that Brutus has done the important work (explaining why Caesar had to die), he will leave to Antony the lesser business of 'tending to' Caesar's positive achievements. Compare I.ii.321–23.

71 **beholding to you** indebted to you. Soon Antony will be holding to them (clutching them) in a way that will turn them into the instruments of his retaliation against Caesar's murderers.

74 **here?** Most editions replace the Folio's question mark with an exclamation mark. But the Fourth Plebeian may be speaking with uncertainty in his voice, seeking confirmation from his fellow citizens before he commits himself unequivocally to Brutus' point of view.

With this I depart, that as I slew my best
Lover for the good of Rome, I have the same
Dagger for my self, when it shall please my
Country to need my Death.

ALL Live, Brutus, live, live.

FIRST Bring him with Triumph home unto his House.

SECOND Give him a Statue with his Ancestors.

THIRD Let him be Caesar.

FOURTH Caesar's better parts
Shall be crown'd in Brutus.

FIRST We'll bring him to his House with Shouts and Clamours.

BRUTUS My Countrymen.

SECOND Peace, silence, Brutus speaks.

FIRST Peace, ho.

BRUTUS Good countrymen, let me depart alone,
And, for my sake, stay here with Antony.
Do grace to Caesar's Corpse, and grace his Speech
Tending to Caesar's Glories, which Mark Antony,
By our permission, is allow'd to make.
I do entreat you, not a man depart,
Save I alone, till Antony have spoke. *Exit.*

FIRST Stay, ho, and let us hear Mark Antony.

THIRD Let him go up into the public Chair,
We'll hear him. – Noble Antony, go up.

[*Antony goes up to the Pulpit.*]

ANTONY For Brutus' sake, I am beholding to you.

FOURTH What does he say of Brutus?

THIRD He says, for Brutus' sake
He finds himself beholding to us all.

FOURTH 'Twere best he speak no harm of Brutus here?

FIRST This Caesar was a Tyrant.

THIRD Nay, that's certain:
We are blest that Rome is rid of him.

SECOND Peace, let us hear what Antony can say.

ANTONY You gentle Romans –

79 **lend me** let me borrow. Compare III.i.298.

82 **interred** buried; here pronounced as a three-syllable word.

86 **grievously** Antony means both (a) terribly, and (b) pitiably, with play on the sense that relates to a *grievance*, injury or injustice.
answer'd paid for.

87 **under leave of** with the permission of.

92–93 **But . . . Man** Here Antony is parodying the appeal with which Brutus began his own funeral address (lines 15–16). The logic implicit in Brutus' argument has been that (a) Brutus is a man of honour, so (b) his assassination of Caesar was an honourable deed. By repeatedly setting this justification in juxtaposition with evidence that Caesar was a man who didn't deserve execution, Antony will suggest a different logic: (a) what Brutus and his companions did was not an honourable deed, so (b) perhaps Brutus and his companions are not such honourable men after all. Whereas Brutus spoke in direct, straightforward prose, Antony addresses the audience in a subtly modulated verse and proceeds in a meandering, indirect fashion to a conclusion that remains more implicit than explicit. Rather than tell the audience what to think and how to feel about Caesar, he paints a series of mini-portraits, so that eventually the crowd is led inductively to a conclusion that it would almost appear to have arrived at on its own. See the notes to lines 23–24.

95 **general Coffers** public treasury. Compare III.i.171

98 **sterner stuff** hardier material: more 'manly' and less subject to the kinds of 'weakness' characteristic of women.

103 **Which . . . refuse** Antony makes no mention of Caesar's anger (I.ii.180).

110 **brutish Beasts** Antony is probably punning on *Brutus* here. *Cause* (lines 108–9) echoes line 13.

ALL Peace, ho, let us hear him.
ANTONY Friends, Romans, Countrymen, lend me your Ears:
I come to bury Caesar, not to praise him.
The Evil that men do lives after them,
The Good is oft interred with their Bones:
So let it be with Caesar. The Noble Brutus
Hath told you Caesar was Ambitious:
If it were so, it was a grievous Fault,
And grievously hath Caesar answer'd it.
Here, under leave of Brutus and the rest
(For Brutus is an Honourable Man,
So are they all, all Honourable Men),
Come I to speak in Caesar's Funeral.
He was my Friend, faithful and just to me;
But Brutus says he was Ambitious,
And Brutus is an Honourable Man.
He hath brought many Captives home to Rome,
Whose Ransoms did the general Coffers fill:
Did this in Caesar seem Ambitious?
When that the Poor have cried, Caesar hath wept;
Ambition should be made of sterner stuff,
Yet Brutus says he was Ambitious:
And Brutus is an Honourable Man.
You all did see that on the Lupercal
I thrice presented him a Kingly Crown,
Which he did thrice refuse. Was this Ambition?
Yet Brutus says he was Ambitious:
And sure he is an Honourable Man.
I speak not to disprove what Brutus spoke,
But here I am, to speak what I do know.
You all did Love him once, not without Cause;
What Cause withholds you then to Mourn for him?
– O Judgement, thou art fled to brutish Beasts,

111 **Bear with me** At this moment, whatever he truly feels about Caesar, Antony seems to be pretending when he pauses to regain control over his emotions. Unlike Brutus, Antony has no desire to come across as a man whose life is ruled by reason alone. No Stoic, Antony is under no illusion that men are better off if they try to deny their feelings, and in the preceding scene he has appeared genuinely moved by Caesar's slaughter. At the same time, however, Antony is capable of using his reason, as he does here, to manipulate the feelings of others.

114 **Me thinks . . . Sayings** Antony may indeed have a better argument than Brutus. But of course his primary appeal is less to the crowd's 'Reason' than to its emotions.

120 **If it be found so** if it be so determined.
dear abide it pay for it dearly. Compare III.i.95–96.

122 **There's . . . Antony** Among other things, Antony is at pains to persuade the crowd that a truly 'Noble Man' is not a man of stern rectitude and rationality, but one who is capable of compassion for a fellow human being. For Brutus, 'Pity' is largely an abstraction, something that applies to 'the general Wrong of Rome' (III.i.171), but something that must be purged from one's heart when it pertains to a man who threatens to do 'general Wrong'.

124 **But** only.

126 **And . . . Reverence** and no one poor enough to look up to him and accord him respect in death.

127 **Maisters** masters (from the Latin *magister*).

135 **Closet** private study.

136 **Commons** the common people, the plebeians.
Testament bequest, will. In Plutarch, Caesar's will is read (at Mark Antony's urging) publicly in the Senate before Antony speaks. Shakespeare saw that the will could be the rhetorical climax of Antony's oration. According to Plutarch, 'when Caesar's testament was read openly among them, whereby it appeared that he bequeathed unto every citizen of Rome seventy-five drachmas a man, and that he left his gardens and arbours unto the people, . . . the people then loved him and were marvellous sorry for him.'

137 **Which pardon me** which, I hope you'll forgive me.

And Men have lost their Reason. – Bear with me,
My Heart is in the Coffin there with Caesar,
And I must pause till it come back to me.

FIRST Me thinks there is much Reason in his Sayings.

SECOND If thou consider rightly of the matter,
Caesar has had great Wrong.

THIRD Has he, Masters?
I fear there will a Worse come in his place.

FOURTH Mark'd ye his Words? He would not take the Crown,
Therefore 'tis certain, he was not Ambitious.

FIRST If it be found so, some will dear abide it.

SECOND Poor soul, his Eyes are red as Fire with Weeping.

THIRD There's not a Nobler Man in Rome than Antony.

FOURTH Now mark him, he begins again to speak.

ANTONY But yesterday, the Word of Caesar might
Have stood against the World: now lies he there,
And none so poor to do him Reverence.
O Maisters! If I were dispos'd to stir
Your Hearts and Minds to Mutiny and Rage,
I should do Brutus wrong, and Cassius wrong,
Who, you all know, are Honourable Men.
I will not do them wrong: I rather choose
To wrong the Dead, to wrong my self and you,
Than I will wrong such Honourable Men.
But here's a Parchment, with the Seal of Caesar,
I found it in his Closet, 'tis his Will:
Let but the Commons hear this Testament,
Which pardon me, I do not mean to read,
And they would go and kiss dead Caesar's Wounds,

139 **Napkins** handkerchiefs. *Kiss* (line 138) recalls III.i.52.

143 **Issue** offspring. Compare III.i.293–97.

147 **meet** fit, suitable.

148 **You . . . Men** Antony is saying that you are not the unfeeling creatures the Stoics would have you be, but men with passions. In the opening scene (I.i.41–42), Murellus has accused the Roman commoners of being precisely what Antony now tells them they are not.

150 **mad** insane. But here the context also gives the word an implication identical to its usual modern American meaning, 'angry'. Antony plays on the sense of *Wood* (line 148), that means 'insane'; compare *A Midsummer Night's Dream*, II.i.192, and *King Lear*, II.ii.199.

155 **stay** wait.

156 **o'ershot my self** gone beyond what I was authorized to do here.

157–58 **the . . . Caesar** Here Antony's irony approaches sarcasm. At this point, however, his intention seems limited to presenting what appears to be an innocent juxtaposition of 'Honourable Men' with a deed that is no longer easy to associate with honour and virtue.

162 **You will compel me** Antony has worked the commoners into such a frenzy that they are now 'forcing' him to drive them to the conclusion his remarks have been designed to compel.

164 **shew** show.

167 **Stand from** stand back from.
Hearse bier.

And dip their Napkins in his Sacred Blood,
Yea, beg a Hair of him for Memory,
And dying, mention it within their Wills,
Bequeathing it as a rich Legacy
Unto their Issue.

FOURTH We'll hear the Will, read it, Mark Antony.

ALL The Will, the Will; we will hear Caesar's Will.

ANTONY Have Patience, gentle Friends, I must not read it.
It is not meet you know how Caesar lov'd you:
You are not Wood, you are not Stones, but Men;
And being Men, hearing the Will of Caesar,
It will inflame you, it will make you mad.
'Tis good you know not that you are his Heirs,
For if you should, O what would come of it?

FOURTH Read the Will, [we'll hear it, Antony:
You shall read us the Will,] Caesar's Will.

ANTONY Will you be Patient? Will you stay awhile?
I have o'ershot my self to tell you of it,
I fear I wrong the Honourable Men,
Whose Daggers have stabb'd Caesar: I do fear it.

FOURTH They were Traitors: Honourable Men?

ALL The Will, the Testament.

SECOND They were Villains, Murderers: the Will, read the Will.

ANTONY You will compel me, then, to read the Will:
Then make a Ring about the Corpse of Caesar,
And let me shew you him that made the Will.
Shall I descend? And will you give me leave?

ALL Come down.

SECOND Descend.

THIRD You shall have leave.

FOURTH A Ring,
Stand round. [*Antony comes down from the Pulpit.*]

FIRST Stand from the Hearse, stand from the Body.

SECOND Room for Antony, most Noble Antony.

171 **If . . . now** Compare *A Midsummer Night's Dream*, I.ii.25–28.

172 **Mantle** Shakespeare is probably referring to a cloak similar to that worn by military officers in the Renaissance. The historical Caesar would have been attired in a toga. *Mantle* is a word with biblical resonance. In 2 Kings 2:8–15, Elisha inherits the prophet Elijah's spiritual gifts along with his mantle. Compare Job 1:20, Psalm 109:29.

175 **the Nervii** a fierce Gallic tribe whom Caesar had defeated in 57 BC. Caesar had demonstrated great personal bravery on this occasion, so Antony's mention of it is a telling reminder of the slain leader's virtue and patriotism.

176 **in this place** Antony points to particular incisions and identifies each with a particular assassin. Since Shakespeare has made it clear that Antony was led away from the scene prior to the assault, the audience (though not the Roman crowd) realizes that he actually has no way of knowing which sword caused which cut.

177 **Rent** tear. This word echoes Luke 23:44–45, 'And it was about the sixth hour, and there was a darkness over all the earth until the ninth hour. And the sun was darkened, and the veil of the temple was rent in the midst.' Compare II.iv.23.

180–82 **Mark . . . no** Here Antony personifies Caesar's blood as a way of emphasizing how shocked the innocent Caesar was to discover the loving Brutus among his enemies. Here *unkindly* means both (a) brutally, and (b) seemingly out of character (kind). And *knock'd* is a wonderfully apt euphemism, one that contrasts Brutus' gentle address with his violent actions. Compare Revelation 3:20, and see the note to *Macbeth*, II.ii.70.

181 **to be resolv'd** to have all doubts removed.

183 **Angel** Antony's implicit point is that Brutus only appeared to be 'an angel of light' (2 Corinthians 11:14).

185 **unkindest** (a) most uncharacteristic of the 'kind' of man Caesar thought Brutus to be (see the note to III.i.226), (b) most unnatural and inhuman, (c) most brutally ungentle. *Cut* recalls III.i.102, 163.

ANTONY Nay press not so upon me, stand far off.
ALL Stand back: room, bear back.
ANTONY If you have Tears, prepare to shed them now.
You all do know this Mantle. I remember
The first time ever Caesar put it on,
'Twas on a Summer's Evening in his Tent,
The Day he overcame the Nervii.
Look, in this place ran Cassius' Dagger through;
See what a Rent the envious Casca made;
Through this the well-beloved Brutus stabb'd,
And as he pluck'd his cursed Steel away
Mark how the Blood of Caesar follow'd it,
As rushing out of doors to be resolv'd
If Brutus so unkindly knock'd, or no:
For Brutus, as you know, was Caesar's Angel.
– Judge, O you Gods, how dearly Caesar lov'd him.
– This was the most unkindest Cut of all.
For when the Noble Caesar saw him stab,

187 **Ingratitude** Antony presents Brutus as a man who not only had no personal reason to dislike Caesar, but who had received numerous benefits from him. According to Plutarch, Caesar not only forgave Brutus for fighting against him as a member of Pompey's army; 'he put a marvellous confidence in him'. He pardoned Cassius for Brutus's sake, and he chose Brutus over the more experienced Cassius to be Praetor. See the note to I.ii.32. Compare the reference to *Ingratitude* in *King Lear*, I.iv.273–75.

189 **muffling up** covering up. Antony is implying that Caesar could not bear to see such a hideous sight as Brutus' unmerited cruelty. *Mantle* echoes line 172.

190–91 **Pompey's . . . Blood** Antony's implication is that even Pompey, Caesar's defeated rival, showed pity for Caesar's plight. In Plutarch, by contrast, we are told that the statue 'took just revenge of Pompey's enemy'. See the note to III.i.116.

193 **Then . . . down** Earlier Cassius accused Caesar of imposing the 'Falling Sickness' (I.ii.255) on Rome's populace. Here Antony says that it is Caesar's assassins who have brought about the downfall of the Republic.

194 **flourish'd** an aptly chosen adjective that evokes the bloody swords being brandished over the assassins' heads (III.i.110), while at the same time conveying the idea that Treason is now prospering, indeed swaggering, in Rome.

196 **dint** stroke or impression.

197 **what** Here the word probably means 'why'. But it is also possible that Shakespeare intended *what* to be followed by a pause (and thus a comma in the printed text) and function as an interjection.

198 **Vesture** mantle, cloak. This word recalls Matthew 25:35, 'And they crucified him, and partook his garments, casting lots: that it might be fulfilled which was spoken by the prophet, They parted my garments among them, and upon my vesture did they cast lots' (quoting Psalm 22:18).

210 **private Griefs** Here Antony implies that, whatever their public reasons for the assassination, the conspirators were motivated primarily by unstated private animosities. This is yet another means of undercutting their credibility as 'Honourable Men' who acted solely out of a concern for the good of their country.

Dundrum Library

Items that you have checked out

Title: Julius Caesar / William Shakespeare ; edited by John F. Andrews ; foreword by Sir John Gielgud.
ID: DLR23000057453
Due: 20/11/2021

Title: King Lear / William Shakespeare ; edited with a commentary by George Hunter ; introduced by Kiernan
ID: DLR23000057454
Due: 20/11/2021

Title: The art of dramatic writing.
ID: DLR20000159459
Due: 20/11/2021

Title: Writing a play / Lesley Bown and Ann Gawthorpe.
ID: DLR20000056614
Due: 20/11/2021

Total items: 4
Account balance: 0.00 EUR
30/10/2021
Checked out: 4
Overdue: 0
Hold requests: 0
Ready for collection: 0

Thank you for visiting us today

Ingratitude, more strong than Traitors' Arms,
Quite vanquish'd him: then burst his Mighty Heart,
And in his Mantle, muffling up his Face,
Even at the Base of Pompey's Statue,
Which all the while ran Blood, great Caesar fell.
O what a Fall was there, my Countrymen?
Then I, and you, and all of us fell down,
Whilst bloody Treason flourish'd over us.
O now you weep, and I perceive you feel
The dint of Pity: these are gracious Drops.
Kind Souls, what weep you when you but behold
Our Caesar's Vesture wounded? Look you here,
Here is Himself, marr'd as you see with Traitors.

FIRST O piteous Spectacle!

SECOND O Noble Caesar!

THIRD O woeful Day!

FOURTH O Traitors, Villains!

FIRST O
Most Bloody Sight!

SECOND We will be Reveng'd:
Revenge about, seek, burn, fire, kill, slay,
Let not a Traitor live.

ANTONY Stay, Countrymen.

FIRST Peace there, hear the Noble Antony.

SECOND We'll hear him, we'll follow him, we'll die with him.

ANTONY Good Friends, sweet Friends, let me not stir you up
To such a sudden Flood of Mutiny:
They that have done this Deed are Honourable.
What private Griefs they have, alas I know not,
That made them do it: they are Wise and Honourable,
And will no doubt with Reasons answer you.
I come not, Friends, to steal away your Hearts.

214 **I am no Orator, as Brutus is** This is a splendidly ironic line. Antony is, of course, right: he is no orator of the type that Brutus is, and he has the 'Hearts' (line 213) of the populace in the palm of his hand as a result of it. See the notes to lines 23–24, 92–93.

215 **a plain, blunt Man** Antony has won the crowd largely because of his success in presenting himself as a man without artifice, a man who expresses his feelings openly and honestly, a man who can be depended on to speak the simple, unvarnished truth. His performance in this role is a nice reminder of the old adage that the hardest part of acting is sincerity: once you learn to fake that, you've got it made.

218 **Writ** Here the word probably means 'authority', authorization. But it also means 'prepared written text'.

220 **right on** directly with no equivocation, hesitation, or detours. Compare III.i.218. Now that 'right-on!' has established itself as a linguistic legacy of the 1960s, Mark Antony seems prophetic in ways that even Shakespeare could not have anticipated.

225 **ruffle up** rouse to fury.

226–27 **that . . . Stones** Here the force of Antony's image is 'move even the stones'. Elizabethans would have heard an echo of Luke 19:37–40, where Jesus tells the Pharisees who urge him to silence his disciples that 'if these should hold their peace, the stones would immediately cry out'. These words allude to Genesis 4:10, where God tells Cain, the first murderer, that 'the voice of thy brother's blood crieth unto me from the ground'. Compare *Macbeth*, II.i.55–59, and *King Lear*, I.iv.195–98.

232 **Why . . . what** This sentence echoes II.iv.1–20, where the anxious Portia tells Lucius to 'run to the Senate-house' but doesn't tell him what he should do. It also recalls III.i.233, where Cassius tells Brutus, 'You know not what you do.' For related instances of confusion or misdirection, see I.i.1–65, I.ii.64–68, 81–82, 269–72, I.iii.33–36, II.i.60–68, 200–9, II.ii.48–50, II.iii.9.

233 **Wherein** in what respect, for what reason.

I am no Orator, as Brutus is,
But, as you know me all, a plain, blunt Man
That love my Friend, and that they know full well
That gave me public Leave to speak of him.
For I have neither Writ nor Words, nor Worth,
Action, nor Utterance, nor the power of Speech,
To stir Men's Blood. I only speak right on:
I tell you that which you your selves do know,
Shew you sweet Caesar's Wounds, poor poor Dumb
  Mouths,
And bid them speak for me. But were I Brutus,
And Brutus Antony, there were an Antony
Would ruffle up your Spirits, and put a Tongue
In every Wound of Caesar, that should move
The Stones of Rome, to rise and Mutiny.

ALL We'll Mutiny.

FIRST We'll burn the House of Brutus.

THIRD Away then, come seek the Conspirators.

ANTONY Yet hear me, Countrymen, yet hear me speak.

ALL Peace, ho, hear Antony, most Noble Antony.

ANTONY Why Friends, you go to do you know not
  what.
Wherein hath Caesar thus deserv'd your Loves?

235 **You have forgot the Will** Antony has spoken of the will, of course, but he has 'allowed' himself to be distracted into digressions about Caesar's mantle and Caesar's corpse. Only now, as his final incitement to the crowd, does he bring the will forth.

239 **Drachmaes** Originally a Greek coin, the drachma was the standard currency of classical Rome. See the note to line 136.

244 **Orchards** gardens.

246 **common Pleasures** pleasure grounds to be enjoyed in common by all Romans, regardless of rank or status. In line 247 the phrase *recreate your selves* (replenish your health with entertainment) recalls I.i.14–16, II.i.308–32.

251 **with the Brands fire** with the embers set afire.

253 **Forms** long benches.
Windows shutters. According to Plutarch, when Antony delivered his funeral oration and 'saw that the people were very glad and desirous also to hear Caesar spoken of and his praises uttered, he mingled his oration with lamentable words, and by amplifying of matters did greatly move their hearts and affections unto pity and compassion. In fine, to conclude his oration, he unfolded before the whole assembly the bloody garments of the dead, thrust through in many places with their swords, and called the malefactors cruel and cursed murderers. With these words he put the people into such a fury that they presently took Caesar's body and burnt it in the market-place with such tables and forms as they could get together. Then, when the fire was kindled, they took firebrands and ran to the murderers' houses to set them a fire and to make them come out to fight.'

258 **He . . . House** Having just dramatized the unleashing of the Roman mob, Shakespeare now draws the scene to a close with a foreshadowing of the new order that will soon be moving into power: the triumvirate of Octavius Caesar, Mark Antony, and Marcus Aemilius Lepidus.

Alas you know not, I must tell you then:
You have forgot the Will I told you of.

ALL Most true, the Will, let's stay and hear the Will.

ANTONY Here is the Will, and under Caesar's Seal:
To every Roman Citizen he gives,
To every several Man, seventy-five Drachmaes.

SECOND Most Noble Caesar, we'll Revenge his Death.

THIRD O Royal Caesar.

ANTONY Hear me with Patience.

ALL Peace, ho.

ANTONY Moreover, he hath left you all his Walks,
His private Arbours, and new-planted Orchards,
On this side Tiber, he hath left them you,
And to your Heirs for ever: common Pleasures
To walk abroad and recreate your selves.
Here was a Caesar: when comes such another?

FIRST Never, never: come, away, away.
We'll burn his Body in the Holy Place,
And with the Brands fire the Traitors' Houses.
Take up the Body.

SECOND Go fetch Fire.

THIRD Pluck
Down Benches.

FOURTH Pluck down Forms, Windows, any thing.

Exit Plebeians [*with Caesar's Body*].

ANTONY Now let it work: Mischief, thou art afoot,
Take thou what Course thou wilt.

Enter Servant.

– How now, Fellow?

SERVANT Sir, Octavius is already come to Rome.

ANTONY Where is he?

SERVANT He and Lepidus are at Caesar's House.

ANTONY And thither will I straight, to visit him:

260 **He comes upon a Wish** I had been hoping for his arrival. In fact, the historical Antony did not welcome Octavius' arrival in Rome (which occurred some six weeks after the assassination), because he saw him as a rival. And it was not until a year and a half later that Antony and Lepidus (who had formed an alliance in the meantime) settled their differences with Octavius and formed the Triumvirate. Typically, Shakespeare telescopes events and adjusts motivations as necessary for maximum dramatic effect.
merry mischievous, playful, disposed to mirth (see I.iii.33, I.ii.313–14, III.i.178–79, III.ii.127–30).

261 **Mood** *Mood* frequently means 'anger' or 'fury' in Shakespeare, and in this line the word probably refers as much to the mood of the mob as to the mood of Fortune. Antony's words have driven the Body Politic into a collective frenzy.

263 **rid** both (a) ridden, and (b) gotten rid of. Plutarch says that as a result of the tumult Antony raised, Brutus 'and his accomplices, for safety of their persons, were driven to fly the city'.

265 **moved** This word echoes Plutarch (see the note to line 253); it also recalls line 226 and III.i.59–60, 235.

III.iii This brief scene takes place on a street in Rome.

1 **I . . . Caesar** Like other dreams in this play, Cinna's proves prophetic. Compare the use of *to night* here with that in III.i.287.

2 **unluckily** unhappily.
charge burden.
Fantasy imagination.

3–4 **I . . . foorth** Shakespeare depicts a similar sense of foreboding in *Titus Andronicus*, II.iii.193–97.

He comes upon a Wish. Fortune is merry,
And in this Mood will give us any thing.

SERVANT I heard him say Brutus and Cassius
Are rid like Madmen through the Gates of Rome.

ANTONY Belike they had some notice of the People,
How I had moved them. Bring me to Octavius.

Exeunt.

Scene 3

Enter Cinna the Poet, and after him the Plebeians.

CINNA I dreamt to night that I did Feast with Caesar,
And things unluckily charge my Fantasy:
I have no Will to wander foorth of Doors,
Yet Something leads me foorth.

FIRST PLEBEIAN What is your name?

6 **Whether . . . going?** Here as in line 13, *Whether* combines the meanings of 'Whither' and 'Where'. The Plebeian's question echoes what Cinna has said in lines 1–4; it also recalls III.i.232, where a man who has come to 'steal away' the 'Hearts' of the people (line 213) tells them 'you go to do you know not what.' In Plutarch Shakespeare would have read that Cinna 'dreamed, the night before, that Caesar bade him to supper with him and that, he refusing to go, Caesar was very importunate with him and compelled him, so that at length he led him by the hand into a great dark place, where, being marvellously afraid, he was driven to follow him in spite of his heart. This dream put him all night into a fever. And yet, notwithstanding, the next morning when he heard that they carried Caesar's body to burial, being ashamed not to accompany his funerals, he went out of his house, and thrust himself into the press of the common people that were in a great uproar.'

9 **directly** both (a) immediately, and (b) straightforwardly. Compare I.i.12–13.

10 **I** Both 'I' (me), and 'Ay' (yes). So also in lines 11–12. Compare I.ii.123, 213, 295.

12 **you were best** if you know what's good for you.

19 **bear a Bang** receive a blow.

21 **Directly** In addition to the senses applicable to line 9, Cinna also means 'in a direct line', without meanders or detours. His words will soon be fulfilled in an indirect figurative sense. See the note to line 6.

31 **Tear him for his bad Verses** Here the Fourth Plebeian seems to be assuming that Cinna is both a conspirator and a poet. His verses are 'bad' because they have been used in the service of treason and murder.

34 **It is no matter** Now that the Fourth Plebeian has made up his mind that Cinna must be executed, he no longer cares whether the poet is a conspirator. If he writes bad verses, that alone will justify his slaughter. Shakespeare's point, of course, is that the people who have been incited to riot by Mark Antony are anything but rational in their indiscriminate violence. This is a mob with a mood of its own.

SECOND Whether are you going?
THIRD Where do you dwell?
FOURTH Are you a Married Man, or a Bachelor?
SECOND Answer every Man directly.
FIRST I, and briefly.
FOURTH I, and wisely.
THIRD I, and truly you were best.
CINNA What is my name? Whether am I going? Where do I dwell? Am I a Married Man, or a Bachelor? Then to answer every Man, directly and briefly, wisely and truly: wisely I say, I am a Bachelor.
SECOND That's as much as to say 'They are Fools that marry.' You'll bear a Bang for that, I fear. Proceed directly.
CINNA Directly I am going to Caesar's Funeral.
FIRST As a Friend or an Enemy?
CINNA As a Friend.
SECOND That matter is answer'd directly.
FOURTH For your Dwelling: briefly.
CINNA Briefly, I dwell by the Capitol.
THIRD Your name, Sir, truly.
CINNA Truly, my name is Cinna.
FIRST Tear him to pieces: he's a Conspirator.
CINNA I am Cinna the Poet, I am Cinna the Poet.
FOURTH Tear him for his bad Verses, tear him for his bad Verses.
CINNA I am not Cinna the Conspirator.
FOURTH It is no matter, his name's Cinna, pluck

34–35 **Pluck . . . Heart** The 'Surgeon' who speaks these lines will 'mend' a 'bad' poet in a way that suggests exorcism; compare I.i.1–31, II.i.319–22. *Name* echoes I.ii.86–87, 139–47, 194–97, 319–24, I.iii.72–78, II.i.148–50, 314–15, and anticipates IV.i.1, IV.ii.62, V.iv.3. 'What's in a Name?' For Cinna the Poet and others in *Julius Caesar*, a great deal. *Heart* recalls line 128 and III.i.283. See the note to III.i.170.

35 **turn him going** send him on his way [to 'Caesar's Funeral', line 21]. Compare IV.i.25.

38 **Brutus** like *Cassius* and *Ligarius* (lines 38, 40), this word can be construed as possessive. The context strongly suggests, but does not require, that interpretation. See the Plutarch quotation in the note to III.ii.253.

but his Name out of his Heart, and turn him going.

THIRD Tear him, tear him. Come, Brands ho,
Firebrands: to Brutus, to Cassius, burn all.
Some to Decius' House, and some to Casca's;
some to Ligarius. Away, go. *Exeunt.*

IV.i This scene takes place some time later, in Antony's house.

1 **prick'd** marked or ticked with a small 'prick' on a list. The new rulers of Rome are planning a purge to solidify their hold on the reigns of power. Compare III.i.217. *Names* echoes III.iii.34–35.

2 **Your Brother** Following the assassination of Caesar, Lepidus' brother, Lucius Aemilius Paulus, joined the party of Brutus, Cassius, and the other republicans. Meanwhile, he proclaimed that Lepidus was an enemy of the Roman people because of his decision to form an alliance with Antony. In retaliation, Lepidus put his name on a list of those to be proscribed (executed). According to North's Plutarch, though the new Triumvirs 'were easily agreed and did divide all the Empire of Rome between them, as if it had been their inheritance', they initially found it hard to 'agree whom they would put to death. . . . Yet at length, giving place to their greedy desire to be revenged of their enemies, they spurned all reverence of blood and holiness of friendship' and executed even their own relatives.

4 **Publius** The historical Antony had no nephew of this name. According to Plutarch, however, he did have an uncle, Lucius Caesar, who was put on the Triumvirs' proscription list.

6 **with a Spot I damn him** As he says this, Antony probably places a prick beside Publius' name. What Publius has done to merit proscription is left to the audience to imagine. But there can be no doubt that, for all the 'heart' he has shown in the previous act of the play, this Antony is anything but a sentimental soul. Unlike Brutus, who had spared Antony to avoid having the conspirators appear 'too Bloody' (II.i.160), Antony comes across in this scene as a man who will unblinkingly sacrifice his own kin if that is the expedient thing to do. *Spot* is a word with strong biblical echoes, among them 1 Peter 1:19 where believers are reminded that they were redeemed 'with the precious blood of Christ, as of a lamb without blemish and without spot'.

9 **How . . . Legacies** Caesar's will was very convenient in the Funeral Oration. But now its 'charge' (cost) is a bother. The words *cut off* recall III.i.163, III.ii.185.

12 **Man** Antony's term suggests that Lepidus is little better than a servingman (the 'man' to a master), hardly the kind of man (*vir* in Latin) to be a triumvir.

ACT IV

Scene 1

Enter Antony, Octavius, and Lepidus.

ANTONY These many then shall die, their Names are prick'd.
OCTAVIUS Your Brother too must die: consent you, Lepidus?
LEPIDUS I do consent.
OCTAVIUS Prick him down, Antony.
LEPIDUS Upon condition Publius shall not live,
Who is your Sister's Son, Mark Antony.
ANTONY He shall not live; look, with a Spot I damn him.
But Lepidus, go you to Caesar's House:
Fetch the Will hither, and we shall determine
How to cut off some charge in Legacies.
LEPIDUS What? Shall I find you here?
OCTAVIUS Or here, or at the Capitol. *Exit Lepidus.*
ANTONY This is a slight unmeritable Man,

13 **Meet** suitable. Compare I.ii.167, 314, II.i.153, III.ii.147, IV.ii.54.

14 **three-fold World** By now the Empire was divided into three parts, with Antony in control of Gaul, Lepidus of Spain, and Octavius of Africa, Sardinia, and Sicily.

16 **took his Voice** accepted his vote. Compare III.i.179, 263.

17 **black Sentence** Here *black* may refer either to (a) death, or (b) the prick marks beside the proscribed names.

20 **sland'rous Loads** burdens (such as unpopular policies) with which neither Antony nor Octavius wishes to be identified.

25 **take we down his Load** we remove his load.
turn him off send him on his way. Compare III.iii.34–36.

26 **shake his Ears** a characteristic gesture for asses.

27 **in Commons** on public pasture-land. *Commons* recalls III.ii.137, 246–47.

30 **appoint him store of Provender** provide him a supply of feed. *Provender* calls to mind the image of Bottom in IV.i.33–36 of *A Midsummer Night's Dream.*

32 **To wind** to turn or wheel.
to . . . on Antony's phrasing echoes III.ii.220, III.iii.9–24.

33 **Corporal Motion** bodily movements.

34 **in some taste** to some extent.

36–38 **one . . . Men** one who is satisfied with second-hand goods, ideas, and other scraps that better men have left behind. *Stal'd* recalls I.ii.70–72.

40 **Property** a tool. Antony may be thinking of a theatre property, an object to be moved around the stage or removed from the scene as needed by the actors in a play. *Fashion* (line 39) recalls II.i.218.

41 **Listen great things** attend to important things (as distinguished from the matter of what to do with Lepidus).

42 **levying Powers** gathering armies.
straight make head immediately raise an army of our own.

43 **combin'd** solidified, strengthened.

Meet to be sent on Errands: is it fit,
The three-fold World divided, he should stand
One of the three to share it?

OCTAVIUS So you thought him,
And took his Voice who should be prick'd to die
In our black Sentence and Proscription.

ANTONY Octavius, I have seen more Days than you,
And though we lay these Honours on this Man,
To ease our selves of divers sland'rous Loads,
He shall but bear them, as the Ass bears Gold,
To groan and sweat under the Business,
Either led or driven, as we point the way:
And having brought our Treasure where we will,
Then take we down his Load, and turn him off,
Like to the empty Ass, to shake his Ears,
And graze in Commons.

OCTAVIUS You may do your Will:
But he's a tried and valiant Soldier.

ANTONY So is my Horse, Octavius, and for that
I do appoint him store of Provender.
It is a Creature that I teach to fight,
To wind, to stop, to run directly on,
His corporal Motion govern'd by my Spirit,
And, in some taste, is Lepidus but so:
He must be taught, and train'd, and bid go forth,
A barren-spirited Fellow, one that feeds
On Objects, Arts, and Imitations,
Which, out of Use and stal'd by other Men,
Begin his fashion. Do not talk of him
But as a Property: and now, Octavius,
Listen great things. Brutus and Cassius
Are levying Powers: we must straight make head.
Therefore let our Alliance be combin'd,

44 **made** mustered.
stretch'd extended, augmented.

45 **presently** forthwith.

46 **How . . . disclos'd** to determine how matters that lie hidden from us may be best uncovered.

47 **And . . . answered** and manifest dangers most surely dealt with.

48 **at the Stake** tied to the stake like bears in a bear-baiting arena. Compare *Macbeth*, V.vii.1–2, *King Lear*, III.vii.52, *Twelfth Night*, III.i.127–29, 2 *Henry VI*, V.i.144, *Troilus and Cressida*, III.iii.219–20, and *Hamlet*, IV.iv.50–53.

49 **bayed about** surrounded by barking attack dogs. *Bayed* echoes III.i.205–8. Lines 49–50 recall II.i.76–84, 222–25, II.ii.124–29, III.i.35–55, 225–27, III.ii.178–85. Compare *Hamlet*, I.v.106–8.

IV.ii This scene occurs near Brutus' tent at his army camp near Sardis. Lucius is no doubt to be thought of as included in '*the Army*'. See the note to lines 45–47.

5 **He . . . well** He sends a worthy man to greet me.

6–9 **In . . . satisfied** Brutus is telling Lucilius that either Cassius has changed or he has been badly represented by his officers; in either case, Brutus wants to have the matter resolved if Cassius is at hand. Just as the previous scene has shown us signs of instability in the Triumvirate at Rome, this one begins with indications that all is not well between the leaders of the republican faction. *Cause* recalls III.ii.108–9. Here *ill* can mean either (a) evil, or (b) incompetent. Compare lines 127–29. *Satisfied* (resolved of my doubts) recalls III.ii.1.

9–11 **I . . . Honour** Pindarus responds to Brutus' accusation by saying that he is sure that Cassius will emerge blameless, with unblemished honour and with warm regard for Brutus. In this speech *appear* means both (a) arrive, and (b) show himself to be. Pindarus' phrasing anticipates V.v.20–25.

12 **A word, Lucilius** As he speaks this line, Brutus probably draws Lucilius aside to speak privately until Cassius enters after line 29. Compare II.i.98, III.i.232.

13 **be resolv'd** have my questions answered.

15 **familiar Instances** indications of familiarity, informality.

Our best Friends made, our Means stretch'd,
And let us presently go sit in Council,
How Covert Matters may be best disclos'd,
And Open Perils surest answered.

OCTAVIUS Let us do so: for we are at the Stake,
And bayed about with many Enemies,
And some that smile have in their Hearts, I fear,
Millions of Mischiefs. *Exeunt.*

Scene 2

Drum. Enter Brutus, Lucilius, and the Army. Titinius and Pindarus meet them.

BRUTUS Stand ho.

LUCILIUS Give the word ho, and stand.

BRUTUS What now, Lucilius, is Cassius near?

LUCILIUS He is at hand, and Pindarus is come
To do you Salutation from his Master.

BRUTUS He greets me well. – Your Master, Pindarus,
In his own Change, or by ill Officers,
Hath given me some worthy Cause to wish
Things done undone; but if he be at hand
I shall be satisfied.

PINDARUS I do not doubt
But that my Noble Master will appear
Such as he is, full of Regard and Honour.

BRUTUS He is not doubted. – A word, Lucilius,
How he receiv'd you: let me be resolv'd.

LUCILIUS With Courtesy, and with Respect enough,
But not with such familiar Instances,

16 **Conference** conversation.

17 **us'd of old** exhibited in the past. Compare I.ii.30–34.

20 **enforced Ceremony** strained manner. Compare I.i.69–70, I.ii.11, II.i.193–95, II.ii.13, III.i.241–43.

21 **Tricks** artifices, games.

22 **hot at hand** lively at the start when they are under restraint.

25 **fall their Crests** let fall the ridges of their necks in the manner of 'Jades' (old, weary horses) with no spirit.

26 **Sink in the Trial** let their riders down when severely tested.

28 **Horse in general** cavalry, horsemen.

30 **gently** slowly, deliberately.

Stand ho stand to attention. After Cassius gives this command to his men, Brutus commands his officers to pass the word through the ranks of his army.

33 **wrong . . . Enemies?** Brutus is so secure in his own sense of integrity that he maintains that it is impossible for him to do wrong to anyone, even his enemies. According to North's Plutarch, Brutus 'was rightly framed unto virtue. So that his very enemies which wish him most hurt, because of his conspiracy against Julius Caesar, if there were any noble attempt done in all this conspiracy, they refer it wholly unto Brutus, and all the cruel and violent acts unto Cassius, who was Brutus' familiar friend but not so well given and conditioned as he.' Later Plutarch says that, whereas Cassius was 'choleric and cruel, who sought to rule men by fear rather than with lenity', Brutus 'in contrary manner, for his virtue and valiantness was well-beloved of the people and his own, esteemed of noblemen, and hated of no man, not so much as of his enemies; because he was a marvellous lowly and gentle person, noble minded, and would never be in any rage, nor carried away with pleasure and covetousness'.

35 **Sober Form** dignified manner. *Sober* also means 'free of levity or drunkenness'.

36 **be content** calm down.

Nor with such free and friendly Conference,
As he hath us'd of old.
BRUTUS Thou hast describ'd
A hot Friend cooling: ever note, Lucilius,
When Love begins to sicken and decay
It useth an enforced Ceremony.
There are no Tricks in plain and simple Faith:
But Hollow Men, like Horses hot at hand,
Make gallant Shew and Promise of their Mettle,
Low March within.
But when they should endure the bloody Spur
They fall their Crests, and like deceitful Jades
Sink in the Trial. Comes his Army on?
LUCILIUS They mean this Night in Sardis to be quarter'd:
The greater part, the Horse in general,
Are come with Cassius.

Enter Cassius and his Powers.

BRUTUS Hark, he is arriv'd:
March gently on to meet him.
CASSIUS Stand ho.
BRUTUS Stand ho,
Speak the word along.
[FIRST SOLDIER] Stand.
[SECOND] Stand.
[THIRD] Stand.
CASSIUS Most Noble Brother, you have done me wrong.
BRUTUS – Judge me, you Gods; wrong I mine Enemies?
And if not so, how should I wrong a Brother?
CASSIUS Brutus, this Sober Form of yours hides Wrongs,
And when you do them –
BRUTUS Cassius, be content,

37 **I do know you well** Brutus' implication seems to be that there is no need for Cassius to shout. But he also suggests that he knows Cassius to be the kind of man who, in Plutarch's words, is 'too familiar with his friends'.

41 **enlarge your Griefs** spell out your grievances at leisure.

43 **Charges** soldiers under their command. *Audiences* echoes III.ii.2.

44 **this ground** this immediate vicinity.

45–47 **let . . . Door** Most of today's editions transpose the names *Lucilius* and *Lucius* in these lines. But Lucilius seems to be Brutus' second in command in this scene.

46 **done our Conference** finished our conversation. Compare lines 14–17.

48 **doth appear in this** is clear from this. Most editions begin a new scene (IV.iii) with this line. But the stage is never cleared, and the action continues uninterrupted. Precisely how Brutus' 'Tent' (line 46) would have been represented on the Elizabethan stage is unclear. The same holds true for the 'Door' (line 47) to be guarded by Lucius and Titinius. In all likelihood these characters simply stand to one side (or to either side) of the stage after Lucilius and the other officers and soldiers exit. Compare II.i.310, where Brutus tell Lucius, 'Boy, stand aside.' When the 'Conference' is interrupted by the 'Poet' after line 167, the intruder may be accompanied by Lucilius, vainly attempting to dissuade him from approaching the 'Door' guarded by Lucius and Titinius.

49 **noted** publicly shamed, called to the notice of others.

51 **praying on his side** pleading his case, requesting leniency.

52 **slighted off** treated as if of no consequence.

55 **nice** petty.
bear his Comment be subjected to discipline. Here *his* means 'its'. Plutarch says that Cassius 'greatly reproved Brutus for being so strait and severe, in such a time as was meeter to bear a little than to take things at the worst'.

57 **much . . . Palm** widely accused of having your hand out for bribes. Plutarch described Cassius as a man 'that would oftentimes be carried away from justice for gain' and a man who 'put himself into sundry dangers, more to have absolute power and authority than to defend the liberty of his country'.

Speak your Griefs softly, I do know you well.
Before the Eyes of both our Armies here,
Which should perceive no thing but Love from us,
Let us not wrangle. Bid them move away:
Then in my Tent, Cassius, enlarge your Griefs,
And I will give you Audience.

CASSIUS Pindarus,
Bid our Commanders lead their Charges off
A little from this ground.

BRUTUS Lucilius, do you the like, and let no man
Come to our Tent till we have done our Conference.
Let Lucius and Titinius guard our Door.

Exeunt. Manent Brutus and Cassius.

CASSIUS That you have wrong'd me doth appear in this:
You have condemn'd, and noted Lucius Pella
For taking Bribes here of the Sardians;
Wherein my Letters, praying on his side
Because I knew the Man, was slighted off.

BRUTUS You wrong'd your self to write in such a Case.

CASSIUS In such a Time as this it is not meet
That every nice Offence should bear his Comment.

BRUTUS Let me tell you, Cassius, you your self
Are much condemn'd to have an itching Palm,

58 **mart your Offices** market your duties and services.

61 **were else your last** would otherwise be your last.

62 **The . . . Corruption** Because it is Cassius who commits it, this corruption is treated with the honour due to Cassius' name. What Brutus is being careful not to say too directly here and in line 63 is that he would chastise Cassius' corruption if anyone else were guilty of it. He also seems to be implying that Cassius' example encourages lesser men to feel that they can accept bribes at no cost to their integrity or honour.

67–68 **What . . . Justice?** Brutus' point is that Cassius' behaviour is becoming almost as reprehensible as Caesar's.

68 **Us** This word is capitalized for emphasis in the Folio text.

70 **But . . . Robbers** only for providing sustenance for robbers. Just what Brutus means here is not clear. Plutarch tells us that Caesar 'was a favourer and suborner of all them that did rob and spoil, by his countenance and authority'. But this is Brutus' first mention of corruption as a motive for the assassination. Perhaps we are to assume that it looms large now solely because of Brutus' need to maintain a clear distinction between the evils that characterized Caesar and the purity of the lives that need to be conducted by those who took it upon themselves to judge and execute him.

72 **the mighty space of our large Honours** Brutus wants to contrast the vastness of his and Cassius' honours with the petty insignificance of the 'Trash' for which Cassius seems willing to sell or barter such riches.

73 **grasped thus** Brutus probably gestures in such a way as to show that what Cassius is trading his honours for is so trifling that it can be clutched in one grasping hand.

75 **bait not me** Cassius picks up on Brutus' baying image and warns Brutus not to try pinning him to the stake like a bear. Compare IV.i.48–52.

79 **make Conditions** manage day-to-day affairs, such as the matter with Lucius Pella. Lines 77–79 echo IV.i.18. Plutarch refers to Cassius as 'the elder man' and says that 'men reputed him commonly to be very skilful in wars'.

Go to an expression of dismissal, here spoken scornfully. The phrase *not Cassius* can mean either (a) not the Cassius I know, or (b) not, Cassius (as most modern editions render it). Compare II.i.253.

To sell and mart your Offices for Gold
To Undeservers.

CASSIUS I, an itching Palm?
You know that you are Brutus that speaks this,
Or by the Gods, this Speech were else your last.

BRUTUS The name of Cassius honours this Corruption,
And Chastisement doth therefore hide his Head.

CASSIUS Chastisement?

BRUTUS Remember March, the Ides of March remember:
Did not great Julius bleed for Justice' sake?
What Villain touch'd his Body, that did stab,
And not for Justice? What? Shall one of Us,
That struck the Foremost Man of all this World
But for supporting Robbers, shall we now
Contaminate our Fingers with base Bribes?
And sell the mighty space of our large Honours
For so much Trash as may be grasped thus?
I had rather be a Dog, and bay the Moon,
Than such a Roman.

CASSIUS Brutus, bait not me,
I'll not endure it: you forget your self
To hedge me in. I am a Soldier, I,
Older in Practice, abler than your self
To make Conditions.

BRUTUS Go to: you are not Cassius.

CASSIUS I am.

BRUTUS I say you are not.

CASSIUS Urge me no more, I shall forget my self.
Have mind upon your Health: tempt me no farther.

83 **Slight** Brutus probably means 'insignificant'. But Plutarch describes Cassius as 'sickly of body', and that sense is pertinent too. Brutus may also be alluding to what Cassius said in line 52.

85 **rash Choler** irrational outburst of anger. See the note to line 33. Brutus is saying that Cassius has fallen under the sway of the humour known as Choler, thought to be caused by an excess of yellow bile. *Room* recalls I.ii.153–54 and III.i.289–90.

88 **I** It is not clear whether Brutus means 'Ay' (yes) or 'I' (myself). Compare III.iii.10–12.

90 **bouge** budge, yield.

93 **Spleen** The spleen was considered the source of the impulsive passions. Here Brutus is saying that because he will not yield to Cassius' choler and refuses to be intimidated by it, Cassius will have to hold his bile in and digest it until it splits his sides.

95 **I'll use you for my Mirth** I'll laugh at you. Brutus is treating Cassius with utter contempt. For him, Cassius is not only a 'Slight Man' (line 36) but a laughing-stock. Compare I.ii.70, where Cassius says how Brutus should 'hold' him if he is proven 'a common Laughter'.

98 **make your Vaunting true** Make good on all your bragging by proving yourself the better soldier.

104 **durst not** would not have dared. *Mov'd* echoes III.iii.265.

105 **tempted him** put him to the test, challenged him. Compare I.iii.53–56.

BRUTUS Away, Slight Man.
CASSIUS Is't possible?
BRUTUS Hear me, for I will speak.
Must I give way, and room, to your rash Choler?
Shall I be frighted when a Madman stares?
CASSIUS O ye Gods, ye Gods, must I endure all this?
BRUTUS All this? I more: fret till your proud Heart break.
Go shew your Slaves how choleric you are,
And make your Bondmen tremble. Must I bouge?
Must I observe you? Must I stand and crouch
Under your Testy Humour? By the Gods,
You shall digest the Venom of your Spleen
Though it do split you. For, from this Day forth,
I'll use you for my Mirth, yea for my Laughter,
When you are Waspish.
CASSIUS Is it come to this?
BRUTUS You say you are a better Soldier:
Let it appear so; make your Vaunting true,
And it shall please me well. For mine own part,
I shall be glad to learn of Noble Men.
CASSIUS You wrong me every way, you wrong me, Brutus.
I said an Elder Soldier, not a Better.
Did I say Better?
BRUTUS If you did, I care not.
CASSIUS When Caesar liv'd, he durst not thus have mov'd me.
BRUTUS Peace, peace, you durst not so have tempted him.
CASSIUS I durst not.
BRUTUS No.
CASSIUS What? Durst not tempt him?
BRUTUS For your Life, you durst not.
CASSIUS Do not presume too much upon my Love,
I may do that I shall be sorry for.

112 **Honesty** integrity.

114 **respect not** both (a) ignore (paying it no 'respect', attention), and (b) view contemptuously.

114–20 **I . . . Indirection** Having just accused Cassius of taking bribes and tolerating corruption in his subordinates, Brutus now levels another charge: Cassius has refused to supply Brutus with the gold he requested. Brutus' 'Honesty' has prevented him from stooping to the 'Vile Means' that Cassius and his officers have used to raise money, so he has turned to Cassius for the supplies he needs. It doesn't seem to have occurred to Brutus that Cassius has to obtain gold from somewhere else in order to provide it to Brutus. Nor does Brutus seem inclined to be overly scrupulous about the source of the 'Gold' supplied to him. Plutarch says of Brutus that 'all that he could rap and rend of his side he had bestowed it in making so great number of ships, that by means of them they should keep all the sea at their commandment'.

119 **Trash** refuse (compare lines 246–48). This word recalls line 73 and I.iii.108–11. *Vile*, a strong word for Romans such as the high-minded Brutus, recalls I.iii.111, II.i.263, III.ii.35–36, and anticipates V.i.39–40, 99–106, V.v.36–38.

122 **denied me** Plutarch says that 'Cassius' friends hindered this request and earnestly dissuaded him from it, persuading him that it was no reason that Brutus should have the money which Cassius had gotten together by sparing and levied with great evil will of the people their subjects, for him to bestow liberally upon his soldiers and by this means to win their good wills by Cassius' charge. This notwithstanding, Cassius gave him the third part of his total sum.'

125 **Rascal Counters** worthless (or counterfeit) coins. Assuming that Cassius has an abundance of money, Brutus accuses him of being 'Covetous' (line 124). But it is equally likely that Cassius was under the same fiscal pressures that were straining Brutus' resources. If so, that may have been part of what the 'Fool' who brought Cassius' 'Answer back' (line 129) said to Brutus. Here as elsewhere, Cassius allows himself to be awed by Brutus.

129 **riv'd** split. Compare I.iii.5–6.

BRUTUS You have done that you should be sorry for.
There is no Terror, Cassius, in your Threats:
For I am arm'd so strong in Honesty
That they pass by me, as the idle Wind,
Which I respect not. I did send to you
For certain sums of Gold, which you denied me,
For I can raise no Money by Vile Means:
By Heaven, I had rather Coin my Heart,
And drop my Blood for Drachmaes, then to wring
From the hard Hands of Peasants their vile Trash
By any Indirection. I did send
To you for Gold to pay my Legions,
Which you denied me: was this done like Cassius?
Should I have answer'd Caius Cassius so?
When Marcus Brutus grows so Covetous,
To lock such Rascal Counters from his Friends,
Be ready, Gods, with all your Thunderbolts,
Dash him to pieces.
CASSIUS I denied you not.
BRUTUS You did.
CASSIUS I did not. He was but a Fool
That brought my Answer back. Brutus hath riv'd my Heart:

130 **bear** both (a) tolerate, and (b) share the burden of. Cassius' phrasing echoes 1 Corinthians 13:7, where Elizabethans would have read that love 'Beareth all things, believeth all things, hopeth all things, endureth all things'. It also recalls Matthew 7:1–15, where Jesus says, 'Judge not that ye be not judged', and asks: 'why beholdest thou the mote that is in thy brother's eye, but considerest not the beam that is in thine own eye? . . . Thou hypocrite, first cast out the beam out of thine own eye; and then shalt thou see clearly to cast out the mote out of thy brother's eye.'

132 **practise them on me** make me the victim of them.

136 **As huge as high Olympus** Once again, Brutus is suggesting that Cassius' flaws are gigantic. Earlier he has called Cassius a 'Madman' (line 86) with a 'proud Heart' (line 88) and a 'Testy Humour' (line 92). Now he implies that Cassius' faults are so enormous that they encroach on the seat of the Olympian Gods themselves. Compare III.i.75.

138 **alone on Cassius** on Cassius alone of the conspirators.

140 **brav'd** taunted. The modern word *bravado* retains this sense.

141 **Check'd** rebuked. *Bondman* (slave, indentured servant) recalls I.iii.101, 113; III.ii.31–32, and IV.ii.89–90; it anticipates V.i.42, V.iii.55. For a Roman, vigilantly jealous of his liberty, a bondman was the most abject of creatures.
observ'd noted.

142 **conn'd by rote** mastered by rote memorization.

146 **Dearer than Pluto's Mine** worth more than the gold mine of the God of Wealth. In Greek mythology the God of Wealth was known as Plutus. By Shakespeare's time, however, he had become indistinguishable from Pluto, God of the Underworld.

152 **it shall have Scope** it (your anger) shall be allowed to range as widely as it wishes.

153 **Dishonour shall be Humour** if you do something dishonourable, it shall be attributed to a humour and thereby excused.

154 **Lamb** a proverbially placid animal, the opposite of the lion, the conventional symbol of wrath.

A Friend should bear his Friend's Infirmities;
But Brutus makes mine greater than they are.
BRUTUS I do not, till you practise them on me.
CASSIUS You love me not.
BRUTUS I do not like your Faults.
CASSIUS A Friendly Eye could never see such Faults.
BRUTUS A Flatterer's would not, though they do appear
As huge as high Olympus.
CASSIUS – Come, Antony, and young Octavius, come,
Revenge your selves alone on Cassius,
For Cassius is a-weary of the World:
Hated by one he loves, brav'd by his Brother,
Check'd like a Bondman, all his Faults observ'd,
Set in a Notebook, learn'd, and conn'd by rote
To cast into my Teeth. – O I could weep
My Spirit from my Eyes. There is my Dagger,
And here my naked Breast: within, a Heart
Dearer than Pluto's Mine, richer than Gold.
If thou beest a Roman, take it forth.
I that denied thee Gold, will give my Heart.
Strike as thou didst at Caesar: for I know,
When thou didst hate him worst, thou lov'dst him better
Than ever thou lovedst Cassius.
BRUTUS Sheathe your Dagger.
Be angry when you will, it shall have Scope;
Do what you will, Dishonour shall be Humour.
O Cassius, you are yoked with a Lamb

155 **That . . . Fire** that harbours Anger for just as long as the Flint carries Fire (that is, for no more than an instant). *Flint* (echoing II.i.36) was proverbial for its hardness and coldness. Brutus is excusing and forgiving Cassius' 'Anger'; but he does so in a way that demeans Cassius' manhood.

156 **enforced** provoked. This word is the first hint in this speech that Brutus accepts any responsibility for Cassius' outbursts. Otherwise Brutus' language is so abstract and disembodied that one can hardly tell that he is accepting Cassius' submission and admitting any faults of his own. Even in reconciliation, Brutus must retain the upper hand. Compare lines 17–20.

159 **Blood ill temper'd** passion inadequately controlled. Line 158 echoes line 95.

164 **rash Humour** disposition to be a 'hasty Spark' (line 156). *Rash* echoes line 85.

165 **forgetful** negligent; forgetting to exercise self-control.

166 **over-earnest** overwrought, subject to 'rash Humour' (line 164).

167 **chides** scolds, rebukes. Compare II.i.169–75, where Brutus describes a psychological mechanism that 'dis-joins Remove from Power' (II.i.18–19).

leave you so Brutus probably means 'allow you to be that way'. But his phrasing suggests a dismissive, flint-like abandonment.

169 **meet** fitting (as in line 54 and in IV.i.13). According to Plutarch, the man here depicted as a 'Poet' was 'one Marcus Faonius, that had been a friend and follower of Cato' and 'took upon him to counterfeit a philosopher not with wisdom and discretion but with a certain bedlam and frantic motion'. Adopting the 'bold manner . . . of the Cynic philosophers (as who would say "dogs")', Faonius broke in upon the quarrelling generals. Cassius fell a-laughing at him. But Brutus thrust him out of the chamber, and called him dog and counterfeit Cynic. Howbeit his coming in brake their strife at that time; and so they left each other.'

173 **what do you mean?** what do you mean to do? Compare II.i.232, II.ii.9.

176 **vildly** vilely. Line 175 echoes lines 116–20.

Cynic The Cynics were a school of philosophers who tended to an acerbic view of life and prided themselves on being plain, blunt men (III.ii.215). Compare the disguised Kent in *King Lear*, I.iv, II.ii.

That carries Anger as the Flint bears Fire,
Who, much enforced, shews a hasty Spark,
And straight is Cold again.

CASSIUS Hath Cassius liv'd
To be but Mirth and Laughter to his Brutus,
When Grief and Blood ill temper'd vexeth him?

BRUTUS When I spoke that, I was ill temper'd too.

CASSIUS Do you confess so much? Give me your Hand.

BRUTUS And my Heart too.

CASSIUS O Brutus!

BRUTUS What's the matter?

CASSIUS Have not you Love enough to bear with me,
When that rash Humour which my Mother gave me
Makes me forgetful.

BRUTUS Yes, Cassius, and from henceforth
When you are over-earnest with your Brutus,
He'll think your Mother chides, and leave you so.

Enter a Poet.

POET Let me go in to see the Generals:
There is some Grudge between 'em, 'tis not meet
They be alone.

LUCILIUS You shall not come to them.

POET Nothing but Death shall stay me.

CASSIUS How now? What's the matter?

POET For shame, you Generals: what do you mean?
Love and be Friends, as two such Men should be,
For I have seen more Years, I'm sure, than ye.

CASSIUS Ha, ha, how vildly doth this Cynic rime?

176–77 **Ha, ha . . . hence** It seems likely that Shakespeare's reason for introducing the Poet into this scene is to provide an occasion for the contrasting responses the old man receives from Cassius (who laughs at him good-naturedly) and Brutus (who rebukes him for a gesture that is clearly well-intended).

179 **his Time** the proper time for such eccentric behaviour.

183 **to night** Compare III.iii.1.

186 **I . . . angry** Cassius is probably referring to Brutus' intemperate outburst to the Poet rather than to the anger he showed during the altercation that preceded it.

188 **Philosophy** Brutus was widely known to be a dedicated Stoic. His father-in-law Cato was a Stoic philosopher. And Plutarch tells us that Brutus also valued 'the Grecian philosophers', and above all others 'Plato's sect'. According to Plutarch, at supper the evening of the quarrel between Cassius and Brutus, 'Faonius made no ceremony, but thrust in amongst the midst of them, and made all the company laugh at him. So they were merry all supper-time and full of their philosophy.'

189 **accidental Evils** misfortunes that come by chance. Again, it seems most likely that Cassius is thinking about the irritating interruption by the Poet, and is suggesting that Brutus' reaction to it was excessive.

BRUTUS Get you hence, Sirrah: saucy Fellow, hence.
CASSIUS Bear with him, Brutus, 'tis his Fashion.
BRUTUS I'll know his Humour, when he knows his Time:
What should the Wars do with these Jigging Fools?
– Companion, hence.
CASSIUS Away, away, be gone. *Exit Poet.*
BRUTUS Lucilius and Titinius, bid the Commanders
Prepare to lodge their Companies to night.
CASSIUS And come your selves, and bring Messala with you
Immediately to us. [*Exeunt Lucilius and Titinius.*]
BRUTUS Lucius, a bowl of Wine. [*Exit Lucius.*]
CASSIUS I did not think you could have been so angry.
BRUTUS O Cassius, I am sick of many Griefs.
CASSIUS Of your Philosophy you make no use,
If you give place to accidental Evils.

190–91 **No . . . dead** The dialogue in lines 184–237 has no source in Plutarch, though Shakespeare does derive several details from the 'Life of Brutus'. Had he chosen to do so, Shakespeare could have made the revelation of Portia's death a moment that would restore some of the audience's sympathy to Brutus. Instead, he arranges the sequence in such a way that Brutus appears to invoke the news of Portia's death not to elicit Cassius' sympathy for her, and not even to elicit Cassius' sympathy for Brutus himself, but to refute Cassius' suggestion that Brutus is less than the paragon of Roman virtue he claims to be. To some degree, the response Brutus receives from Cassius is the one he wishes. Cassius marvels that Brutus didn't kill him when he, Cassius, 'cross'd' him (line 192). And Cassius is deeply touched by a loss that a man with less Stoic fortitude than Brutus possesses would find 'insupportable' (line 193). But, unlike Brutus, Cassius also seems to focus his emotions on Portia herself (line 208).

194–98 **Impatient . . . Fire** The phrase *Impatient of* here means 'Impatience over'. It is clear from the circumstances of Portia's death that 'Cato's Daughter' has finally proven unequal to the 'accidental Evils' that confronted her. Overwhelmed by her passions, she has been unable to maintain the Stoic stance that would have won her husband's approval. See the note to II.iv.9.

201 **In . . . Cassius** In *The Merry Wives of Windsor*, a similar reconciliation occurs when Page says, 'I hope we shall drink down all Unkindness' (I.i.202–3).

207 **call in question our Necessities** determine what our needs are.

208 **Portia . . . you** Presumably these remarks are to be exchanged privately. If we are to assume that Messala hears them, or overhears them, the exchanges that occur in lines 223–37 take on a 'strange' (but not inconceivable) character indeed.

BRUTUS No man bears Sorrow better. Portia
Is dead.
CASSIUS Ha? Portia?
BRUTUS She is dead.
CASSIUS How scap'd I killing, when I cross'd you so?
O insupportable and touching Loss!
Upon what Sickness?
BRUTUS Impatient of my Absence,
And Grief, that young Octavius with Mark Antony
Have made themselves so strong: for with her Death
That Tidings came. With this she fell distract,
And, her Attendants absent, swallow'd Fire.
CASSIUS And died so?
BRUTUS Even so.
CASSIUS O ye immortal Gods!

Enter Boy with Wine, and Tapers.

BRUTUS Speak no more of her. – Give me a bowl of
Wine.
– In this I bury all Unkindness, Cassius.
Drinks.
CASSIUS My Heart is thirsty for that Noble Pledge.
– Fill, Lucius, till the Wine o'erswell the Cup:
I cannot drink too much of Brutus' Love.
[*Drinks. Exit Lucius.*]

Enter Titinius and Messala.

BRUTUS Come in, Titinius. – Welcome, good Messala.
Now sit we close about this Taper here,
And call in question our Necessities.
CASSIUS Portia, art thou gone?
BRUTUS No more, I pray you.
– Messala, I have here received Letters,
That young Octavius and Mark Antony

212 **Bending their Expedition** directing their speedy course.
Philippi Here as elsewhere, the metrical position dictates an accent on the second syllable.

213 **Tenure** tenor, import.

215 **Proscription** decrees of execution.
Bills of Outlawry decrees that certain citizens are now to be considered enemies of the State. Shakespeare drew the phrasing in this line from North's Plutarch.

223–37 **Had . . . so** In this passage Messala gives Brutus the same information Brutus has just imparted to Cassius. Many critics assume that this passage represents an earlier piece of writing and that Shakespeare had marked it for deletion in the final, revised version of the play. Perhaps so: the scene holds together perfectly well without the passage. On the other hand, the fact is that the passage was included in the First Folio and retained in subsequent editions. And it has a logic in terms of the characterization of Brutus that makes it seem to many to be a part of the playwright's design. The premise of this edition is that the passage does belong in the final version of the play.

227 **ought** anything.

232–34 **Why . . . now** If Brutus were receiving the news of his wife's death for the first time, this response would seem remarkably unfeeling, even for a Stoic. And it is difficult to imagine that Shakespeare could have written it with that situation in mind, owing in part to the fact that the Brutus we see here is not even interested enough to ask Messala to explain by what 'strange Manner' Portia died. What seems most likely, then, is that Shakespeare wished to portray Brutus as a man who is willing to let Messala tell him what he already knows so that Brutus can demonstrate how a true Roman receives bad news. Messala's response is probably more satisfying to Brutus than Cassius' had been a few minutes earlier. For Messala, Brutus' reaction to the news validates Brutus' credentials as a great man who provides a worthy example for lesser men to learn from and imitate. Compare III.i.99–106.

236–37 **I . . . so** Cassius' comment suggests that, while he admires the 'Art' with which Brutus performs his role, he finds it difficult to imagine the 'Nature' that could 'bear it so'. Brutus exemplifies the 'formal Constancy' he commends in the 'Roman Actors' he cites in II.i.222–25. *Bear* echoes lines 130, 164.

Come down upon us with a mighty Power,
Bending their Expedition toward Philippi.

MESSALA My self have Letters of the self-same Tenure.

BRUTUS With what Addition?

MESSALA That by Proscription, and Bills of Outlawry,
Octavius, Antony, and Lepidus
Have put to death an hundred Senators.

BRUTUS Therein our Letters do not well agree:
Mine speak of seventy Senators that died
By their Proscriptions, Cicero being one.

CASSIUS Cicero one?

MESSALA Cicero is dead,
And by that order of Proscription.
– Had you your Letters from your Wife, my Lord?

BRUTUS No, Messala.

MESSALA Nor nothing in your Letters writ of her?

BRUTUS Nothing, Messala.

MESSALA That me thinks is strange.

BRUTUS Why ask you? Hear you ought of her in yours?

MESSALA No, my Lord.

BRUTUS Now as you are a Roman tell me true.

MESSALA Then like a Roman, bear the Truth I tell,
For certain she is dead, and by strange Manner.

BRUTUS Why farewell Portia. We must die, Messala:
With meditating that she must die once,
I have the Patience to endure it now.

MESSALA Even so great Men great Losses should endure.

CASSIUS I have as much of this in Art as you,
But yet my Nature could not bear it so.

238 **our Work alive** the work we have to do in the world of the living. Brutus' implication is that we've now spent enough time talking about death.

239 **presently** right away.

246 **this ground** our present position. Compare lines 42–44.

248 **grudg'd us Contribution** This line suggests that, despite his high-mindedness, Brutus has in fact tried to 'wring / From the hard Hands of Peasants their vile Trash' (lines 118–19).

251 **new added** reinforced.

252 **cut him off** This phrase recalls IV.i.9.

255 **Under your pardon** Begging your pardon. Brutus interrupts Cassius before he can offer a counter-argument.

256 **tried . . . Friends** exacted as much assistance from our friends as we are likely to get. *Utmost* recalls II.i.211–12. *Cause* (line 257) recalls line 7.

261 **at the Flood** at the highest point. *Tide* recalls III.i.257–58, and it hints that the 'Tide of Times' may belong to Caesar and his forces rather than to the overconfident Brutus.

262 **Omitted** if this opportunity is missed.

266 **loose** both (a) loose (release, forfeit), and (b) lose.
Then . . . on For the third time, Cassius allows himself to be overruled by Brutus on a crucial decision. *Will* recalls II.ii.60–82. According to North's Plutarch, 'Cassius was of opinion not to try this war at one battle, but rather to delay time and draw it out in length, considering that they were the stronger in money and the weaker in men and armours. But Brutus in contrary manner did alway before, and at that time also, desire nothing more than to put all to the hazard of battle, as soon as might be possible, to the end he might quickly restore his country to her former liberty, or rid him forthwith of this miserable world.' Compare lines 137–39, V.v.33–42.

267 **We'll . . . them** Here *We'll* refers to Cassius' forces; *them* refers to the forces of Antony and Octavius.

BRUTUS Well, to our Work alive. What do you think
Of marching to Philippi presently.
CASSIUS I do not think it good.
BRUTUS Your Reason?
CASSIUS This it is:
'Tis better that the Enemy seek us,
So shall he waste his Means, weary his Soldiers,
Doing himself Offence, whilst we, lying still,
Are full of Rest, Defence, and Nimbleness.
BRUTUS Good Reasons must of force give place to Better.
The People 'twixt Philippi and this ground
Do stand but in a forc'd Affection:
For they have grudg'd us Contribution.
The Enemy, marching along by them,
By them shall make a fuller Number up,
Come on refresh'd, new added, and encourag'd:
From which Advantage shall we cut him off,
If at Philippi we do face him there,
These People at our back.
CASSIUS Hear me, good Brother.
BRUTUS Under your pardon. You must note beside
That we have tried the utmost of our Friends:
Our Legions are brim full, our Cause is ripe,
The Enemy increaseth every Day,
We at the Height are ready to decline.
There is a Tide in the Affairs of Men,
Which taken at the Flood, leads on to Fortune:
Omitted, all the Voyage of their Life
Is bound in Shallows and in Miseries.
On such a full Sea are we now afloat,
And we must take the Current when it serves,
Or loose our Ventures.
CASSIUS Then with your Will go on:
We'll along our selves, and meet them at Philippi.
BRUTUS The deep of Night is crept upon our Talk,

270 **niggard** buy off as cheaply as possible. Brutus is saying that, though our natures need a long rest, we will give them only a short one. Plutarch says that Brutus 'was a careful man and slept very little. . . . He never slept in the day time, and in the night no longer than the time he was driven to be alone, and when everyone else took their rest.' See the note to II.i.4.

272 **hence** proceed hence. Compare *to morrow* with *to night* in line 183.

276 **ill** evil, bad. Compare IV.ii.6, 159–60.

277 **Never** never again.

283 **o'er-watch'd** overtired from waiting up for your Master. This word recalls II.i.97. Compare *King Lear*, II.ii.166, where Kent refers to himself as 'All weary and o'erwatch'd'.

And Nature must obey Necessity,
Which we will niggard with a little Rest:
There is no more to say.

CASSIUS No more, good night;
Early to morrow will we rise, and hence.

Enter Lucius.

BRUTUS Lucius, my Gown. [*Exit Lucius.*]
– Farewell, good Messala.
– Good night, Titinius. – Noble, Noble Cassius,
Good night, and good Repose.

CASSIUS O my dear Brother,
This was an ill Beginning of the Night:
Never come such Division 'tween our Souls;
Let it not, Brutus.

Enter Lucius with the Gown.

BRUTUS Every thing is well.

CASSIUS Good night, my Lord.

BRUTUS Good night, good Brother.

TITINIUS, MESSALA Good night, Lord Brutus.

BRUTUS Farewell, every one.
Exeunt. [*Manent Brutus and Lucius.*]
– Give me the Gown. Where is thy Instrument?

LUCIUS Here in the Tent.

BRUTUS What, thou speak'st drowsily?
Poor Knave, I blame thee not, thou art o'er-watch'd.
Call Claudio and some other of my Men,
I'll have them sleep on Cushions in my Tent.

LUCIUS Varrus and Claudio.

Enter Varrus and Claudio.

VARRUS Calls my Lord?

291 **watch your pleasure** stay awake awaiting your orders. Compare line 283.

297 **Bear with me** be patient with my demands and lapses. *Bear* recalls I.ii.33–34, 110–13, 128–29, 317; I.iii.99–100; II.i.28–31, 117–22, 213, 223–25, 299–300; II.ii.60–62; III.i.158–60; III.ii.111–13, 170; III.iii.19–20; IV.i.21; IV.ii.54–55, 130–31, 178, 230, 236–37.

300 **I** both (a) I [am], and (b) Ay. Compare III.iii.10–12.
an't if it.

301 **I trouble thee too much** I demand too much of you.

303 **Might** strength.

304 **young Bloods** the constitutions of young people.

310 **Leaden Mace** A 'Mace' is a rod of office; here it is 'Leaden' because the officer employing it to make his arrest is Slumber, who has made Lucius' eyelids heavy.

311 **Knave** boy, page.

315 **Leaf** Like the clock references in the play, this word is anachronistic; in Brutus' time books were in scroll form. See the note to II.i.190.

S.D. **Ghost of Caesar** This stage direction is our only indication that the apparition is the Ghost of Caesar. Nothing that Brutus says here indicates that he recognizes or acknowledges it as such. Later, however, he says that 'The Ghost of Caesar hath appear'd to me / Two several times by Night' (V.v.17–18). In Plutarch the apparition is identified only as Brutus' 'evil spirit' (see line 324), never as Caesar's ghost.

317 **ill** poorly, faintly. But in line 330, *Ill* means 'Evil' (line 324). Compare line 276.

BRUTUS I pray you, Sirs, lie in my Tent and sleep;
It may be I shall raise you by and by
On business to my brother Cassius.
VARRUS So please you, we will stand, and watch your pleasure.
BRUTUS I will not have it so: lie down, good Sirs;
It may be I shall otherwise bethink me.
[*Varrus and Claudio lie down.*]
– Look, Lucius, here's the Book I sought for so;
I put it in the pocket of my Gown.
LUCIUS I was sure your Lordship did not give it me.
BRUTUS Bear with me, good Boy, I am much forgetful.
Canst thou hold up thy heavy Eyes awhile,
And touch thy Instrument a strain or two.
LUCIUS I, my Lord, an't please you.
BRUTUS It does, my Boy:
I trouble thee too much, but thou art Willing.
LUCIUS It is my Duty, Sir.
BRUTUS I should not urge thy Duty past thy Might,
I know young Bloods look for a time of Rest.
LUCIUS I have slept, my Lord, already.
BRUTUS It was well done, and thou shalt sleep again:
I will not hold thee long. If I do live,
I will be good to thee. *Music, and a Song.*
This is a sleepy Tune. – O murd'rous Slumber!
Layest thou thy Leaden Mace upon my Boy,
That plays thee Music? – Gentle Knave, good night:
I will not do thee so much wrong to wake thee.
If thou dost nod, thou break'st thy Instrument:
I'll take it from thee, and, good Boy, good night.
– Let me see, let me see; is not the Leaf turn'd down
Where I left reading? Here it is, I think.

Enter the Ghost of Caesar.

How ill this Taper burns. – Ha! Who comes here?

319 **monstrous** portentous, ominous. Compare I.iii.68, 71, II.i.78–80.

320 **Art thou any thing?** Brutus' question is whether the apparition is simply a product of his own sick mind or something that has an existence separate from himself. After the Ghost disappears, Brutus awakens the others in his tent in the hope that what he saw was a product of their dreams.

322 **stare** stand on end.

333 **false** out of tune.

344 **commend me** send my greetings.

– I think it is the weakness of mine Eyes
That shapes this monstrous Apparition.
It comes upon me. – Art thou any thing?
Art thou some God, some Angel, or some Divel,
That mak'st my Blood cold, and my Hair to stare?
Speak to me, what thou art.

GHOST Thy Evil Spirit, Brutus?

BRUTUS Why com'st thou?

GHOST To tell thee thou shalt see me at Philippi.

BRUTUS Well: then I shall see thee again?

GHOST I, at Philippi.

BRUTUS Why I will see thee at Philippi then.
[*Exit Ghost.*]
Now I have taken Heart, thou vanishest.
Ill Spirit, I would hold more Talk with thee.
– Boy, Lucius, Varrus, Claudio, Sirs: awake,
Claudio.

LUCIUS The Strings, my Lord, are false.

BRUTUS He thinks he still is at his Instrument.
– Lucius, awake.

LUCIUS My Lord.

BRUTUS Didst thou dream, Lucius, that thou so criedst out?

LUCIUS My Lord, I do not know that I did cry.

BRUTUS Yes, that thou didst. Didst thou see any thing?

LUCIUS Nothing, my Lord.

BRUTUS Sleep again, Lucius. – Sirrah Claudio,
– Fellow, thou: awake.

VARRUS My Lord.

CLAUDIO My Lord.

BRUTUS Why did you so cry out, Sirs, in your Sleep?

BOTH Did we, my Lord?

BRUTUS Ay: saw you any thing?

VARRUS No, my Lord, I saw nothing.

CLAUDIO Nor I, my Lord.

BRUTUS Go and commend me to my brother Cassius:

345 **betimes** early, right away. Compare II.i.114–15

Bid him set on his Pow'rs betimes before,
And we will follow.

BOTH
It shall be done, my Lord.

Exeunt.

V.i This scene occurs on the Plains of Philippi.

1 **answered** fulfilled.

4 **Battailes** battalions; often spelled, and probably pronounced, *battles*. So also in line 16.

5 **warn** summon to battle.

6 **Answering** responding.

7 **I am in their Bosoms** I know what is in their hearts.

8 **Wherefore** why.

8–9 **They . . . places** They could content themselves with deploying their main forces elsewhere (while merely feigning an intention to attack us here). See the second note to IV.ii.266.

10 **fearful Bravery** bravado, a dazzling show of strength intended to frighten. See the note to line 13. *Bravery* echoes IV.ii.140. *Fearful* recalls I.ii.77–78, 86–87, 192–97, 207–8, 247–49; I.iii.22–25, 53–56, 59–78, 126–27, 137; II.i.181–82, 188, 200, 245–47; II.ii.25–26, 35–37, 41–43, 50–51, 105–6; II.iv.31–33; III.i.17–19, 102–6, 130, 144–47; III.ii.117, 157–58; III.iii.19–20; IV.i.48–51. It anticipates lines 102–6.
Face pretence.

12 **But 'tis not so** Antony's point is that he and Octavius are not fooled. What he is referring to, however, is somewhat ambiguous: (a) whether 'they have Courage', (b) whether they have managed to 'fasten in our Thoughts' the idea that they have courage, or (c) whether Brutus and Cassius are merely using this 'warning' as a 'Face' to disguise their real strategy. What is not ambiguous is that Antony, like Octavius, reads the military situation in the same way that Cassius does.

13 **Shew** appearance, spectacle. Plutarch says that, 'for bravery and rich furniture, Brutus' army far excelled Caesar's. For the most part of their armours were silver and gilt, which Brutus had bountifully given them, although in all other things he taught his captains to live in order without excess.'

14 **bloody Sign of Battle** The Romans displayed a red flag to signal that a battle was at hand.

16 **softly** slowly (perhaps stealthily).

ACT V

Scene 1

Enter Octavius, Antony, and their Army.

OCTAVIUS Now Antony, our Hopes are answered.
You said the Enemy would not come down,
But keep the Hills and Upper Regions.
It proves not so: their Battailes are at hand,
They mean to warn us at Philippi here:
Answering before we do demand of them.

ANTONY Tut, I am in their Bosoms, and I know
Wherefore they do it. They could be content
To visit other places, and come down
With fearful Bravery, thinking by this Face
To fasten in our Thoughts that they have Courage;
But 'tis not so.

Enter a Messenger.

MESSENGER Prepare you, Generals,
The Enemy comes on in gallant Shew;
Their bloody Sign of Battle is hung out,
And something to be done immediately.

ANTONY Octavius, lead your Battaile softly on
Upon the left hand of the even Field.

OCTAVIUS Upon the right hand I, keep thou the left.

19 **cross me in this Exigent** oppose me at this critical juncture. Octavius insists on the more important wing; Plutarch says nothing about such an argument between Antony, the more experienced soldier, and Octavius. If anything, he suggests the opposite, since Caesar is ill on the day of the battle and stays in his tent.

20 **so** thus. Octavius is saying that he will do as he said he would. In this brief exchange Shakespeare hints at the future conflict between these two members of the Triumvirate; and significantly, he shows Octavius to be the stronger man, despite Antony's position as the older and apparently more assertive battlefield general.

21 **would have Parley** would like to talk. Plutarch says nothing about a pre-battle 'parley'.

24 **answer on their Charge** respond when they attack.

26 **Stir . . . Signal** Octavius speaks to his subordinates.

28 **Not . . . do** Octavius replies to Brutus' greeting with the implication that Brutus and Cassius are cowardly.

29 **Good . . . Octavius** Brutus seems to be implying that if there is any chance of resolving their conflict by 'Good Words', that would be better than doing so with the lives of men.

30 **In . . . Words** Antony alludes to the deceit with which Brutus and his companions tricked Caesar with 'good Words' to set him up for their 'bad Strokes'. Compare III.i.210, IV.i.48–51.

32 **hail Caesar** Antony alludes to 'the most unkindest Cut of all' (III.ii.185). And *hail* recalls the greeting Judas gave Jesus as he betrayed him; see the note to III.i.52.

34 **Hybla** a Sicilian region famous for its honey.

35 **And leave them Honey-less** Cassius is probably reminding Antony of the sweet words he spoke to the conspirators after the assassination.

Not Sting-less too Antony taunts Brutus with the reminder that he stung the conspirators after he sweet-talked them.

37 **Buzzing** Brutus' implication is that Antony is now filling the air with buzzing sounds so incoherent that they can serve only as a brave threat to frighten potential adversaries away before Antony is forced to put his stinger to the test.

ANTONY Why do you cross me in this Exigent?
OCTAVIUS I do not cross you: but I will do so. *March.*

Drum. Enter Brutus, Cassius, and their Army.

BRUTUS They stand, and would have Parley.
CASSIUS Stand fast, Titinius, we must out and talk.
OCTAVIUS Mark Antony, shall we give Sign of Battle?
ANTONY No, Caesar, we will answer on their Charge.
Make forth, the Generals would have some Words.
OCTAVIUS Stir not until the Signal.
BRUTUS Words before Blows: is it so, Countrymen?
OCTAVIUS Not that we love Words better, as you do.
BRUTUS Good Words are better than bad Strokes, Octavius.
ANTONY In your bad Strokes, Brutus, you give good Words:
Witness the Hole you made in Caesar's Heart,
Crying 'Long live, hail Caesar.'
CASSIUS Antony,
The posture of your Blows are yet unknown;
But for your Words, they rob the Hybla Bees,
And leave them Honey-less.
ANTONY Not Sting-less too.
BRUTUS O yes, and Sound-less too:
For you have stol'n their Buzzing, Antony,
And very wisely threat before you sting.
ANTONY Villains, you did not so when your Vile Daggers
Hack'd one another in the Sides of Caesar:

41 **shew'd . . . Apes** smiled the way apes do before they bite.

44 **Flatterers** As this speech illustrates, *flatterer* was a much stronger term in Shakespeare's time than it is in our own. Here a flatterer is a person who plays on a victim's vanity and cunningly deceives him into a false sense of well-being or security that sets him up for the kill. Compare III.i.35–49.

46 **to day** Compare IV.ii.272.

48 **the Cause** the case at hand, the issue to be resolved. Octavius is using *cause* (Latin *causa*) in the legal sense. Compare IV.ii.257.

49 **The Proof of it** the issue of it (the resulting battle), the judicial test that will decide the matter.
redder Drops drops of blood (as opposed to drops of sweat).

50 **Look . . . Conspirators** Octavius probably draws his sword.

51 **goes up again** is put away. Compare *Romeo and Juliet*, IV.iii.184, 211–13.

52 **three . . . Wounds** In Plutarch Caesar receives, 'three-and-twenty wounds'. Shakespeare may have changed the number to add another allusion to the Crucifixion; Jesus was said to have died at the age of thirty-three.

53–54 **or . . . Traitors** or till the swords of traitors have added another Caesar to their list of slaughters.

57 **borne** both (a) carried, and (b) born. Compare III.ii.114 and line 71.

61 **a Masker and a Reveller** another reference to Mark Antony's reputation for licentious, undisciplined behaviour. A masker was a person who enjoyed masquerades and other wild parties.

64 **to day** echoes line 46, and anticipates line 92.

65 **Stomachs** guts, appetites for battle. Then as now, the abdomen was considered the seat of valour.

67 **on the Hazard** at stake. The metaphor is from a game of chance played with dice. A hazard was a wager on the throw.

You shew'd your Teeths like Apes, and fawn'd like Hounds,
And bow'd like Bondmen, kissing Caesar's Feet;
Whilst damned Casca, like a Cur, behind
Strook Caesar on the Neck. O you Flatterers.
CASSIUS Flatterers? – Now Brutus, thank your self:
This Tongue had not offended so to day
If Cassius might have rul'd.
OCTAVIUS Come, come, the Cause. If Arguing make us sweat,
The Proof of it will turn to redder Drops.
Look, I draw a Sword against Conspirators:
When think you that the Sword goes up again?
Never till Caesar's three and thirty Wounds
Be well aveng'd, or till another Caesar
Have added Slaughter to the Sword of Traitors.
BRUTUS Caesar, thou canst not die by Traitors' Hands
Unless thou bring'st them with thee.
OCTAVIUS So I hope:
I was not borne to die on Brutus' Sword.
BRUTUS O if thou wert the Noblest of thy Strain,
Young Man, thou couldst not die more Honourable.
CASSIUS A peevish Schoolboy, worthless of such Honour,
Join'd with a Masker and a Reveller.
ANTONY Old Cassius still.
OCTAVIUS Come Antony, away.
– Defiance, Traitors, hurl we in your Teeth.
If you dare fight to day, come to the Field;
If not, when you have Stomachs.
Exeunt Octavius, Antony, and Army.
CASSIUS Why now blow Wind, swell Billow, and swim Bark:
The Storm is up, and all is on the Hazard.
BRUTUS Ho, Lucilius, hark, a word with you.
Lucilius and Messala stand forth.
LUCILIUS My Lord.

71 **borne** born.

73 **As Pompey was** Before the battle of Pharsalia Pompey allowed himself to be swayed, against his better judgement, into venturing all his fortunes on one encounter. Cassius fears that the outcome at Philippi will be the same for him as the outcome at Pharsalia was for Pompey. See the note to IV.ii.266.

75 **held Epicurus strong** adhered to the belief that Epicurus was the wisest sage. Epicurus was a Greek philosopher (342–270 BC) who believed that the Gods took no interest in human affairs and thus that there were no such things as omens to signal divine intervention.

77 **partly . . . presage** believe to some degree that there are things that 'presage' (foretell) the future. Plutarch says that several ominous signs (among them the ones Cassius mentions here) 'began somewhat to alter Cassius' mind from Epicurus' opinions, and had put the soldiers also in a marvellous fear'.

78 **our former Ensign** our frontmost banner; the flag in the vanguard of our army.

79 **fell** descended from the sky.

81 **consorted** accompanied, came with.

83 **steeds** steads, places.
Kites preying hawks. The three birds listed in this line are all eaters of carrion, and thus birds of ill omen.

85 **sickly Prey** moribund carrion-to-be. Cassius' imagery echoes I.i.14–16, 27–29; I.ii.108–29, 209–10, 240–55; II.i.170–72, 231–68, 308–32; II.ii.23–26, 65, 111–13; II.iv.40–41; IV.ii.187–204, 317.

86 **most fatal** portending a bad fate. *Ghost* recalls the stage direction following IV.ii.316.

90 **constantly** unchangingly, resolutely. Compare II.i.222–25, 297–99, II.iv.6, III.i.22, 60–74.

92 **The . . . Friendly** Here Cassius puts up a brave front. The Gods may 'stand Friendly' to 'day', but that does not necessarily mean that they will prove friendly today to Cassius. Compare line 64.

93 **lead . . . Age** live to old age.

CASSIUS Messala.
MESSALA What says my General?
CASSIUS Messala,
This is my Birth-day, as this very Day
Was Cassius borne. Give me thy Hand, Messala:
Be thou my Witness that against my Will,
As Pompey was, am I compell'd to set
Upon one Battle all our Liberties.
You know that I held Epicurus strong,
And his Opinion: now I change my Mind,
And partly credit things that do presage.
Coming from Sardis, on our former Ensign
Two mighty Eagles fell, and there they perch'd,
Gorging and feeding from our Soldiers' Hands,
Who to Philippi here consorted us:
This Morning are they fled away and gone,
And in their steeds do Ravens, Crows, and Kites
Fly o'er our Heads, and downward look on us
As we were sickly Prey; their Shadows seem
A Canopy most fatal, under which
Our Army lies, ready to give up the Ghost.
MESSALA Believe not so.
CASSIUS I but believe it partly,
For I am fresh of Spirit, and resolv'd
To meet all Perils very constantly.
BRUTUS Even so, Lucilius.
CASSIUS Now, most Noble Brutus,
The Gods to day stand Friendly, that we may,
Lovers in Peace, lead on our Days to Age.

94 **rests still Incertain** are ever uncertain.

95 **reason with** come to terms with.

96 **Battaile** both (a) battalion, army, and (b) battle. So also in line 107.

98 **determined** resolved.

99 **Even . . . of** according to the dictates of.

100 **Cato** Cato the Younger (Portia's father), who killed himself in Africa in 46 BC rather than allow himself to fall into the hands of Julius Caesar.

101 **I know not how** Brutus is usually taken to mean that he is unable to understand how a Stoic such as Cato could do something the Stoics considered 'Cowardly and Vile' (line 102); but the Folio punctuation suggests that 'I know not how' refers to the means by which Cato committed suicide. See the note to lines 109–11 for the account of this conversation Shakespeare would have found in North's Plutarch. *Vile* (line 102) recalls I.iii.111, II.i.263, III.ii.35–36, IV.ii.116–20, 176, V.i.39–40, and anticipates V.v.36–38.

103–4 **prevent . . . Life** cut short life's natural duration.

108 **In Triumph** as a captive in a triumphal procession.

But since the Affairs of Men rests still Incertain,
Let's reason with the worst that may befall.
If we do lose this Battaile, then is this
The very last time we shall speak together:
What are you then determined to do?

BRUTUS Even by the Rule of that Philosophy
By which I did blame Cato for the Death
Which he did give himself, I know not how:
But I do find it Cowardly and Vile,
For Fear of what might fall, so to prevent
The Time of Life, arming my self with Patience
To stay the Providence of some high Powers
That govern us below.

CASSIUS Then if we loose
This Battaile, you are contented to be led
In Triumph thorough the Streets of Rome.

109–11 **No . . . Mind** Brutus has just said that he believes Cato to have been a failure in his renunciation of 'Patience' (line 104), or endurance. But now, pushed to the wall by Cassius' question about what *he* will do if confronted by the same choice Cato was faced with, Brutus admits that he will take the same course that Cato took. For Brutus, however, this will not represent a defeat, because 'He bears too great a Mind'. In North's Plutarch Brutus says, 'Being but a young man and not over greatly experienced in the world, I trust (I know not how) a certain rule of philosophy by the which I did greatly blame and reprove Cato for killing of himself, as being no lawful nor godly act, touching the gods, nor, concerning men, valiant; not to give place and yield to divine providence, and not constantly and patiently to take whatsoever it pleaseth him to send us, but to draw back and fly. But being now in the midst of the danger, I am of a contrary mind. For, if it be not the will of God that the battle fall out fortunate for us, I will look no more for hope, neither seek any new supply for war again, but will rid me of this miserable world, and content me with my fortune. For I gave up my life for my country in the Ides of March, for the which I shall live in another more glorious world.' In Plutarch Brutus comes across as a counterpart to Cassius, a man who alters his philosophy in the light of experience (see the note to line 77); in Shakespeare Brutus appears to be a man who is too puffed up with pride and self-righteousness to see how contradictory his statements are.

123 **it sufficeth** it is enough.

124 **Come ho, away** Brutus probably shouts this line as a command to the two armies.

V.ii This scene occurs on the field of battle near Philippi.

1 **Bills** written orders.

S.D. **Alarum** a trumpet call to battle.

BRUTUS No, Cassius, no. Think not, thou Noble Roman,
That ever Brutus will go bound to Rome:
He bears too great a Mind. But this same Day
Must end that Work the Ides of March begun,
And whether we shall meet again I know not.
Therefore our everlasting Farewell take:
For ever, and for ever, farewell, Cassius.
If we do meet again, why we shall smile;
If not, why then this Parting was well made.

CASSIUS For ever, and for ever, farewell, Brutus.
If we do meet again, we'll smile indeed;
If not, 'tis true, this Parting was well made.

BRUTUS Why then lead on. O that a Man might know
The end of this Day's Business ere it come:
But it sufficeth that the Day will end,
And then the End is known. Come ho, away.

Exeunt.

Scene 2

Alarum. Enter Brutus and Messala.

BRUTUS Ride, ride, Messala, ride and give these Bills
Unto the Legions on the other side. *Loud Alarum.*
Let them set on at once: for I perceive

4 **Cold Demeanour** a lack of fighting spirit.
Octavio's Wing Octavius' side of the opposing forces. According to Plutarch, 'Brutus prayed Cassius that he might have the leading of the right wing, the which men thought was far meeter for Cassius, both because he was the elder man, and also for that he had the better experience. But yet Cassius gave it him, and willed that Messala, who had charge of one of the warlikest legions they had, should be also in that wing with Brutus.' Shakespeare makes no mention of this passage here, but he seems to have drawn upon it for the brief flare-ups between Cassius and Brutus in IV.ii.75–110 and Antony and Octavius in V.i.16–20.

6 **let them all come down** tell all to attack at once.

V.iii This scene takes place in another part of the battlefield.

1 **fly** flee. Cassius is referring to his own forces, which are retreating without having been ordered to do so.

3 **Ensign** standard-bearer, bearer of the army's colours.

5 **Brutus . . . early** Brutus gave the command for his wing to attack prematurely. Once again, Brutus' judgement has proven defective. In Plutarch's words, 'Brutus had conquered all on his side, and Cassius had lost all on the other side. For nothing undid them but that Brutus went not to help Cassius, thinking he had overcome them, as he himself had done; and Cassius on the other side tarried not for Brutus, thinking he had been overthrown, as himself was.'

7 **fell to Spoil** stopped fighting and began looting the fallen enemy for trophies of battle.

9 **fly futher off** flee to a spot more distant from the lines than this.

15 **hide thy Spurs in him** dig your spurs into his sides; in other words, ride as quickly as you can.

17 **here again** back here.

But Cold Demeanour in Octavio's Wing,
And sudden push gives them the Overthrow.
Ride, ride, Messala, let them all come down.

Exeunt.

Scene 3

Alarums. Enter Cassius and Titinius.

CASSIUS O look, Titinius, look, the Villains fly.
My self have to mine own turn'd Enemy:
This Ensign here of mine was turning back,
I slew the Coward, and did take it from him.

TITINIUS O Cassius, Brutus gave the Word too early,
Who, having some Advantage on Octavius,
Took it too eagerly: his Soldiers fell to Spoil,
Whilst we by Antony are all enclos'd.

Enter Pindarus.

PINDARUS Fly further off, my Lord; fly further off,
Mark Antony is in your Tents, my Lord;
Fly therefore, Noble Cassius, fly far off.

CASSIUS This Hill is far enough. Look, look, Titinius,
Are those my Tents where I perceive the Fire?

TITINIUS They are, my Lord.

CASSIUS Titinius, if thou lovest me,
Mount thou my Horse, and hide thy Spurs in him,
Till he have brought thee up to yonder Troops
And here again, that I may rest assur'd

21 **My . . . thick** my eyesight has always been blurred. Plutarch says that 'Cassius himself saw nothing, for his eyesight was very bad, saving that he saw, and yet with much ado, how his enemies spoiled his camp before his eyes. He also saw a troop of horsemen whom Brutus sent to aid him, and thought that they were his enemies that followed him.' For Shakespeare, Cassius' inability to see clearly has a symbolic quality that parallels Caesar's deafness (compare I.ii.56–60, 207–10); it is another manifestation of 'the Falling Sickness' (I.ii.253–55) that afflicts most of Rome's leaders.

regard Titinius keep an eye on Titinius.

23–24 – **This . . . end** Cassius' life has come full circle. Such a pattern was often regarded as a symbol of completion, fulfilment. But it could also be interpreted as a symbol of futility and defeat, an indication that there has been no forward movement or progress. What Shakespeare did not know as he extrapolated from Plutarch and wrote these lines for Cassius was that he himself would die on or nearly on the day of his birth, 23 April.

25 **run his Compass** completed the circuit defined by a rotating compass. *Run* also suggests the sands flowing through an hourglass.

28 **make to him** run up to him.

30 **light** alight, dismount.

31 **ta'en** taken.

34 **To see** to be alive for. Literally, of course, Cassius does not *see* Titinius taken. The distinction proves significant. In Plutarch, Cassius refers to Titinius as 'one of my best friends'.

37 **swore thee** made thee swear.

saving of thy Life as the condition for my sparing your life.

40 **Freeman** that is, a man no longer bound to Cassius as a slave.

41 **search** probe (by penetrating it with this sword).

42 **Stand not to answer** don't pause to answer. *Stand* occurs more often in *Julius Caesar* than in any other Shakespearean play. For other instances see I.ii.3; I.iii.131; II.i.51, 140, 165, 310; II.iii.13; II.iv.25; III.i.84, 88, 99–101, 206, 285; III.ii.166–70; IV.i.13–15; IV.ii.1, 30–31, 91–92, 246–47, 291; V.i.21–22, 92; V.v.72–74.

Whether yond Troops are Friend or Enemy.
TITINIUS I will be here again, even with a Thought. *Exit.*
CASSIUS Go, Pindarus, get higher on that Hill,
My Sight was ever thick: regard Titinius,
And tell me what thou not'st about the Field.
[*Pindarus goes above.*]
– This Day I breathed first, Time is come round,
And where I did begin, there shall I end;
My Life is run his Compass. – Sirrah, what News?
PINDARUS *above* O my Lord.
CASSIUS What News?
PINDARUS Titinius is enclosed round about
With Horsemen, that make to him on the Spur,
Yet he spurs on. Now they are almost on him:
Now Titinius. Now some light: O he
Lights too. He's ta'en. *Shout.*
And hark, they shout for joy.
CASSIUS Come down, behold no more. [*Exit Pindarus above.*]
– O Coward that I am, to live so long,
To see my best Friend ta'en before my Face.

Enter Pindarus.

– Come hither, Sirrah.
In Parthia did I take thee Prisoner,
And then I swore thee, saving of thy Life,
That whatsoever I did bid thee do,
Thou shouldst attempt it. Come now, keep thine Oath,
Now be a Freeman, and with this good Sword,
That ran through Caesar's Bowels, search this Bosom.
Stand not to answer: here, take thou the Hilts,
And when my Face is cover'd, as 'tis now,

44–45 – **Caesar . . . thee** North's Plutarch says that Cassius 'slew himself with the same sword, with the which he strake Caesar'.

46 **so** thus, in this way.

46–47 **yet . . . Will** Here Pindarus appears to be saying that if he had been brave enough he would have slain himself rather than obey his master's order. He has failed to acquit himself like a real 'Roman', so he will now run away and hide rather than bear the shame of having a true Roman 'take note of him' (line 49). In IV.xiv of *Antony and Cleopatra*, Eros does what Pindarus now wished he had dared to do. According to Plutarch, 'casting his cloak over his head and holding out his bare neck unto Pindarus', Cassius 'gave him his head to be stricken off. But after that time Pindarus was never seen more. Whereupon, some took occasion to say that he had slain his master without his commandment.' *Durst* echoes IV.ii.104–7; *note* recalls IV.ii.48–52.

50 **Change** exchange. Brutus has overcome Octavius, but Antony has overcome Cassius, so the balance of forces remains unchanged. Neither side has gained an advantage.

60 **to Night** towards night. Compare V.i.64.

64 **Mistrust of my Success** doubts as to how I fared in my mission. Here *Success* refers only to one's having completed a sequence. Messala adds the necessary qualifier in the next line when he says 'good Success'. Plutarch says that when Cassius 'sent Titinius' to locate Brutus' troops, 'Brutus' horsemen saw him coming afar off, whom when they knew that he was one of Cassius' chiefest friends, they shouted out for joy; and they that were familiarly acquainted with him lighted from their horses, and went and embraced him. The rest compassed him in round about a-horseback, with songs of victory and great rushing of their harness, so that they made all the field ring again for joy. But this marred all. For Cassius [thought] indeed that Titinius was taken of his enemies.' Compare lines 27–31.

66 **Error, Melancholy's Child** A man under the influence of Melancholy (a humour resulting from an excess of black bile in the system) could be expected to make errors of judgement; his despondency made his sight 'thick' (line 21).

Guide thou the Sword – [*Pindarus thrusts him.*]
– Caesar, thou art reveng'd,
Even with the Sword that kill'd thee. [*Dies.*]

PINDARUS So I am Free, yet would not so have been
Durst I have done my Will. – O Cassius,
Far from this Country Pindarus shall run,
Where never Roman shall take note of him. [*Exit.*]

Enter Titinius and Messala.

MESSALA It is but Change, Titinius: for Octavius
Is overthrown by Noble Brutus' Power,
As Cassius' Legions are by Antony.

TITINIUS These Tidings will well comfort Cassius.

MESSALA Where did you leave him?

TITINIUS All disconsolate,
With Pindarus his Bondman, on this Hill.

MESSALA Is not that he that lies upon the ground?

TITINIUS He lies not like the Living: O my Heart!

MESSALA Is not that he?

TITINIUS No, this was he, Messala,
But Cassius is no more. – O setting Sun,
As in thy red Rays thou doest sink to Night,
So in his red Blood Cassius' Day is set.
The Sun of Rome is set; our Day is gone;
Clouds, Dews, and Dangers come; our Deeds are done.
Mistrust of my Success hath done this Deed.

MESSALA Mistrust of good Success hath done this Deed.
O hateful Error, Melancholy's Child,

67 **apt Thoughts of Men** Here *apt* means 'eager' and refers to a proneness to error. Compare II.ii.97, III.i.160–61.

68–70 **O Error . . . thee** Messala completes his little allegory by saying that when Melancholy gives birth to Error, the child's emergence is fatal to the mother. Compare I.iii.33–35, II.i.28–32. The phrase *things that are not* echoes 1 Corinthians 1:27–29, where the Apostle Paul says that 'God hath chosen the foolish things of the world to confound the wise and God hath chosen the weak things of the world, to confound the mighty things, And vile things of the world and things which are despised, hath God chosen, and things which are not, to bring to nought things that are, That no flesh should rejoice in his presence' (1560 Geneva Bible).

75 **Steel, and Darts** swords and arrows.
envenomed poisoned; here to be pronounced as a four-syllable word.

83 **misconstrued** misinterpreted; here pronounced as a three-syllable word with the stress on the second syllable. See the notes to lines 21, 68–70, as well as to I.ii.43, 160, 313, I.iii.34–35, II.i.305, IV.iii.130.

86 **apace** quickly.

87 **regarded** revered.

88 **a Roman's Part** a role befitting a noble Roman.

Why dost thou shew to the apt Thoughts of Men
The things that are not? O Error, soon conceiv'd,
Thou never com'st unto a happy Birth,
But kill'st the Mother that engend'red thee.
TITINIUS What, Pindarus? Where art thou, Pindarus?
MESSALA Seek him, Titinius, whilst I go to meet
The Noble Brutus, thrusting this Report
Into his Ears; I may say thrusting it,
For piercing Steel, and Darts envenomed,
Shall be as welcome to the Ears of Brutus
As Tidings of this Sight.
TITINIUS Hie you, Messala,
And I will seek for Pindarus the while.
[*Exit Messala.*]
– Why didst thou send me forth, brave Cassius?
Did I not meet thy Friends, and did not they
Put on my Brows this Wreath of Victory,
And bid me give it thee? Didst thou not hear their
Shouts?
Alas, thou hast misconstrued every thing.
But hold thee, take this Garland on thy Brow;
Thy Brutus bid me give it thee, and I
Will do his bidding. – Brutus, come apace,
And see how I regarded Caius Cassius.
– By your leave, Gods: this is a Roman's Part.
– Come, Cassius' Sword, and find Titinius' Heart. *Dies.*

Alarum. Enter Brutus, Messala, young Cato, Strato, Volumnius, and Lucilius.

BRUTUS Where, where, Messala, doth his Body lie?
MESSALA Lo yonder, and Titinius mourning it.
BRUTUS Titinius' Face is upward.
CATO He is slain.
BRUTUS O Julius Caesar, thou art Mighty yet:
Thy Spirit walks abroad, and turns our Swords

95 **own proper** own. Here it may be that *proper* (which often means 'own') is not merely redundant: Brutus' line suggests that it is 'proper' (fitting) that the conspirators' swords should be directed against the conspirators themselves. At this moment Brutus sees Caesar's spirit as an avenging angel; whether Brutus is now ready to conclude that it was a mistake to assassinate Caesar, however, is anything but clear. Compare IV.ii.317–30.

96 **Look where** see whether.

100 **Fellow** equal. Brutus addresses this line to Cassius' corpse.
moe more in number. Shakespeare often uses this form; and frequently, as here, he uses it in a rhyming context. Plutarch says that when Brutus 'was come thither, after he had lamented the death of Cassius, calling him the last of all the Romans, being unpossible that Rome should ever breed again so noble and valiant a man as he, he caused his body to be buried and sent it to the city of Thassos, fearing lest his funerals within the camp should cause great disorder.' Brutus' words over Cassius' corpse recall his remarks about Portia in IV.ii.190–208, 223–37.

103 **Tharsus** Plutarch mentions Thassos (see the note to line 100). Shakespeare may have preferred the sound of 'Tharsus'. But it is also conceivable that he wanted to echo the name of the 'famous city in Cilicia' that an Elizabethan audience would have associated with 'Saul of Tarsus' (Acts 21:39, 9:11), the persecutor of Christians who learned on the road to Damascus that he has 'misconstrued every thing' (see Acts 9:1–31) and became known thereafter as the Apostle Paul.

105 **Least** lest (as in II.i.28, III.i.88, 93).
discomfort discourage, dishearten. See the note to line 100.

107 **Battailes** battalions. Compare V.i.96, 107.

V.iv The scene shifts to another part of the battlefield, later in the day. Plutarch indicates that the second battle took place three weeks later. In the meantime Brutus' naval forces won a great triumph. 'But by ill fortune, rather than through the malice or negligence of the captains, this victory came not to Brutus' ear till twenty days after. For had he known of it before, he would not have been brought to have fought a second battle, considering that he had excellent good provision for his army for a long time, and, besides, lay in a place of great strength.'

In our own proper Entrails. *Low Alarums.*
CATO Brave Titinius,
Look where he have not crown'd dead Cassius.
BRUTUS Are yet two Romans living such as these?
– The last of all the Romans, fare thee well:
It is impossible that ever Rome
Should breed thy Fellow. – Friends, I owe moe Tears
To this dead Man than you shall see me pay.
– I shall find time, Cassius, I shall find time.
– Come therefore, and to Tharsus send his Body:
His Funerals shall not be in our Camp,
Least it discomfort us. – Lucilius, come,
And come, young Cato, let us to the Field:
Labio and Flavio set our Battailes on.
'Tis three a'clock, and Romans, yet ere Night
We shall try Fortune in a second Fight. *Exeunt.*

Scene 4

Alarum. Enter Brutus, Messala, Cato, Lucilius, and Flavius.

BRUTUS Yet Countrymen, O yet hold up your Heads.
[*Exit.*]

2 **What Bastard doth not?** Cato's point is that everyone in Brutus' army is a true Roman; there is no one here who is an illegitimate soldier, a man of lesser breed. Compare I.i.77–80; I.ii.130–58, 169–72, 204–6, 253–55; I.iii.72–115; II.i.51, 110–38.

4–5 **I . . . Friend** Young Cato appeals to his heritage in much the same way that Brutus has done earlier in the play when he invoked the spirit of the ancestral Lucius Junius Brutus.

7 **Lucilius** The Folio provides no speech designation for lines 7–8; it does attribute lines 9–11 to Lucilius, however, and most modern editions (including this one) give the first two lines to him as well. The problem is complicated by the fact that Brutus is given no exit in the Folio text after line 1. What would seem to clinch the argument in favour of having Brutus exit and having Lucilius (rather than Brutus) speak lines 7–8 is what Lucilius says in line 14 after he is captured: 'Kill Brutus, and be honour'd in his Death.' Plutarch says that Lucilius 'seeing a troop of barbarous men making no reckoning of all men else they met in their way, but going all together right against Brutus, he determined to stay them with the hazard of his life, and, being left behind, told them that he was Brutus'; and, because they should believe him, he prayed them to bring him to Antonius, for he said he was afraid of Caesar, and that he did trust Antonius better.'

12 **Onely I yield to die** I yield only on the condition that you kill me. Compare Plutarch's account in the note to line 12.

13 **so much** so much valour in me.
straight immediately.

16 **Room ho** Make way!

24 **or . . . or** either . . . or. Lines 20–25 recall IV.ii.9–11.

CATO What Bastard doth not? Who will go with me?
I will proclaim my Name about the Field:
I am the Son of Marcus Cato, ho,
A Foe to Tyrants, and my Country's Friend.
I am the Son of Marcus Cato, ho.

Enter Soldiers, and fight.

[LUCILIUS] And I am Brutus, Marcus Brutus, I:
Brutus, my Country's Friend; know me for Brutus.
[*Young Cato is killed.*]
– O young and noble Cato, art thou down?
Why now thou diest as bravely as Titinius,
And may'st be honour'd, being Cato's Son.

[1] SOLDIER Yield, or thou diest.

LUCILIUS Onely I yield to die.
There is so much that thou wilt kill me straight:
Kill Brutus, and be honour'd in his Death.

[1] SOLDIER We must not: a Noble Prisoner.

Enter Antony.

2 SOLDIER Room ho: tell Antony Brutus is ta'en.

1 SOLDIER I'll tell thee News; here comes the General.
– Brutus is ta'en, Brutus is ta'en, my Lord.

ANTONY Where is he?

LUCILIUS Safe, Antony, Brutus is safe enough.
I dare assure thee that no Enemy
Shall ever take alive the Noble Brutus:
The Gods defend him from so great a Shame.
When you do find him, or alive or dead,

25 **He . . . Brutus** He will be found to be Brutus (that is, you will see that he is true to his identity). Here Lucilius asserts a Roman military code that seems at odds with the dictates of Stoicism. Whereas the strictest teachings of Stoicism, as Brutus has enunciated them in V.i.99–106, present suicide as a reprehensible escape from trials that should be endured with unyielding patience, the Roman code of military behaviour holds it shameful for a noble Roman to be taken alive. In other words, Brutus is caught between one code that regards suicide as shameful, and another that regards anything other than suicide as shameful in his situation. See the note to V.i.109–11, and compare Lucilius' phrasing with that in II.i.253.

27 **Keep this Man safe** Antony may mean 'keep this man from being harmed by our army', but he probably also means 'keep this man from taking his own life'. In Plutarch, Antony says, 'My companions, I think ye are sorry you have failed of your purpose, and that you think this man hath done you great wrong. But, I do assure you, you have taken a better booty than you followed. For, instead of an enemy, you have brought me a friend; and for my part, if you had brought me Brutus alive, truly I cannot tell what I would have done to him. For I had rather have such men my friends as this man here, than enemies.'

29 **then** Antony means 'than'; but in time many of the 'Men' he now counts as 'Friends' will prove 'Enemies'. Compare III.ii.25, 40, and see II.ii.126–29.

30 **where** whether.

V.v The scene now shifts to the part of the battlefield occupied by Brutus' forces.

1 **poor Remains of Friends** my pitiful number of remaining friends.

He will be found like Brutus, like himself.

ANTONY This is not Brutus, Friend, but I assure you,
A Prize no less in worth. Keep this Man safe,
Give him all kindness. I had rather have
Such Men my Friends, then Enemies. Go on,
And see where Brutus be alive or dead,
And bring us word, unto Octavius' Tent,
How every thing is chanc'd. *Exeunt.*

Scene 5

Enter Brutus, Dardanius, Clitus, Strato, and Volumnius.

BRUTUS Come, poor Remains of Friends, rest on this Rock.

2 **shew'd** showed, displayed. Statilius is a scout who has sent a signal from the enemy front. Plutarch says that in order to determine how many men had been slain in battle, Brutus sent Statilius 'to go through the enemies, for otherwise it was impossible to see their camp, and from thence, if all were well, that he would lift up a torch-light in the air, and then return again with speed to him. The torch-light was lift up as he had promised, for Statilius went thither. . . . But his evil fortune was such that as he came back he lighted in his enemies' hands and was slain.' The reference to the torch indicates to the audience that the battlefield is now dark.

11 **ill** bad, unwelcome. Compare IV.ii.317, 330.

13 **Noble Vessel** Brutus' body.

14 **That** so that.

15 **list** hear, listen to. According to Plutarch, 'the night being far spent, Brutus as he said bowed towards Clitus one of his men and told him somewhat in the ear, the other answered him not, but fell a-weeping. Thereupon he proved Dardanus, and said somewhat also to him. At length he came to Volumnius himself, and, speaking to him in Greek, prayed him, for the study's sake which brought them acquainted together, that he would help him put his hand to his sword, to thrust it in him to kill him. Volumnius denied his request, and so did many others.'

18 **Two several times** on two different occasions.

20 **my Hour is come** Brutus' words echo such New Testament passages as Luke 22:53, where Jesus tells the elders who have come to arrest him 'this is your hour, and the power of darkness', and John 12:27, where Jesus says, 'Now is my soul troubled; and what shall I say? Father, save me from this hour; but for this cause came I unto this hour.'

23 **Pit** Brutus is probably thinking about a trap into which animals were driven by hunters. But the image also suggests the grave. *World* (line 22) echoes I.ii.122, 126–29, 132–33; I.iii.12–13, 98–100; II.ii.28–29; III.i.66–68, 157, 208–9; III.ii.124–26; IV.i.13–15; IV.ii.68–73, 138–39; V.v.72–74.

29 **Office** duty.

31 **Farewell . . . Volumnius** Here Brutus says farewell to Clitus, Dardanius, and Volumnius, who are preparing to flee.

CLITUS Statilius shew'd the Torchlight, but my Lord,
He came not back: he is or ta'en or slain.
BRUTUS Sit thee down, Clitus. Slaying is the Word:
It is a Deed in Fashion. Hark thee, Clitus.
CLITUS What I, my Lord? No, not for all the World.
BRUTUS Peace, then, no Words.
CLITUS I'll rather kill my self.
BRUTUS Hark thee, Dardanius.
DARDANIUS Shall I do such a Deed?
CLITUS O Dardanius.
DARDANIUS O Clitus.
CLITUS What ill Request did Brutus make to thee?
DARDANIUS To kill him, Clitus: look, he meditates.
CLITUS Now is that Noble Vessel full of Grief,
That it runs over even at his Eyes.
BRUTUS Come hither, good Volumnius, list a Word.
VOLUMNIUS What says my Lord?
BRUTUS Why this, Volumnius.
The Ghost of Caesar hath appear'd to me
Two several times by Night: at Sardis once,
And this last Night, here in Philippi Fields.
I know my Hour is come.
VOLUMNIUS Not so, my Lord.
BRUTUS Nay, I am sure it is, Volumnius.
Thou seest the World, Volumnius, how it goes:
Our Enemies have beat us to the Pit. *Low Alarums.*
It is more worthy to leap in our selves
Than tarry till they push us. Good Volumnius,
Thou know'st that we two went to School together:
Even for that our Love of old, I prythee
Hold thou my Sword Hilts, whilest I run on it.
VOLUMNIUS That's not an Office for a Friend, my Lord.
Alarum still.
CLITUS Fly, fly, my Lord, there is no tarrying here.
BRUTUS Farewell to you, and you, and you, Volumnius.

33–42 **Countrymen . . . Hour** Brutus addresses these words to the three soldiers who have just refused to kill him, thereby proving themselves 'True' to him in the sense that they love him too much to take his life. Whether their affection gives Brutus more 'Glory' than Octavius and Mark Antony will obtain by their 'vile Conquest' is open to question, but it does provide Brutus some much-needed consolation at the end of his weary journey. In Plutarch Brutus says, 'It rejoiceth my heart that not one of my friends hath failed me at my need, and I do not complain of my fortune, but only for my country's sake. For, as for me, I think myself happier than they that have overcome, considering that I leave a perpetual fame of courage and manhood, the which our enemies the conquerors shall never attain unto by force nor money, neither can let their posterity to say that they, being naughty and unjust men, have slain good men, to usurp tyrannical power not pertaining to them.'

36 **Loosing** both (a) loosing, releasing (Brutus' optimistic reading of it); and (b) losing. Compare I.ii.122, IV.ii.266.

40 **Live's** Words such as *life*, *knife*, and *wife* usually take the voiced form in Shakespeare's works when they have an *s* ending.

42 **That . . . Hour** In this line, Brutus' world-weariness comes very near despair. See the note to line 20.

45 **Respect** reputation. Compare I.i.10–11, I.ii.56–60, III.ii.15–16, IV.ii.14–17, 111–14, V.v.75–76.

46 **smatch** smattering. Characteristically, Brutus would not wish to have his honour in any way diminished by his selecting for his assistant in death a man unworthy of such an exalted responsibility.

50 **Caesar, now be still** As Brutus dies, it is clear that he feels that his real pursuer has been Caesar, with Antony and Octavius serving only as the agents of Caesar's retribution. Again, however, Brutus' words tell us nothing about whether he feels any remorse or guilt for what he has done. All they indicate is that Brutus has taken upon himself the role of executioner. Plutarch records no last words for Brutus.

54 **Free . . . Messala** Strato is referring to Messala's new status as a member of Octavius' forces. Brutus has killed himself rather than surrender to captivity by the enemy.

– Strato, thou hast been all this while asleep.
Farewell to thee too, Strato. – Countrymen,
My Heart doth joy that yet in all my Life
I found no Man but he was True to me.
I shall have Glory by this Loosing Day
More than Octavius and Mark Antony
By this vile Conquest shall attain unto.
So fare you well at once, for Brutus' Tongue
Hath almost ended his Live's History.
Night hangs upon mine Eyes, my Bones would rest,
That have but labour'd to attain this Hour.

Alarum. Cry within: 'Fly, fly, fly'.

CLITUS Fly, my Lord, fly.
BRUTUS Hence, I will follow.
[*Exeunt all but Brutus and Strato.*]
– I prythee, Strato, stay thou by thy Lord.
Thou art a Fellow of a good Respect;
Thy Life hath had some smatch of Honour in it;
Hold then my Sword, and turn away thy Face
While I do run upon it. Wilt thou, Strato?
STRATO Give me your Hand first. Fare you well, my Lord.
BRUTUS Farewell, good Strato. [*He runs on his Sword.*]
– Caesar, now be still:
I kill'd not thee with half so good a Will.
Dies.

Alarum. Retreat. Enter Antony, Octavius, Messala, Lucilius, and the Army.

OCTAVIUS What Man is that?
MESSALA My Master's Man. – Strato, where is thy Master?
STRATO Free from the Bondage you are in, Messala,

56 **For Brutus onely overcame himself** Strato refers to Brutus' suicide, but his words are applicable to a much broader context. See the notes to I.ii.44, V.iii.21, 83. Compare the uses of *onely* in I.ii.39, 154, II.i.152, III.i.180–81, III.ii.220, V.iv.12, V.v.68, 70.

58 **So Brutus should be found** it is only fitting that Brutus be found thus. Compare V.iv.24–25.

60 **entertain them** give them welcome and take them in.

61 **bestow thy Time with me** employ the rest of your life as my assistant.

62 **prefer me** commend me, vouch for me.

65 **then** therefore. Messala assures Octavius that Strato has passed the highest test for service.

66 **latest** final. According to Plutarch, as soon as Messala presented Strato to Octavius, he said, 'Caesar, behold, here is he that did the last service to my Brutus.'

68 **save onely he** except him. Compare lines 56–57.

70–71 **He . . . them** Antony is saying that Brutus became one of the conspirators only because of an honest concern for the common good. The syntax of this clause is complex. 'He onely' seems at first to mean 'he alone' (thus continuing the contrast Antony has drawn in the previous two lines); but by the end of the clause it has become connected to 'made one of them', with 'in a general honest Thought / And common Good to all' functioning as a phrase to explain why he became one of them. The phrase 'general honest Thought' could be punctuated with a comma after *general*; it means 'a thought deriving from a commitment to the general well-being and reflecting Brutus' personal integrity'. Compare I.ii.83–85, III.i.171, III.ii.95.

72 **gentle** noble, dignified.
Elements the four elements (earth, water, air, and fire) that produced the humours in one's psychological makeup.

75 **use** bestow, treat. Significantly, it is Octavius who has the last words and will preside over the concluding ceremonies.

77 **to night** tonight, but with a suggestion of '[dedicated] to night'. Compare V.i.64, V.iii.60.

The Conquerors can but make a Fire of him:
For Brutus onely overcame himself,
And no Man else hath Honour by his Death.

LUCILIUS So Brutus should be found. – I thank thee, Brutus,
That thou hast prov'd Lucilius' Saying true.

OCTAVIUS All that serv'd Brutus, I will entertain them.
– Fellow, wilt thou bestow thy Time with me?

STRATO I, if Messala will prefer me to you.

OCTAVIUS Do so, good Messala.

MESSALA How died my Master, Strato?

STRATO I held the Sword, and he did run on it.

MESSALA Octavius, then take him to follow thee,
That did the latest Service to my Master.

ANTONY This was the Noblest Roman of them all.
All the Conspirators save onely he
Did that they did in Envy of great Caesar:
He onely in a general honest Thought,
And common Good to all, made one of them.
His Life was gentle, and the Elements
So mixt in him that Nature might stand up
And say to all the World, 'This was a Man.'

OCTAVIUS According to his Virtue let us use him,
With all Respect, and Rites of Burial.
Within my Tent his Bones to night shall lie,
Most like a Soldier ordered honourably.
So call the Field to rest, and let's away,
To part the Glories of this happy Day.

Exeunt omnes.

FINIS

PERSPECTIVES ON JULIUS CAESAR

Although *Julius Caesar* employs figurative language quite sparingly, its occasional resort to wordplay elicited scorn from several eighteenth-century critics. In his eight-volume edition of Shakespeare's complete works, for instance (London, 1747), William Warburton questioned the propriety of Cassius' recollection that on one occasion Caesar's 'Coward lips did from their colour fly' (I.ii.120).

> A plain man would have said the *colour* fled from his lips; not his *lips* from their colour. But the false expression was from as false a piece of Wit: a poor quibble, alluding to a *coward* flying from his *colours*.

A few years later, in his *Elements of Criticism* (London, 1762), Lord Kames objected to Antony's remarks over the corpse of Caesar in III.i.208–11:

> O world! thou wast the forest to this hart:
> And this, indeed, O world, the heart of thee.
> How like a deer, stricken by many princes,
> Dost thou here lie!

'Playing thus with the sound of words,' Kames intoned, 'which is still worse than a pun, is the meanest of all conceits.' Kames also complained about Shakespeare's other extravagances. 'It is a capital fault,' he said, 'to introduce an hyperbole in the description of any thing ordinary or familiar; for in such a case it is altogether unnatural, being destitute of surprise, its only foundation.'

For the most eminent of eighteenth-century commentators, however, *Julius Caesar* was to be faulted less for its excesses than for its stylistic deficiencies. In the notes accompanying his edition of Shakespeare's complete works (London, 1765), Samuel Johnson confessed that

> Of this tragedy many particular passages deserve regard, and the

contention of Brutus and Cassius is universally celebrated; but I have never been strongly agitated in perusing it, and I think it somewhat cold and unaffecting compared with some other of Shakespeare's plays; his adherence to the real story, and to Roman manners, seems to have impeded the natural vigour of his genius.

A well-known contemporary of Johnson's, Horace Walpole, was more enthusiastic about the drama. In a 1773 essay first printed by W. S. Lewis in *Notes by Horace Walpole on Several Characters of Shakespeare* (Farmington, Conn., 1940), Walpole asked:

is it not amazing that as all rules are drawn from the *conduct* of great genius's, not from their *directions*, nobody should have thought of drawing up rules from Shakespeare's plays, rather than of wishing they had been written from rules collected from such subaltern genius's as Euripides and Sophocles? I maintain that it was likely we should have had finer tragedies, if Shakespeare's daring had been laid down for a rule of venturing, than by pointing out his irregularities as faults.

[Joseph] Addison is a glaring proof that pedantry and servility to rules could dishabilitate a man of genius. Compare his *Cato* and Shakespeare's *Julius Caesar*. There is as much difference as between the soul of Julius and the timidity of Addison. A school boy of parts might by 19 have written *Cato*. The other was written by a master of human nature, and by a genius so quick and so intuitive, so penetrating, that Shakespeare from the dregs and obstacles of vile translations has drawn finer portraits of Caesar, Brutus, Cassius, Antony and Casca than Cicero himself has done, who lived with and knew the men. Why? because Cicero thought of what he should say of them; Shakespeare of what they would have said themselves.

But Shakespeare has not only improved on Cicero, but on the founders of his art, Euripides and Sophocles, for he has done what they did not, he has introduced a chorus properly and speaking and acting in character. The Roman mob before whom Brutus and Antony plead, is just. They did plead before the Roman mob, and the mob is made by Shakespeare to display the effect that eloquence has on vulgar minds. . . . Shakespeare never introduces a chorus but with peculiar propriety. Fluellen &c in *Henry 5th* are in effect a chorus: but they are not a parcel of mutes unconcerned in the action, who by the mouth of one representative draw moral and common place reflections from the incidents of the piece. A chorus was the first idea; to incorporate the chorus in the body of the drama, was an improvement wanting. Instead of observing that Shakespeare's enlightened mind had made that improvement, we have had men so absurd as to revert to the original imperfection – just as some men have wished to revive the feudal system – for some men cannot perceive the discrimination between original principles and original usages.

The most influential of the Romantic critics spoke fewer words about *Julius Caesar* than about other Shakespearean tragedies, but in his lectures of 1811–12 Samuel Taylor Coleridge drew upon the play to illustrate his observation that Shakespeare was generally disinclined to depict the emotions and proclivities most demeaning to human nature. Thus, Coleridge observed,

> There was no one character in which Envy was portrayed, excepting in Cassius in *Julius Caesar*; yet even there it is not hateful to you, but he has counterbalanced it by a number of excellent feelings. He leads the reader to suppose that it is rather something constitutional, something derived from his mother which he cannot avoid: throwing the blame from the will of the man to some unavoidable circumstance, rather than fix the attention of the reader on one of those passions which actually debase the mind.

Along similar lines, Coleridge noted that the ineffectuality of the conspiracy in the play derived, not from the plotters' selfish or wicked motives, but from a lack of judgement implicit in their honourable ones:

> the whole design to liberate their country fails from the generous temper and overweening confidence of Brutus in the goodness of their cause and the assistance of others. Thus it has always been.

A member of Coleridge's circle shared his friend's admiration for the psychological portraits to be found in *Julius Caesar*. In a comment dating from 1812 and printed in a collection of his *Dramatic Criticism, 1808–1831* by L. H. and C. W. Houtchens (London, 1949), Leigh Hunt said that

> *Julius Caesar*, with the exception of *Coriolanus*, has perhaps less of the poetical in it than any other tragedy of Shakespeare; but fancy and imagination did not suit the business of the scene; and what is wanting in colour and ornament, is recompensed by the finest contrasts of character. It is of itself a whole school of human nature. The variable impotence of the mob, the imperial obstinacy of Caesar, the courtly and calculating worldliness of Anthony, the vulgar jealousy of Casca, the loftier jealousy and impatient temper of Cassius, the disinterested-

ness and self-centred philosophy of Brutus, seem to bring at once before us the result of a thousand different educations, and of a thousand habits, induced by situation, passion, or reflection. Brutus, however, is clearly the hero of the story, and as Gildon observes, should have given his name to the piece; for Caesar appears but in two short scenes and is dispatched at the beginning of the third act; whereas Brutus, after his first interview with Cassius in the commencement of the play, is the arbiter of all that succeeds, and the predominant spirit to the last.

In *Shakspere: A Critical Study of His Mind and Art* (London, 1875), Edward Dowden responded to critiques such as Hunt's.

Julius Caesar appears in only three scenes of the play. In the first scene of the third act he dies. Where he does appear, the poet seems anxious to insist upon the weakness rather than the strength of Caesar. He swoons when the crown is offered to him, and upon his recovery enacts a piece of stagy heroism; he suffers from the falling-sickness; he is deaf; his body does not retain its early vigour. He is subject to the vain hopes and vain alarms of superstition. His manner of speech is pompous and arrogant; he accepts flattery as a right; he vacillates, while professing unalterable constancy; he has lost in part his gift of perceiving facts, and of dealing efficiently with men and with events. Why is this? And why is the play, notwithstanding, 'Julius Caesar'? Why did Shakspere decide to represent in such a light the chief man of the Roman world?

Dowden's answer was that

Julius Caesar is indeed protagonist of the tragedy; but it is not the Caesar whose bodily presence is weak, whose mind is declining in strength and sure-footed energy, the Caesar who stands exposed to all the accidents of fortune. This bodily presence of Caesar is but of secondary importance, and may be supplied when it actually passes away, by Octavius as its substitute. It is the spirit of Caesar which is the dominant power of the tragedy; against this – the spirit of Caesar – Brutus fought; but Brutus, who forever errs in practical politics, succeeded only in striking down Caesar's body; he who had been weak now rises as pure spirit, strong and terrible, and avenges himself upon the conspirators. The contrast between the weakness of Caesar's bodily presence in the first half of the play, and the might of his spiritual presence in the latter half of the play, is emphasized, and perhaps over-emphasized, by Shakspere. It was the error of Brutus that he failed to perceive wherein lay the true Caesarean power, and acted with short-sighted eagerness and violence. . . .

> The ghost of Caesar (designated by Plutarch only the 'evil spirit' of Brutus), which appears on the night before the battle of Philippi, serves as a kind of visible symbol of the vast posthumous power of the dictator. . . . With strict propriety, therefore, the play bears the name of *Julius Caesar*.

A decade later, in *Shakespeare as a Dramatic Artist* (Oxford, 1885), Richard G. Moulton argued that

> The passion in the play of *Julius Caesar* gathers around the conspirators, and follows them through the mutations of their fortunes. . . . The exact key to the movement of the drama will be given by fixing attention upon the *justification of the conspirators' cause* in the minds of the audience; and it is this which is found to rise gradually to its height in the centre of the play, and from that point to decline to the end. . . .
>
> The stoicism of Brutus, with its suppression of the inner sympathies, arrives practically at the principle – destined in the future history of the world to be the basis of a yet greater crime – that it is expedient that one man should die rather than that a whole people should perish. On the other hand, Antony trades upon the fickle violence of the populace, and uses it as much for personal ends as for vengeance. This demoralisation of both the sides of character is the result of their divorce. Such is the essence of this play if its action be looked at as a whole: but it belongs to the movement of dramatic passion that we see the action only in its separate parts at different times. Through the first half of the play, while the justification of the conspirators' cause is rising, the other side of the question is carefully hidden from us; from the point of the assassination the suppressed element starts into prominence, and sweeps our sympathies along with it to its triumph at the conclusion of the play.

As the nineteenth century drew to a close, Bernhard ten Brink saw the key to Shakespeare's play in 'the idea . . . that was projected into the world by Caesar and represented by him'. In *Five Lectures on Shakespeare*, translated into English by Julia Franklin (London, 1895), ten Brink said that

> In vain do Brutus and his friends combat against [the idea Caesar projects]; they are annihilated in the struggle. And the less adequate its embodiment, the more distinctly does the full significance of the idea as such stand out. Or, to be more explicit, it is embodied not so much in Caesar's person as in his position, his power, in the judgment, the mood, the character, of the people. Hence the significance in this

> tragedy of the gatherings of the populace, scenes which are at once eminently characteristic and intensely dramatic. If Shakespeare be guilty of serious errors as to the outward usages, nay, in individual instances as to the views, the manners, of the Romans, that which is really typical of the time and situation he reproduces with historic fidelity.

The American actor and director Orson Welles updated the 'idea' of *Julius Caesar* and made it the starting point for a famous 1937 production of the play in New York's Mercury Theatre. Welles emphasized what he referred to as the 'political violence' of twentieth-century totalitarianism, and 'the moral duty of the individual in the face of tyranny', and he gave his rendering of the drama the subtitle 'Death of a Dictator'. As Marvin Spevack recalls in the introduction to his edition of *Julius Caesar* for *The New Cambridge Shakespeare* (Cambridge, 1988), Welles'

> almost exclusive concentration on Caesar, Brutus, and the mob produced something even farther removed from the original than its eighteenth- and nineteenth-century predecessors [when *Julius Caesar* was adapted in various ways]. In this political context the masses in all their fickleness, easy persuadability, and unreflecting cruelty acquired an unsurpassed prominence, with the Cinna the Poet scene (3.3) – in a complete reversal of a centuries-long tradition [when it was omitted from performances of the tragedy] – as a haunting experience. Welles obviously had to play in modern dress . . . and, with a sure instinct for producing spectacular impressions, made extensive use of cinematic lighting effects. His production set a precedent never to be forgotten by later directors.

As Mary McCarthy observed in a 1938 review of the Welles *Julius Caesar*, reprinted in her *Theatre Chronicles, 1937–62* (New York, 1962), the purpose of the production 'was to say something about the modern world, to use Shakespeare's characters to drive home the horrors and inanities' of modern police states.

> *Julius Caesar* is about the tragic consequences that befall idealism when it attempts to enter the sphere of action. It is perhaps also a comment on the futility and dangerousness of action in general. In a non-political sense, it is a 'liberal' play, for it has three heroes, Caesar, Antony and Brutus, of whom Brutus is the most large-souled and sympathetic. Shakespeare's 'liberal' formula, which insists on playing fair with all its characters, is obviously in fearful discord with Mr

> Welles's anti-fascist formula, which must have heroes and villains at all costs. . . . Mr Welles has cut the play to pieces; he has very nearly eliminated the whole sordid tragic business of the degeneration and impotence of the republican forces; he has turned the rather shoddy Cassius into a shrewd and jovial comedian whose heart is in the right place; he has made Caesar, whose political stature gave the play dignity and significance, into a mechanical, expressionless robot; he has transformed the showy, romantic, buccaneering Antony into a repulsive and sinister demagogue. If he could do all this and still come out with a play that was consistent and uniformly forceful, the experiment might be forgivable. There were some things, however, which could not be cut or distorted, and these, by their very incongruous presence, destroyed the totality of the play's effect. The most prominent of these unassimilated chunks of Shakespeare was Antony's final speech ('This was the noblest Roman of them all' – too famous, doubtless, to be cut), which in the mouth of the blackshirt monster of the Welles production seemed an unconvincing and even tasteless tribute to the memory of Brutus.

While reviewers debated the merits of the Welles production, many readers were turning anew to the *Prefaces to Shakespeare* (London, 1927–47) of an earlier director. In his remarks on *Julius Caesar*, Harley Granville-Barker spoke with particular eloquence about Shakespeare's characterization of Mark Antony, who

> takes the tide that Brutus loses. He is a born opportunist, and we see him best in the light of his great opportunity. He stands contrasted with both Cassius and Brutus, with the man whom his fellows respect the more for his aloofness, and with such a rasping colleague as Cassius must be. Antony is, above all things, a good sort.
>
> Shakespeare keeps him in ambush throughout the first part of the play. Up to the time when he faces the triumphant conspirators he speaks just thirty-three words. But there have already been no less than seven separate references to him, all significant. . . . And, though we may father him on Plutarch, to English eyes there can be no more typically English figure than the sportsman turned statesman, but a sportsman still. Such men range up and down our history. Antony is something besides, however, that we used to flatter ourselves was not quite so English. He can be, when occasion serves, the perfect demagogue. . . .
>
> [When he greets the assassins who stand in a knot around Caesar's body,] in bitter irony, he caps their [just-completed blood-bathing] ritual with his own. It is the ritual of friendship, but of such a

friendship as the blood of Caesar, murdered by his friends, may best cement. . . . They shall never be able to say he approved their deed; but he is waiting, please, for those convincing reasons that Caesar was dangerous. He even lets slip a friendly warning to Cassius that the prospect is not quite clear. Then, with yet more disarming frankness, comes the challenging request to Brutus to let him speak in the market place. As he makes it, a well-calculated request! For how can Brutus refuse, how admit that the Roman people will not approve this hard service done them? . . .

To what he is to move his hearers we know: and it will be worth while . . . to analyse the famous speech, that triumph of histrionics. For though the actor of Antony must move us with it also – and he can scarcely fail to – Shakespeare has set him the further, harder and far more important task of showing us an Antony the mob never see, of making him clear to us, moreover, even while we are stirred by his eloquence, of making clear to us just by what it is we are stirred. It would, after all, be pretty poor playwriting and acting which could achieve no more than a plain piece of mob oratory, however gorgeous; a pretty poor compliment to an audience to ask of it no subtler response than the mob's. But to show us, and never for a moment to let slip from our sight, the complete and complex Antony, impulsive and calculating, warm-hearted and callous, aristocrat, sportsman and demagogue, that will be for the actor an achievement indeed; and the playwright has given all the material for it.

. . . There is nothing aloof, nothing superior about Antony. He may show a savage contempt for this man or that; he has a sort of liking for men in the mass. He is, in fact, the common man made perfect in his commonness; yet he is perceptive of himself as of his fellows, and, even so, content. . . .

. . . Antony finishes the play in fine form; victorious in battle, politically magnanimous to a prisoner or two, and ready with a resounding tribute to Brutus, now that he lies dead. Not in quite such fine form, though; for the shadow of that most unsportsmanlike young man Octavius is already moving visibly to his eclipse.

In the wake of Welles' production and Granville-Barker's prefaces appeared an unsettling essay by Leo Kirschbaum on 'Shakespeare's Stage Blood and Its Critical Significance' (*Publications of the Modern Language Association*, 1949). In what he described as 'an experiment in trusting Shakespeare', Kirschbaum pointed to evidence in the First Folio text that 'Caesar's blood' is more than what one critic had described as 'a political metaphor, distant from the experience of our senses'. Far from being literary 'metaphors', Kirschbaum insisted, 'The bathing of the hands in Caesar's bloody corpse and the smearing of the swords are . . . naturalistic stage effects . . . deliberately meant by Shakespeare for actual production and undoubtedly achieved at the Globe.' Kirschbaum noted that 'In his text, Pope assigned the "Stoope Romans, stoope," speech to Casca and wrote: "In all the editions this speech is ascribed to Brutus, than which nothing is more inconsistent with his mild and philosophical character." ' Kirschbaum said that 'Theobald thought Pope "more nice than wise" in this change' and defended the Folio speech heading on the grounds that 'Brutus esteemed the death of Caesar a sacrifice to liberty'. Meanwhile, in a comment echoed by a number of later commentators, a scholar named Upton wrote in 1746 that such a ritual

> was agreeable to an ancient and religious custom. So in Aeschylus we read that the seven captains, who came against Thebes, sacrificed a bull, and dipped their hands in the gore, invoking at the same time the gods of war, and binding themselves with an oath to revenge the cause of Eteocles (*Seven Against Thebes*, V, 42). . . . By this solemn action Brutus gives the assassination of Caesar a religious air and turn.

The only problem with Upton's reading of this 'solemn action', Kirschbaum suggested, was

> How the audience is to get the notion of a solemn religious sacrifice from the shocking gory effect. . . . The silence of most editors and critics, the pious explanations of others, seem indicative of some kind of turning away from the unseemly. None of them appears willing to face the scene in its own maculate terms.
>
> The critics are in line with the producers. Eighteenth and nineteenth century productions did not contain the lines and action we have been discussing. . . .
>
> As Knight recognized, there is no warrant in the source for the blood-bathing action. Nevertheless, North's Plutarch may have suggested it. In the life of Brutus, we read that when the conspirators were stabbing Caesar, 'so many swords and daggers lighting upon one body, one of them hurt another, and among them Brutus caught a blow on his hand, because he would make one in murdering of him, and all the rest also were every man of them bloodied.'

The inescapable conclusion, Kirschbaum argued, is that

> Shakespeare invented the blood-bath, deliberately gave the proposal

> for it to Brutus, and followed it with the invention of the bloody handshake with Antony.
>
> What, then, are Shakespeare's intentions? . . . I think we can be fairly sure of the five following glosses: (1) Shakespeare introduces a scene which in its novelty and brutality excites the spectators and grasps their attention. (2) He underscores the fact that the conspirators are bloodthirsty men – even if the audience has already allowed that the motives of some of them were initially respectable. All murder is in the act savage and inhuman, Shakespeare is saying. Whether or not killing ever justifies the doctrine of a bad means serving a good end, the merciless rending of a man is an obscene performance. (3) As Pope saw, that Brutus should suggest the blood-bath comes as a shock. And that is exactly Shakespeare's intention. However they may disagree in particulars, all commentators on Shakespeare's play regard Brutus as a man who does not understand himself or others. That the dignified and gentle Brutus should propose the ghastly procedure of the conspirators bathing their hands in the blood of Caesar's body wrenches the mind. It emphasizes the disorder in the man. . . . (4) The conspirators openly degenerate precisely at that juncture where Antony begins to fashion the ensuing events. As Moulton, seconded by Granville-Barker, points out, the entrance of Antony's servant [at III.i.276] is the turning point of the play. (5) The blood of Caesar begins to spread. As critics have noted, the implications of his death overshadow the rest of the drama. He is mighty yet. The dreadful blood which we see covering the hands of the conspirators, then touching Antony's hand, then staining the exhibited mantle, then turning the witless plebeians into destroyers – this is the symbol and mark of the blood and destruction which is to flow through the rest of the play, overwhelming the conspirators' plans, accomplishing Antony's promise to Caesar's butchered corpse.

A few years later Brents Stirling extended Kirschbaum's insights in an essay focused on Brutus' acknowledgement that the conspirators must have good 'Reasons' for their deed, 'Or else were this a Savage Spectacle' (III.i.224). In *Unity in Shakespearian Tragedy* (New York, 1956), Stirling reminded us that

> Modern readers are prone to find the tragedy of Brutus in his rigid devotion to justice and fair play. Many members of the Globe audience, however, believed that his virtues were complicated by self-deception and doubtful principle. In sixteenth-century views of history the conspiracy against Caesar often represented a flouting of unitary sovereignty, that prime point of Tudor policy, and exemplified the anarchy thought to accompany 'democratic' or constitutional

checks upon authority. . . . Although naturally aware of his disinterested honor and liberality, contemporary audiences could thus perceive in him a conflict between questionable goals and honorable action, a contradiction lying in his attempt to redeem morally confused ends by morally clarified ends. . . .

When a dramatist wishes to present an idea, his traditional method, of course, is to settle upon an episode in which the idea arises naturally but vividly from action and situation. Such an episode in *Julius Caesar* is the one in which Brutus resolves to exalt not only the mission but the tactics of conspiracy: having accepted republicanism as an honorable end, he sets out to dignify assassination, the means, by lifting it to the level of rite and ceremony. In II.i, as Cassius urges the killing of Antony as a necessary accompaniment to the death of Caesar, Brutus declares that 'such a course will seem too bloody. . . , / To cut the head off and then hack the limbs.' With this thought a sense of purpose comes over him: 'Let's be sacrificers, but not butchers, Caius.' Here his conflict seems to be resolved, and for the first time he is more than a reluctant presence among the conspirators as he expands the theme which ends his hesitation and frees his moral imagination. . . .

. . . From the suggestion of Plutarch that Brutus' first error lay in sparing Antony, Shakespeare moves to the image of Antony as a limb of Caesar, a limb not to be hacked because hacking is no part of ceremonial sacrifice. From Plutarch's description of Brutus as high-minded, gentle and disinterested, Shakespeare proceeds to the Brutus of symbolic action. Gentleness and disinterestedness become embodied in the act of 'unwrathful' blood sacrifice. High-mindedness becomes objectified in ceremonial observance. . . .

The vivid assassination scene carries out Brutus' ritual prescription in dramatic detail, for the killing is staged with a formalized approach, ending in kneeling, by one conspirator after another until the victim is surrounded. . . . The conspirators ceremonially bathe their hands in Caesar's blood, and Brutus pronounces upon 'this our lofty scene' with the prophecy that it 'shall be acted over / In states unborn and accents yet unknown!'

The mockery in counterritual now begins as a servant of Antony enters . . . and confronts Brutus. . . . Here [in III.i.124–27] a threefold repetition, 'kneel,' 'fall down,' and 'being prostrate,' brings the ceremonial irony close to satire. Following this worship of the new idol by his messenger, Antony appears in person and with dramatic timing offers himself as a victim. In one speech [III.i.159–64] he evokes both the holy scene which the conspirators so desire and the savagery which underlay it. . . . The murder scene is thus hallowed by Antony in a manner which quite reverses its sanctification by the

> conspirators. Brutus, forbearing, attempts to mollify Antony with his cherished theme of purgation [III.i.170–73]. . . . Antony's response is again one of counterceremony, the shaking of hands in formal sequence which serves to make each conspirator stand alone and unprotected by the rite of blood which had united him with the others. . . . It is then that Antony, addressing the body of Caesar, suddenly delivers his first profanation of the ritual sacrifice [III.i.204–6]. . . . And lest the allusion escape, Shakespeare continues Antony's inversion of Brutus' ceremonial formula: the dish carved for the gods is doubly transformed into the carcass hewn for hounds with further metaphors of Caesar as a hart in the forest and as 'a deer strucken by many princes.'
>
> [Later, in the Forum Scene, III.ii] Antony reenacts the death of Caesar in a ritual of his own, one intended to show that the original 'lofty scene' presented a base carnage. Holding Caesar's bloody mantle as a talisman, he reproduces *seriatim* the sacrificial strokes, but he does so in terms of the 'rent' Casca made and the 'cursed steel' that Brutus plucked away with the blood of Caesar following it. . . . for the second time Antony reminds us of [the conspirators'] ritual bond by recounting each stroke, and his recreation of the rite becomes a mockery of it. Brutus' transformation of blood into the heady wine of sacrifice is reversed both in substance and in ceremony.

Stirling's analysis of the uses and abuses of ritual in the tragedy supported what L. C. Knights had written a few years earlier in 'Shakespeare and Political Wisdom: A Note on the Personalism of *Julius Caesar*' (*Sewanee Review*, 1953).

> An important part of the imaginative impact of *Julius Caesar* lies in our awareness of a contrast between public life and private. . . . Commentators point to the ironic contrast between Caesar the public figure and Caesar the man ('Come on my right hand, for this ear is deaf'). When Brutus, in his 'gown' – the symbol of domestic privacy – speaks gently to his boy, we are told that this 'relieves the strain' of the tragic action. And every account of the characters includes some reference to those aspects of Caesar, Brutus and Cassius that are revealed in their more intimate moments and hidden or disguised in public. What seems not to be recognized is the cumulative effect of these and many other reminders of a more personal life – the important part this pervasive but unobtrusive personalism plays, or should play, in our evaluation of the public action. . . .
>
> . . . We notice . . . how often the verb 'love' appears in this play, how often different characters speak of their love – their 'dear love' or 'their kind love' – for each other, how often they seem to find a special

satisfaction in referring to themselves as 'brothers.' Now the effect of all this is not only one of pathos or simple irony. The focus of our attention is the public world: from the arena of that world, personal life – where truth between man and man resides – is glimpsed as across a gulf. The distance between these two worlds is the measure of the distortion and falsity that takes place in the attempt to make 'politics' self-enclosed. . . .

What the play also makes manifest, however, is that personal feelings, which Brutus tries to exclude from his deliberations on 'the general good,' are in fact active in public life. But they are active in the wrong way. Unacknowledged, they influence simply by distorting. . . .

The moral *dérèglement*, the confusion of values and priorities, issues in a kind of masquerade, as when the forms of friendship are exploited for political ends. It is this that explains our sense of something monstrous in the action, imperfectly symbolized by the storm and prodigies, and made explicit by Brutus in soliloquy when, deserting the actual, he has given himself up to a phantasmagoria of abstractions [II.i.62–68, 76–84].

[The first thing we learn from the tragedy that ensues] is that human actuality is more important than *any* political abstraction, though more difficult to bear. The second is that politics is vitiated and corrupted to the extent to which, as politicians, we lose our sense of the *person* on the other side of the dividing line of class or party or nation.

Knights' comments about abstraction were reinforced a year later by R. A. Foakes in 'An Approach to *Julius Caesar*' (*Shakespeare Quarterly*, 1954). Foakes commenced his study with remarks on a prominent 'rhetorical feature' of the tragedy, the tendency of many characters to refer to themselves in the third person. 'This device puts a distance between the speaker and what he is saying' and 'makes his words impersonal'; and it is a telling sign of Caesar's detachment from his compatriots that he habitually 'speaks in this way'.

Speak; Caesar is turn'd to hear. (I, ii, 17)

Yet Caesar shall go forth; for these predictions
Are to the world in general as to Caesar. (II, ii, 28–29)

But others speak the same way, as Foakes demonstrated by pointing to similar patterns in the phrasing of Brutus, Casca, Cassius, and Antony. Foakes then observed that names are frequently invoked in *Julius Caesar* as 'marks of the lineage and standing of a character' and as indications of 'the qualities and virtues the character ought to have, though not necessarily those he actually possesses'. Thus 'Caesar does not fear Cassius', but if his 'name were liable to fear' there is no man he would sooner avoid.

> . . . Caesar may be afraid in himself, but his name, his reputation, must be impervious to fear. Cassius incites Brutus by comparing his name with Caesar's,
>
> Brutus and Caesar: what should be in that Caesar?
> Why should that name be sounded more than yours?
> Write them together, yours is as fair a name;
> Sound them, it doth become the mouth as well;
> Weigh them, it is as heavy; conjure with 'em,
> Brutus will start a spirit as soon as Caesar. (I, ii, 142–47)
>
> The importance of a man's name is shown vividly when the plebeians seize Cinna the poet in spite of his protests,
>
> *Cinna.* I am not Cinna the conspirator.
> *4th Citizen.* It is no matter, his name's Cinna; pluck but his name out of his heart, and turn him going. (III, iii, 36–39)
>
> So the soldiers who capture Lucillius take the name he gives, Brutus, for the person; the name and the ideal, the reputation and the person, are identified in public, but the differences between them are clear to the audience; Caesar the man is less powerful than his name, and Brutus less honorable than his reputation, or great ancestry. . . .
>
> The names of Caesar and Brutus thus have symbolic qualities, and represent a concept as well as an individual character. Two other names which have much importance are . . . Rome and Roman (72 times in the play), and . . . liberty. . . .
>
> The conspirators, especially Brutus and Cassius, associate themselves with Rome as the home of truth, honor, liberty, and manliness; it is by suggesting that Romans are slaves that Cassius incites Brutus to rebel. . . ; it is for Rome . . . that Brutus joins the conspiracy, and he is conscious of the duties of being a Roman. . . . Romans are free-men, to whom Pompey and Caesar bring slaves, and whose servants are bond-men. . . . It is in the name of freedom that Brutus is persuaded to join the conspiracy against Caesar.

In Foakes' view, Brutus

> acts in the name of one ideal [liberty] to destroy another [Rome], but the action is dishonorable, and the ideal of liberty, an illusion. Cassius too acts and incites Brutus in the name of liberty, but in destroying

> Caesar the conspirators are not destroying tyranny, for Caesar is no tyrant, but rather the force of order in Rome. . . .
>
> . . . The action of the play turns on the distance between the ideals and public symbols for which the names of Caesar, Brutus, and Cassius stand, and their true nature and actions. The three main figures are all noble and yet weak; none has the stature of hero or villain. Brutus and Cassius kill the man Caesar and not his spirit, not what he stands for, what they aim to destroy; it is a treacherous and dishonorable act which brings disorder, loss of the liberty they had sought, and finally civil war. All they had hoped to gain they lose, until they have nothing left but their names, and the opportunity to die bravely, to find [a typically Roman definition of] freedom in suicide. . . . [Theirs is] a tale of frustration and disorder which spreads outwards to involve the mob, the whole nation, in civil destruction. All is the result of a self-deception, an obsession with names and an ignorance of reality, that could lead Brutus to think he was acting honorably in slaying his 'best lover' (III, ii, 49), and Cassius to think the death of one man would bring freedom.

David Daiches brought a less 'royalist' perspective to the play than did Foakes, but in an essay on 'Guilt and Justice in Shakespeare: *Julius Caesar*' in his *Literary Essays* (London, 1956), he too concluded that, paradoxically, 'innocence often achieves evil'.

> If Brutus had been a less simply virtuous man, he would not have helped to kill one of his best friends and brought tyranny to Rome (the opposite of what he intended). . . . A more worldly Brutus, a less morally sensitive Hamlet, a tougher and more cunning Othello, would have done less harm in the world. . . .
>
> Innocence plays into the hands of evil; only the tarnished and sophisticated mind can achieve that approximate good which alone lies within human reach. . . . The case of Brutus is that of the liberal intellectual in a world of *Realpolitik* – a familiar enough case in the modern world. Cassius is the co-hero of the play, and, skilled politician though he is, with little scruple in playing on Brutus's finer feelings, he admires Brutus and cannot help allowing Brutus to achieve moral ascendancy over him, once the murder of Caesar is accomplished. . . . But Cassius is not as unlike Brutus as he thinks he is. Though he is the shrewder and the more practical, he is basically an idealist too, an intellectual, whom Caesar had come to suspect because 'he thinks too much.' . . . In *Julius Caesar* Antony's is the success story; he is the tarnished man who knows how to come to terms with life. He is not

evil – he is generous, noble and kind-hearted – but he lacks innocence: he is post-lapsarian man, who has adapted himself to life after the Fall.

Wherein lies Antony's success? Is it not in his ability to manipulate people, to act the puppeteer and utilize the worthy emotions of innocent people for his own purposes? Cassius does this in a very mild way with Brutus, but Antony is the great puppeteer of the play. . . .

Antony manipulates his self-interest and his ideals into a compromise that is above all practicable. He is too good to be a tragic villain, too bad to be a tragic hero. Are we to say, then, that he is Shakespeare's ideal practical man? Shakespeare answers that question for us in his *Antony and Cleopatra*, which shows us, as Granville-Barker has said, the nemesis of the sensual man. The unstable equilibrium cannot last; Antony in the end surrenders wholly to his passions and loses the political world to young Octavius Caesar, the man whose fortunes he had earlier saved. *There*, perhaps, is Shakespeare's ideal practical man, Octavius Caesar, shrewd, cool-headed, altogether a cold fish. Obviously it is not the ideal practical man who is the glory of the human species, and we do not need Octavius to tell us that practical success was not, for Shakespeare, the greatest thing in life.

For Robert B. Heilman, another term for 'innocence' was 'self-ignorance'. In 'To Know Himself: An Aspect of Tragic Structure' (*A Review of English Literature*, 1964), Heilman observed that

Among three or four characters there is so much awareness of the strengths and vulnerabilities of others, and of the ways in which others must be approached to secure desired responses, that there is a constant air of intellectual melodrama; it is not stupid people who engage in various rhetorical sorties and campaigns. . . . Consciousness implies self-consciousness. Yet in *Julius Caesar* it is rare that anyone holds a mirror up to the self. . . .

[Shakespeare] conceives of Cassius and Brutus in ways that might lead to a drama of consciousness: he presents both as having actual or potential divisions that are the raw material of self-confrontation and self-knowledge. . . . Yet Cassius asks questions only of Brutus . . . not of himself. . . . Cassius' 'Caesar, thou art revenged' (V, iii, 46) is hardly a self-judgement; it is rather an ironic observation reversing the 'he who laughs last' truism.

. . . Out of [Brutus' conflicts] might grow some self-interrogation, some wondering, especially in a man by no means thoughtless. But Shakespeare has chosen to show him as a man of narrower range, with a singular closure against alternative views, and not to criticize that

> narrowness by making dramatic capital of its inadequacy either as a moral fact or as a guide to practical politics. In Brutus he finds a self-assurance that either proscribes self-questioning or assumes that all answers are known. It is a remarkable case of *hubris*, in the realms of both tactics and motives, not brought to book; the play does not really develop the irony that, with slight changes in the characters, the revolt might have worked; much less makes the characters, Brutus above all, realize this fact and find in it a mirror of self. . . .
>
> . . . In taking over from Plutarch the apparition of Caesar's ghost to Brutus, Shakespeare flattens the business out into an almost lifeless formality of revenge. The visitation meant, in North's words, 'that the gods were offended with the murther of Caesar' – an open invitation to introduce, in Brutus, an inquiry into deed and self. Compare the appearance of Banquo's ghost to Macbeth, in whom the intense inner pressures here come to the surface. In *Julius Caesar* there is nothing of the kind; Brutus, though he knows he will not win, still retains inner peace. His suicide has no trace of that self-judgement, incomplete though it may be, that precedes Othello's.

For Heilman, Brutus' failure to achieve self-knowledge could be explained only as a failure on the part of the playwright: 'Shakespeare's imagination [was] not yet carrying him into the inner puzzles of tragic character.' But in recent years a number of scholars have seen Brutus' display of mental and spiritual deficiencies as a conscious, significant aspect of Shakespeare's artistic design.

In '*Julius Caesar*: The Politics of the Hardened Heart' (*Shakespeare Studies*, 1966), John S. Anson locates the thematic centre of the play in 'the image of Rome as a body, an organism in which all the characters function as members'. What makes the action tragic is that in this case the body is dysfunctional.

> Characteristically, . . . the noble Roman finds his identity almost exclusively in what he conceives as his social role and reputation. Brutus lives in the light of his libertarian ancestor, and Caesar 'always is Caesar' (I.ii.212); both alike are Romans, lover-rivals bound in a single *cursus honorum*.
>
> . . . The decade of the fifteen-nineties, when *Julius Caesar* was written, marks the rise of Neo-Stoicism in England. In 1594, Sir John Stradling issued his translation of Justus Lipsius' *Two Bookes of Constancie*, and, four years later, [Guillaume] Du Vair's *The Moral Philosophie of the Stoicks* appeared in an English version by the Oxford scholar Thomas James. The doctrine of self-sufficient impassivity advanced by their works, although it derives from a long and

varied classical tradition, became associated in its more popular redactions principally with Seneca and the ancient Romans. . . . Thus, for the Elizabethans, Neo-Stoicism resuscitated a distinctly Roman ethos; to be a Stoic meant, in effect, to be a Roman. . . .

To many, of course, this Roman creed of constancy, however its authors sought to align it with Christian teaching, seemed, in its blanket condemnation of all emotion, to do a violence to both human nature and conscience. . . . 'The Stoics that condemn passion,' wrote [Sir Thomas] Browne in *Religio Medici*, '. . . could not endure without a groan a fit of the Stone or Colick.' . . . For moral incisiveness, however, nothing surpasses the character of the Senecan hero sketched years before by Erasmus in *The Praise of Folly*:

> 'tis agreed of all hands that our passions belong to Folly; inasmuch as we judge a wise man from a fool by this, that the one is ordered by them, the other by reason: and therefore the Stoics remove from a wise man all disturbance of mind as so many diseases. But these passions do not only the office of a tutor to such as are making towards the port of wisdom, but are in every exercise of virtue as it were spurs and incentives, nay and encouragers to well doing; which though that great Stoic Seneca most strongly denies, and takes from a wise man all affections whatever, yet in doing that he leaves him not so much as a man but rather a new kind of god that was never yet nor ever like to be. Nay, to speak plainer, he sets up a stony semblance of a man, void of all sense and common feeling of humanity. And much good to them with this wise man of theirs; let them enjoy him to themselves. . . . A man dead to all sense of nature and common affections, and no more moved with love or pity than if he were a flint or rock; whose censure nothing escapes; that commits no errors himself, but has a lynx's eyes upon others; measures everything by an exact line, and forgives nothing; pleases himself with himself only; the only rich, the only wise, the only free man, and only king; in brief, the only man that is everything, but in his own single judgment only; that cares not for the friendship of any man, being himself a friend to no man; makes no doubt to make the gods stoop to him, and condemns and laughs at the whole actions of our life? And yet such a beast is this their perfect wise man.

For Anson, *Julius Caesar* is best approached 'as a drama exploring . . . the moral petrification Erasmus diagnosed as the illness of Senecal man'. He notes that

> the quality Caesar most prizes is just that Constancy upon which Lipsius dilates. . . . Whatever its accuracy as self-evaluation, Caesar's boast [when he describes himself in III.i.59–74 as 'Constant as the Northern Star'] reveals at least the ideal of greatness to which,

> presumably, he and his hearers alike subscribe. . . . Fixed, unassailable, godlike, Caesar claims for himself a position of moral supremacy in a social order.
>
> What finally invalidates this claim is not so much its untruth. . . ; rather, its failure lies deeper within its very assumptions, in a falsification of values upon which the claim is constructed. From a world of men who are 'flesh and blood, and apprehensive,' Caesar boasts that he stands apart in an isolation conceived not as the result but the source and quintessence of his greatness. To ensconce himself thus unassailably from humanity, however, he dissevers himself perforce from his own flesh and blood as well. . . . Unthawed, unmelting, Caesar achieves his greatness through the express disowning of his human kind-ness, through the disavowal, above all, of fear and pity, the specifically tragic emotions which mark the awareness of frailty respectively in oneself and in others.

Citing Elizabethan treatises on physiology, Anson argues that one consequence of Caesar's refusal to acknowledge that feelings have any legitimacy in human life is that he inhibits the operations of his own heart. Like other Romans, he suffers from a 'narcosis of the hand' and from a body that has grown 'increasingly "out of touch" '. Meanwhile, the vanity that motivates him to seek self-sufficiency also prompts two other maladies: the epileptic seizures to which Caesar falls victim, and the deafness that medieval commentaries on the New Testament ascribed to a person who refuses to 'hear' or 'confess the Word of God'. Like Falstaff in 2 *Henry IV*, I.ii.122–40, Anson says, Caesar suffers from 'the disease of not list'ning', a handicap that proves fatal when he dismisses the Soothsayer as a 'Dreamer' and refuses to pay heed either to his own prudential fears or to the warnings of those who urge him to proceed cautiously on the Ides of March.

Anson's analysis of Neo-Stoicism in *Julius Caesar* has spawned three articles on the play by Marvin L. Vawter, the most important of which, ' "Division 'tween Our Souls": Shakespeare's Stoic Brutus', appeared in the 1974 volume of *Shakespeare Studies*. Vawter argues that in addition to his knowledge of the Neo-Stoics of his own era, Shakespeare was also familiar with Cicero's *De Finibus*, a Latin treatise addressed to Brutus and calling into question many of the tenets of Roman Stoicism. In the passages Vawter quotes, Cicero tells Brutus that it is foolish and self-defeating to believe that virtue derives from intellect alone: 'Fundamentally, argues Cicero, the Stoics simply do not understand the true nature of human beings.' Anticipating St Augustine, who said that 'The "whole human nature ... is composed of flesh and soul," not just one or the other,' Cicero maintained, in Vawter's words, that 'the man who abjures his own body is a living contradiction and a fool'.

> Knowing [that] the historical Brutus was a Stoic who believed in the self-sufficiency of virtue-reason, Shakespeare portrays Brutus as a cultural elitist shutting out communication with the communal body of his loved ones and countrymen and subjecting his physical body to the totalitarian authority of his mind. In Brutus the 'iarring concord' of which Lipsius speaks becomes a full-scale battle: 'poor Brutus, with himself at war, / Forgets the shows of love to other men' (I.ii.45–46). As Brutus's 'genius' plans 'the acting of a dreadful thing,' the murder of a man he says he loves, his 'mortal instruments,' the emotional and physical half of his soul or 'state,' resists this hideous deed. Brutus 'suffers then / The nature of an insurrection' (II.i.64–69). But the sensitive half of Brutus's soul is no match for his tyrannous mind.
>
> ... Because he is a Stoic, his inflated mind tyrannizes over his body and the emotional feeling within that body. That is, his mind is the tyrant, and his heart is the bondslave.
>
> ... Not only does he neglect 'the shows of love' to Cassius – and later to Caesar – he has also forgotten how to love Portia. ... his sick mind is brutalizing his body with the result that there is nothing 'wholesome' about him [II.i.262). ...
>
> Montaigne, in the context of attacking the Stoic Wise Man's pretensions to 'constancy,' provides an important Renaissance point of view on such men as Shakespeare's Brutus. ...
>
> > The body hath a great part in our being, and therein keeps a speciall rancke. ... Such as goe about to sunder our two principall parts, and separat them one from another, are much to blame: They ought rather to be coupled and joyned fast together. The soule must be enjoined not ... to despise and leave the body ... but ought to combine and cling fast unto him. ... Christians have a particular instruction concerning this bond, for they know that Gods justice ... embraceth the conjunction of body and soule. ... God beholds the whole man.
>
> Condemning the man whose mind is obsessed with 'dissociating hir selfe from the body,' Montaigne issues a significant warning:
>
> > It is mere folly, insteade of transforming themselves into Angels, they transchange themselves into beastes: in lieu of advancing, they abase themselves. ...
>
> Though mentally and morally sick, Brutus nonetheless believes Fate

has chosen him to be physician to a political body corrupted by a malignant head. As he prepares to 'cut the head off' (II.i.163), Brutus, only a partial man himself, can yet speak of performing 'A piece of work that will make sick men whole.' Caius Ligarius, seizing the other half of the paradox, retorts, 'But are not some whole that we must make sick?' Ligarius' rejoinder exposes the shallowness of Brutus's medicinal metaphor.

. . . Brutus, far from being the healer of the state, is rather a carrier of the disease. . . . he infects Portia with the constancy that will eventually cause her death.

. . . In the belief that his own personal sense of virtue-reason is 'self-sufficient for a happy life' the Stoic Wise Man deliberately cuts himself off from all ties with a less perfect humanity. He is an absolutist . . . and he believes himself incapable of misjudgment or moral error. Conversely, in accordance with the Stoic paradox that 'all offences are equal,' he has no forbearance for the faults or shortcomings of others. . . .

In the quarrel between Brutus and Cassius, which occurs immediately before Portia's suicide is revealed, Brutus piously accuses Cassius of taking bribe money – money he will demand from Cassius minutes later for his own uses. At this moment, we can understand how 'the eye' of the Stoic Wise Man 'sees not itself.' 'You love me not,' says Cassius in response to Brutus's undocumented charges. 'I do not like your faults,' retorts Brutus. But Cassius replies, 'A friendly eye could never see such faults.' . . .

. . . But the most important aspect of this scene is the extent to which Brutus's attack on Cassius mirrors his indictment of Caesar. He admitted that he knew 'no personal cause to spurn' Caesar (II.i.20–21), but, to justify the assassination in his own mind, Brutus also makes Caesar's 'infirmities greater than they are' by saying to himself: 'what he is, augmented, / Would run to these and these extremities' (II.i.30–31). Furthermore, he does not kill Caesar because he has seen Caesar 'practise' an offense; he murders him '*lest* he may' (II.i.28, my italics). . . .

In *Julius Caesar*, Shakespeare attempts to reunite the sensitive and rational souls of his audience so that they will realize that Brutus commits, not a sacrificial ritual of cultural salvation, but a savage felony of cultural assassination. Even though his Stoic philosophy makes him a man alone, his disembodied mind brings chaos to an entire social order. In the disparity between Brutus's claim, 'let no man abide this deed / But we the doers' (III.i.94–95), and the actuality that Shakespeare dramatizes – the destruction of Cinna the poet, of Portia,

> and of Rome itself – lies the truth of Stoic self-sufficiency and the reality of the 'noble Brutus.'

In a 1993 article for *Shakespeare Quarterly* (' "A Thing Unfirm": Plato's *Republic* and Shakespeare's *Julius Caesar*') Barbara L. Parker adduces an even earlier classical source for the playwright's most popular Roman play.

> Central to the *Republic* is the concept of the founding of the state on reason. Because rational government is achievable only by rational men, or philosophers, democracy is to be eschewed; the ruler must govern by virtue of knowledge of truth, a knowledge the base, irrational masses cannot possess. Accordingly, Plato's republic is rigidly stratified; it is comprised of three hierarchically ordered classes: the Workers, or populace, at the bottom; the Auxiliaries, or militia, over them; and the Guardian or Guardians at the top. The state's integrity lies in the accepted subordination of the lower to the higher, justice – the real subject of the *Republic* – depending upon each class maintaining its bounds and function. Injustice, conversely, results when, in a meddling and restless spirit, one class infringes the bounds and vocation of another. . . . The three classes correspond to man's appetites, his will, and his reason. Like the state, man must be ruled by reason if he is to achieve that justice of the soul whereby each faculty performs its appointed task. . . .
>
> The condition of the commonwealth thus mirrors the soul of its ruler, and Plato devotes Books 8 and 9 of his *Republic* to the perversions of the ruling principle in the state. Oligarchy, for example, reflects an uneven distribution of wealth, with political power resting on property valuation. An impoverished populace results. The people then procure a champion and eventually expel the rich to establish democracy. But the inordinate love of liberty that characterizes democracy leads inevitably to tyranny, as the power-seeking champion discards pretence and effects a coup d'état. This descent corresponds to that of the soul when reason, vitiated, yields progressive sway to appetite and will.
>
> Understanding fully the role of the *Republic* in *Julius Caesar* requires viewing the play in the context of such political degeneration, a degeneration that begins in *The Rape of Lucrece*, continues in *Coriolanus*, and culminates in *Julius Caesar*. It is initiated in *Lucrece* by abolition of the monarchy, which, together with the instatement of the consulate, paves the way for popular control. In *Coriolanus*, Rome has lapsed into oligarchy, with consequences precisely paralleling those defined in the *Republic*. Because the condition of oligarchy is an uneven distribution of wealth, this form of government produces

'inevitable division': 'such a State is not one, but two. . . , the one of poor, the other of rich men; and they are living on the same spot and always conspiring against one another.' . . . Thus in *Coriolanus* the famished and seditious masses seek revenge on the surfeiting patricians, who in turn enact 'piercing statutes daily to chain up and restrain the poor'. . . . With the establishment of the tribunate, however, democracy progressively displaces oligarchy as the plebeians continue to amass power. In *Julius Caesar* the degenerative process is complete: democracy has passed into tyranny, both in the ruler and in the state. . . .

Plato devotes an extended portion of the *Republic* to discussion of the corruption of the philosophic nature, a discussion he prefaces with a description of the metals that theoretically comprise the human soul. The Workers are framed of brass and iron, the Auxiliaries of silver, and the Guardians of gold. . . . Because the masses are unavoidably corrupt, the philosopher must keep to his own environment, since all seeds, when deprived of 'proper nutriment or climate or soil, in proportion to their vigour,' will be tainted. The noblest natures are most prone to such injury; thus the philosopher, in 'alien soil, becomes the most noxious of all weeds' and the author 'of the greatest evil to States and individuals'. . . .

Parker notes that Plato describes

the tyrant as the man in whom 'the basest elements of human nature have set up an absolute despotism . . . over the higher.' . . . Eventually, the protector becomes a wolf: 'having a mob entirely at his disposal, he is not restrained from shedding the blood of kinsmen,' killing some and banishing others. The rich begin to hate him. 'And if they are unable to expel him, . . . they conspire to assassinate him.' . . .

Shakespeare's Caesar – partially deaf, figuratively blind, sustained by mass adulation, and ruled by a populace he should theoretically command – markedly resembles the captain in Socrates' parable of the ship of state. This captain 'is taller and stronger than any of the crew, but he is a little deaf and has a similar infirmity in sight, and his knowledge of navigation is not much better.' The sailors quarrel about his steering, each believing 'he has a right to steer, though he has never learned the [pilot's art]. . . , and they are ready to cut in pieces any one who says the contrary. They throng about the captain, . . . praying him to commit the helm to them.' At length 'they mutiny and take possession of the ship,' having first 'chained up the noble captain's senses with . . . some narcotic drug'. . . . The resemblance is the more striking in that no mention of Caesar's deafness appears in any of Shakespeare's known sources. . . .

As the *Republic* informs Shakespeare's characterization of Caesar, so too it informs the characterization of Brutus. Brutus is not merely Caesar's parallel; Brutus figuratively *becomes* Caesar through a like process of reverse alchemy that morally debases and destroys him. In Gary Miles's words, 'this implicit convergence of personalities and roles' is underscored by 'the apparition that is simultaneously the ghost of Caesar and Brutus' own "evil spirit",' by the shout, 'Let him be Caesar,' and by the plebeian's punning assertion that 'Caesar's better parts / Shall be crown'd in Brutus' (3.2.51–52). It is perhaps further underscored by the fact that 'Caesar' had by Shakespeare's time become a generic term for a dictator or absolute monarch.

FURTHER READING

Many of the works quoted in the preceding survey, or excerpts from those works, can be found in modern collections of criticism. Of particular interest are three anthologies:

Bloom, Harold (ed.), *William Shakespeare's 'Julius Caesar': Modern Critical Interpretations*, New York: Chelsea House, 1988 (9 entries, all from books or articles listed separately in this bibliography).

Charney, Maurice (ed.), *Discussions of Shakespeare's Roman Plays*, Boston: D. C. Heath and Co., 1964 (6 entries that deal with *Julius Caesar*, among them the essays quoted above by Edward Dowden and Richard G. Moulton, and a superb article on 'Shakespeare and the Elizabethan Romans' by T. J. B. Spencer).

Dean, Leonard F. (ed.), *Twentieth Century Interpretations of 'Julius Caesar'*, Englewood Cliffs, N.J.: Prentice-Hall, 1968 (18 entries, including the essays quoted above by David Daiches, R. A. Foakes, Harley Granville-Barker, Robert B. Heilman, Leo Kirschbaum, L. C. Knights, and Brents Stirling).

Other studies of Shakespeare that include valuable discussions of *Julius Caesar*:

Andrews, John F., 'Was the Bard Behind It? Old Light on the Lincoln Assassination', *Atlantic Monthly*, October 1990, pp. 26, 28, 32.

Barroll, J. Leeds, 'Shakespeare and Roman History', *Modern Language Review*, 53 (1958), 327–43.

Barton, Anne, '*Julius Caesar* and *Coriolanus*: Shakespeare's Roman War of Words', in *Shakespeare's Craft*, ed. Philip H. Highfill, Carbondale, Ill.: Southern Illinois University Press, 1982.

Battenhouse, Roy, *Shakespearean Tragedy: Its Art and Its Christian Premises*, Bloomington: Indiana University Press, 1969.

Blits, Jan H., *The End of the Ancient Republic: Essays on 'Julius Caesar'*, Durham, N.C.: Carolina Academic Press, 1982.

Bonjour, Adrien, *The Structure of 'Julius Caesar'*, Liverpool: University Press of Liverpool, 1958.

Booth, Stephen, 'The Shakespearean Actor as Kamikaze Pilot', *Shakespeare Quarterly*, 36 (1985), 553–70 (a wise and witty discussion of why so many of the actors who play Brutus do, and should, 'go down in flames' when critics review their performances).

Bulman, James C., *The Heroic Idiom of Shakespearean Tragedy*, Newark, Del.: University of Delaware Press, 1985.

Burckhardt, Sigurd, *Shakespearean Meanings*, Princeton: Princeton University Press, 1968.

Calderwood, James L., *Shakespearean Metadrama*, Minneapolis: University of Minnesota Press, 1971.

Cantor, Paul, *Shakespeare's Rome: Republic and Empire*, Ithaca, N.Y.: Cornell University Press, 1976.

Charlton, H. B., *Shakespearian Tragedy*, Cambridge: Cambridge University Press, 1948.

Charney, *Shakespeare's Roman Plays*, Cambridge, Mass.: Harvard University Press, 1961.

Clarke, M. L., *The Noblest Roman: Marcus Brutus and his Reputation*, Ithaca, N.Y., 1981.

Danson, Lawrence, *Tragic Alphabet*, New Haven: Yale University Press, 1974.

Dorsch, T. S. (ed.), *The Arden Edition of 'Julius Caesar'*, London: Methuen, 1955.

Drakakis, John, ' "Fashion it thus": *Julius Caesar* and the Politics of Theatrical Representation', *Shakespeare Survey*, 44 (1992), 65–74.

Frye, Northrop, *Fools of Time*, London: Oxford University Press, 1965.

Garber, Marjorie, *Dream in Shakespeare*, New Haven: Yale University Press, 1974.

Goldberg, Jonathan, *James I and the Politics of Literature*, Baltimore: Johns Hopkins University Press, 1983.

Honigmann, E. A. J., *Shakespeare: Seven Tragedies*, Macmillan, 1976.

Humphreys, A. R., *The Oxford Shakespeare: 'Julius Caesar'*, Oxford: Clarendon Press, 1984.

Kaula, David, ' "Let Us Be Sacrificers": Religious Motifs in *Julius Caesar*', *Shakespeare Studies*, 14 (1981), 197–213 (shows, among other things, that many of the references to Rome in the play would have been interpreted by Elizabethan Protestants as allusions to the Roman Catholic Church and its rituals, and that much of the play's imagery would have been coloured by Renaissance commentaries comparing the Pope of Rome to the Antichrist).

Knight, G. Wilson, *The Imperial Theme*, London: Oxford University Press, 1931.

Leggatt, Alexander, *Shakespeare's Political Drama: The History Plays and the Roman Plays*, London: Methuen, 1988.

Liebler, Naomi Conn, ' "Thou Bleeding Piece of Earth": The Ritual Ground of *Julius Caesar*', *Shakespeare Studies*, 14 (1981), 175–96.

Long, Michael, *The Unnatural Scene*, London: Methuen, 1976.
MacCallum, M. W., *Shakespeare's Roman Plays and Their Background*, London: Macmillan, 1910.
Maxwell, J. C., 'Shakespeare's Roman Plays: 1900–1956', *Shakespeare Survey*, 10 (1957), 1–11.
Miola, Robert S., *Shakespeare's Rome*, Cambridge: Cambridge University Press, 1983.
Monsarrat, Gilles D., *Light from the Porch: Stoicism and English Renaissance Literature*, Paris: Didier-Erudition, 1984.
Nuttall, A. D., *A New Mimesis*, London: Methuen, 1983.
Palmer, John, *Political Characters of Shakespeare*, London: Macmillan & Co., 1945.
Paster, Gail Kern, ' "In the spirit of men there is no blood": Blood as Trope of Gender in *Julius Caesar*', *Shakespeare Quarterly*, 40 (1989), 284–98.
Pickup, Ronald, '*Julius Caesar*', in *Shakespeare in Perspective*, ed. Roger Sales, Vol. II, London: BBC Publications, 1982.
Proser, Matthew N., *The Heroic Image in Five Shakespearean Tragedies*, Princeton: Princeton University Press, 1965.
Rabkin, Norman, *Shakespeare and the Common Understanding*, New York: Free Press, 1967.
Rebhorn, Wayne A., 'The Crisis of the Aristocracy in *Julius Caesar*', *Renaissance Quarterly*, 43 (1990), 75–111.
Ribner, Irving, *Patterns in Shakespearean Tragedy*, London: Methuen, 1960.
Richmond, Hugh M., *Shakespeare's Political Plays*, New York: Random House, 1967.
Righter, Anne, *Shakespeare and the Idea of the Play*, London: Chatto & Windus, 1962.
Ripley, John, *'Julius Caesar' on Stage in England and America, 1599–1973*, Cambridge: Cambridge University Press, 1980.
Rose, Mark, 'Conjuring Caesar: Ceremony, History, and Author in 1599', *English Literary Renaissance*, 19 (1989), 291–304.
Schanzer, Ernest, *The Problem Plays of Shakespeare*, London: Routledge & Kegan Paul, 1963.
Sewall, Arthur, *Character and Society in Shakespeare*, Oxford: Clarendon Press, 1951.
Siemon, James R., *Shakespearean Iconoclasm*, Berkeley: University of California Press, 1985.
Simmons, J. L., *Shakespeare's Pagan World: The Roman Tragedies*, Charlottesville: University Press of Virginia, 1973.
Smith, Warren D., 'The Duplicate Revelation of Portia's Death', *Shakespeare Quarterly*, 4 (1953), 153–61.

Spencer, T. J. B., *Shakespeare's Plutarch*, Harmondsworth: Penguin, 1964 (the source for all the Plutarch quotations in this volume).
—— 'Shakespeare and the Elizabethan Romans', *Shakespeare Survey*, 10 (1957), 27–38.
Spevack, Marvin (ed.), *The New Cambridge Shakespeare: 'Julius Caesar'*, Cambridge: Cambridge University Press, 1988.
Stewart, J. I. M., *Character and Motive in Shakespeare*, London: Longmans, Green, 1949.
Traversi, Derek, *Shakespeare: The Roman Plays*, London: Hollis & Carter, 1963.
Van Doren, Mark, *Shakespeare*, New York: Henry Holt, 1939.
Vawter, Marvin L., ' "After their Fashion": Cicero and Brutus in *Julius Caesar*', *Shakespeare Studies*, 9 (1976), 205–19.
Velz, John W., 'Clemency, Will, and Just Cause in *Julius Caesar*', *Shakespeare Survey*, 22 (1969), 109–18.
—— 'Orator and Imperator in *Julius Caesar*', *Shakespeare Studies*, 15 (1982), 55–75.
—— *Shakespeare and the Classical Tradition: A Critical Guide to Commentary, 1660–1960*, Minneapolis: University of Minnesota Press, 1968.
Walker, Roy, 'Unto Caesar: A Review of Recent Productions', *Shakespeare Survey*, 10 (1957), 27–38.
Whitaker, Virgil K., *The Mirror Up to Nature: The Technique of Shakespeare's Tragedies*, San Marino, Cal.: Huntington Library, 1965.

Background studies and useful reference works:

Abbott, E. A., *A Shakespearian Grammar*, New York: Haskell House, 1972 (information on how Shakespeare's grammar differs from ours).
Allen, Michael J. B., and Kenneth Muir (eds), *Shakespeare's Plays in Quarto: A Facsimile Edition*, Berkeley: University of California Press, 1981.
Andrews, John F. (ed.), *William Shakespeare: His World, His Work, His Influence*, 3 vols, New York: Scribners, 1985 (articles on 60 topics).
Barroll, Leeds, *Politics, Plague, and Shakespeare's Theater*, Ithaca: Cornell University Press, 1992.
Bentley, G. E., *The Profession of Player in Shakespeare's Time, 1590–1642*, Princeton: Princeton University Press, 1984.
Blake, Norman, *Shakespeare's Language: An Introduction*, New York: St Martin's Press, 1983 (general introduction to all aspects of the playwright's language).
Bullough, Geoffrey (ed.), *Narrative and Dramatic Sources of Shakespeare*, 8 vols, New York: Columbia University Press, 1957–75 (printed sources, with helpful summaries and comments by the editor).

Campbell, O. J., and Edward G. Quinn (eds), *The Reader's Encyclopedia of Shakespeare*, New York: Crowell, 1966.

Cook, Ann Jennalie, *The Privileged Playgoers of Shakespeare's London*: Princeton: Princeton University Press, 1981 (argument that theatre audiences at the Globe and other public playhouses were relatively well-to-do).

De Grazia, Margreta, *Shakespeare Verbatim: The Reproduction of Authenticity and the Apparatus of 1790*, Oxford: Clarendon Press, 1991 (interesting material on eighteenth-century editorial practices).

Eastman, Arthur M., *A Short History of Shakespearean Criticism*, New York: Random House, 1968.

Gurr, Andrew, *Playgoing in Shakespeare's London*, Cambridge: Cambridge University Press, 1987 (argument for changing tastes, and for a more diverse group of audiences than Cook suggests).

—— *The Shakespearean Stage, 1574–1642*, 2nd edn, Cambridge: Cambridge University Press, 1981 (theatres, companies, audiences, and repertories).

Hinman, Charlton (ed.), *The Norton Facsimile: The First Folio of Shakespeare's Plays*, New York: Norton, 1968.

Muir, Kenneth, *The Sources of Shakespeare's Plays*, New Haven: Yale University Press, 1978 (a concise account of how Shakespeare used his sources).

Onions, C. T., *A Shakespeare Glossary*, 2nd edn, London: Oxford University Press, 1953.

Partridge, Eric, *Shakespeare's Bawdy*, London: Routledge & Kegan Paul, 1955 (indispensable guide to Shakespeare's direct and indirect ways of referring to 'indecent' subjects).

Schoenbaum, S., *Shakespeare: The Globe and the World*, New York: Oxford University Press, 1979 (lively illustrated book on Shakespeare's world).

—— *Shakespeare's Lives*, 2nd edn, Oxford: Oxford University Press, 1992 (readable, informative survey of the many biographers of Shakespeare, including those believing that someone else wrote the works).

—— *William Shakespeare: A Compact Documentary Life*, New York: Oxford University Press, 1977 (presentation of all the biographical documents, with assessments of what they tell us about the playwright).

Spevack, Marvin, *The Harvard Concordance to Shakespeare*, Cambridge, Mass.: Harvard University Press, 1973.

Whitaker, Virgil, K., *Shakespeare's Use of Learning*, San Marino, Cal.: Huntington Library, 1963.

Wright, George T., *Shakespeare's Metrical Art*, Berkeley: University of California Press, 1988.

PLOT SUMMARY

1.1 In Rome, on a street, two tribunes, Flavius and Murellus, disperse a crowd of Commoners who plan to celebrate the triumphant return of Julius Caesar. The tribunes leave to remove the symbols of Caesar's victory which have been placed on statues.

1.2 In a public place, Caesar, his wife and many others, are on their way to attend a race, part of a holy festival. A soothsayer warns Caesar to beware of the ides of March. Caesar dismisses the warning, and departs with his company, leaving only Brutus and Cassius behind.

Brutus confesses to Cassius that he is troubled, which Cassius suggests is because he is worried that Caesar may become the King of Rome. Cassius declares that he will never be another man's subject.

Caesar and his company briefly return, Caesar warning Antony to beware of lean, thinking-men such as Cassius. Brutus finds out from Casca that Antony, urged on by the people, had offered Caesar a coronet three times. Caesar refused each offer. He then had an epileptic fit. Casca also tells how the tribunes have been 'put to silence' for their actions.

Left alone, Cassius reveals how he hopes to persuade Brutus to oppose Caesar.

1.3 As a terrible storm rages that night, Casca meets Cicero in a street. Casca describes the prodigies he has just witnessed. After Cicero leaves, Cassius enters, and tells Casca that he believes the prodigies to be warnings against Caesar's increasing power. He persuades Casca to join his party. One of that party, Cinna, arrives, and Cassius tells him where to leave various anonymous messages for Brutus.

2.1 Before dawn on the ides of March, the sleepless Brutus, out in his garden, considers justifications for killing Caesar. His servant, a boy named Lucius, brings him a message which has been left in his study. It urges him to take action.

Cassius and the other conspirators arrive. They discuss how they are to kill Caesar that day at the Capitol. Brutus insists that Antony should not be harmed. After they leave, Brutus's wife, Portia, enters, and asks him to tell her what he is planning. He says he will, but is interrupted by the arrival of a visitor. He promises Portia that he will tell her after the visitor has left. Ligarius enters, and agrees to help Brutus, whatever he plans to do.

2.2 While the storm continues, Caesar is persuaded by Calphurnia, his wife, not to leave his house. Decius, one of the conspirators, enters and in turn persuades Caesar to go to the Capitol as he originally planned. Other Roman nobles arrive, most of whom are conspirators.

2.3 Artemidorus waits on a street near the Capitol to give Caesar a written message warning him about the conspiracy.

2.4 In front of Brutus's house, Portia, impatient for news of the progress of the conspirators, sends Lucius, a servant, to the Capitol. The Soothsayer enters, on his way to take up a place somewhere along Caesar's route to the Captiol.

3.1 Before the Capitol, Caesar greets the Soothsayer. Artemidorus gives Caesar his message. Caesar delays reading it since it contains information concerning him personally. Instead he enters the Capitol where he is stabbed to death by the conspirators.

As the conspirators prepare to go to tell the people what has happened, Antony arrives. Brutus tells him that he has no need to fear, and that they will explain their actions after the people have been calmed. Antony asks to be allowed to give a funeral speech over Caesar's body in the market-place. Brutus agrees, against Cassius's advice, on the conditions that Antony speaks after Brutus's own speech to the people (explaining why Caesar had to die) and that Antony speak only in praise of Caesar.

After the conspirators have set off for the market-place, Antony declares his hatred of them, and prophesies a civil war. With a servant, he takes up Caesar's body to carry it to the market-place where he intends, through his funeral speech, to test the people's response to Caesar's death.

3.2 In the forum, Brutus tells the people why Caesar was killed. The people praise him. But then Antony gives his funeral speech, during which he shows the people Caesar's punctured cloak and corpse, and reads out Caesar's will, which contains many gifts to the people. He turns the people against the conspirators and they leave to burn the conspirators' houses. Antony goes to meet Octavius and Lepidus.

3.3 Cinna the poet is found by the crowd and killed for having the same name as one of the conspirators.

4.1 Sometime later, in his house, Antony, in partnership with Octavius and Lepidus, finalizes the list of the people the three want killed. Lepidus leaves, and Antony tells Octavius that Brutus and Cassius are raising armies against them.

4.2 In his camp near Sardis, their armies present, Brutus, standing outside his tent, meets with Cassius. Inside the tent, the two discuss and finally resolve some financial grievances. Brutus tells Cassius the news of Portia's suicide.

Two friends enter, and the group discuss news of events at Rome, and their tactics for the forthcoming battle with Octavius and Antony. Brutus decides they shall march to Philippi and fight there. The others leave and Brutus calls in two soldiers to sleep in his tent, in case he should need to use them as messengers. He asks Lucius to play to him, but the boy soon falls asleep. The ghost of Caesar then appears, telling Brutus that he will visit him again at Philippi.

5.1 On the plains of Philippi, Octavius and Antony meet with Brutus and Cassius in front of their respective armies. The two sides separate, and Brutus and Cassius say their farewells to each other.

5.2 The battle begun, Brutus issues orders.

5.3 Cassius, his army defeated by Antony's, mistakenly believes the battle lost and orders Pindarus, his servant, to kill him. Brutus, whose forces have overwhelmed Octavius's, arrives to find Cassius dead. He leaves to begin a second battle.

5.4 Roman noblemen on Brutus's side are killed and captured.

5.5 Brutus, his army beaten and in retreat, kills himself. He is found by Antony and Octavius, who praise him and order that he be given an honourable burial. They leave to celebrate their victory.